Handbook of Dinosaurs

Compiled by

Silvia Herbert

Scribbles

Year of Publication 2018

ISBN : 9789352979240

Book Published by

Scribbles

(An Imprint of Alpha Editions)

email - alphaedis@gmail.com

Produced by: PediaPress GmbH
Limburg an der Lahn
Germany
http://pediapress.com/

Contents

Introduction

Dinosaur

<indicator name="pp-default"> 🔒 </indicator>

Dinosaurs	
Temporal range: Late Triassic–Present, 233.23 – 0 Mya	
PreꞒꞒ OSD C P T J K PₘN	

A collection of fossil dinosaur skeletons. Clockwise from top left: *Microraptor gui* (a winged theropod), *Apatosaurus louisae* (a giant sauropod), *Edmontosaurus regalis* (a duck-billed ornithopod), *Triceratops horridus* (a horned ceratopsian), *Stegosaurus stenops* (a plated stegosaur), *Pinacosaurus grangeri* (an armored ankylosaur)

Scientific classification 🖉	
Kingdom:	Animalia
Phylum:	Chordata
Clade:	Dinosauriformes
Clade:	**Dinosauria** Owen, 1842
Major groups	

- †*Eodromaeus*
- †Herrerasauria
- †Ornithischia
- †Sauropodomorpha
- Theropoda

Dinosaurs are a diverse group of reptiles[1] of the clade **Dinosauria**. They first appeared during the Triassic period, between 243 and 233.23 million years ago, although the exact origin and timing of the evolution of dinosaurs is the subject of active research. They became the dominant terrestrial vertebrates after the Triassic–Jurassic extinction event 201 million years ago; their dominance continued through the Jurassic and Cretaceous periods. Reverse genetic engineering[2] and the fossil record both demonstrate that birds are modern feathered dinosaurs, having evolved from earlier theropods during the late Jurassic Period. As such, birds were the only dinosaur lineage to survive the Cretaceous–Paleogene extinction event 66 million years ago. Dinosaurs can therefore be divided into *avian dinosaurs*, or birds; and *non-avian dinosaurs*, which are all dinosaurs other than birds. This article deals primarily with non-avian dinosaurs.

Dinosaurs are a varied group of animals from taxonomic, morphological and ecological standpoints. Birds, at over 10,000 living species, are the most diverse group of vertebrates besides perciform fish. Using fossil evidence, paleontologists have identified over 500 distinct genera and more than 1,000 different species of non-avian dinosaurs. Dinosaurs are represented on every continent by both extant species (birds) and fossil remains. Through the first half of the 20th century, before birds were recognized to be dinosaurs, most of the scientific community believed dinosaurs to have been sluggish and cold-blooded. Most research conducted since the 1970s, however, has indicated that all dinosaurs were active animals with elevated metabolisms and numerous adaptations for social interaction. Some were herbivorous, others carnivorous. Evidence suggests that egg-laying and nest-building are additional traits shared by all dinosaurs, avian and non-avian alike.

While dinosaurs were ancestrally bipedal, many extinct groups included quadrupedal species, and some were able to shift between these stances. Elaborate display structures such as horns or crests are common to all dinosaur groups, and some extinct groups developed skeletal modifications such as bony armor and spines. While the dinosaurs' modern-day surviving avian lineage (birds) are generally small due to the constraints of flight, many prehistoric dinosaurs (non-avian and avian) were large-bodied—the largest sauropod dinosaurs are estimated to have reached lengths of 39.7 meters (130 feet) and heights of 18 meters (59 feet) and were the largest land animals of all time. Still, the idea that non-avian dinosaurs were uniformly gigantic is a misconception based in part on preservation bias, as large, sturdy bones are more likely to last until they are fossilized. Many dinosaurs were quite small: *Xixianykus*, for example, was only about 50 cm (20 in) long.

Since the first dinosaur fossils were recognized in the early 19th century, mounted fossil dinosaur skeletons have been major attractions at museums around the world, and dinosaurs have become an enduring part of world culture. The large sizes of some dinosaur groups, as well as their seemingly monstrous and fantastic nature, have ensured dinosaurs' regular appearance in bestselling books and films, such as *Jurassic Park*. Persistent public enthusiasm for the animals has resulted in significant funding for dinosaur science, and new discoveries are regularly covered by the media.

Etymology

The taxon **Dinosauria** was formally named in 1841 by paleontologist Sir Richard Owen, who used it to refer to the "distinct tribe or sub-order of Saurian Reptiles" that were then being recognized in England and around the world. The term is derived from Ancient Greek δεινός *(deinos)*, meaning 'terrible, potent or fearfully great', and σαῦρος *(sauros)*, meaning 'lizard or reptile'. Though the taxonomic name has often been interpreted as a reference to dinosaurs' teeth, claws, and other fearsome characteristics, Owen intended it merely to evoke their size and majesty.

Other prehistoric animals, including mosasaurs, ichthyosaurs, pterosaurs, plesiosaurs, and *Dimetrodon*, while often popularly conceived of as dinosaurs, are not taxonomically classified as dinosaurs.

Definition

Under phylogenetic nomenclature, dinosaurs are usually defined as the group consisting of the most recent common ancestor (MRCA) of *Triceratops* and Neornithes, and all its descendants. It has also been suggested that Dinosauria be defined with respect to the MRCA of *Megalosaurus* and *Iguanodon*, because these were two of the three genera cited by Richard Owen when he recognized the Dinosauria. Both definitions result in the same set of animals being defined as dinosaurs: "Dinosauria = Ornithischia + Saurischia", encompassing ankylosaurians (armored herbivorous quadrupeds), stegosaurians (plated herbivorous quadrupeds), ceratopsians (herbivorous quadrupeds with horns and frills), ornithopods (bipedal or quadrupedal herbivores including "duckbills"), theropods (mostly bipedal carnivores and birds), and sauropodomorphs (mostly large herbivorous quadrupeds with long necks and tails).

Birds are now recognized as being the sole surviving lineage of theropod dinosaurs. In traditional taxonomy, birds were considered a separate class that

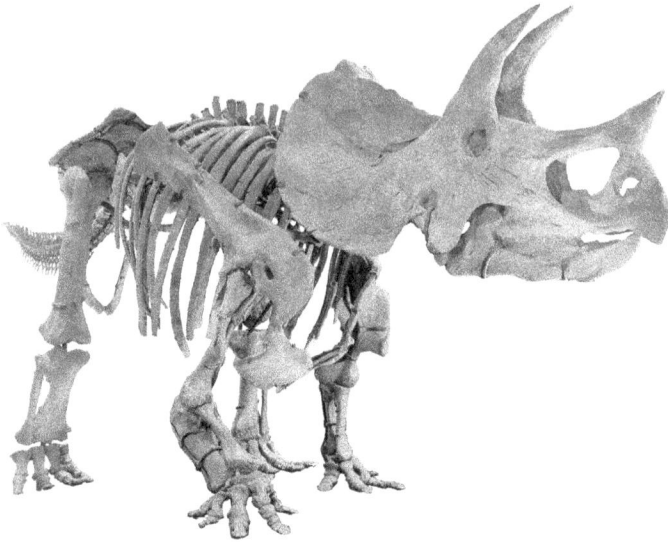

Figure 1: *Triceratops skeleton, Natural History Museum of Los Angeles County*

had evolved from dinosaurs, a distinct superorder. However, a majority of contemporary paleontologists concerned with dinosaurs reject the traditional style of classification in favor of phylogenetic taxonomy; this approach requires that, for a group to be natural, all descendants of members of the group must be included in the group as well. Birds are thus considered to be dinosaurs and dinosaurs are, therefore, not extinct. Birds are classified as belonging to the subgroup Maniraptora, which are coelurosaurs, which are theropods, which are saurischians, which are dinosaurs.[3]

Research by Matthew Baron, David B. Norman, and Paul M. Barrett in 2017 suggested a radical revision of dinosaurian systematics. Phylogenetic analysis by Baron *et al.* recovered the Ornithischia as being closer to the Theropoda than the Sauropodomorpha, as opposed to the traditional union of theropods with sauropodomorphs. They resurrected the clade Ornithoscelida to refer to the group containing Ornithischia and Theropoda. Dinosauria itself was redefined as the last common ancestor of *Triceratops horridus*, *Passer domesticus*, *Diplodocus carnegii*, and all of its descendants, to ensure that sauropods and kin remain included as dinosaurs.

Figure 2: *In phylogenetic taxonomy, birds are included in the group Dinosauria.*

General description

Using one of the above definitions, dinosaurs can be generally described as archosaurs with hind limbs held erect beneath the body. Many prehistoric animal groups are popularly conceived of as dinosaurs, such as ichthyosaurs, mosasaurs, plesiosaurs, pterosaurs, and pelycosaurs (especially *Dimetrodon*), but are not classified scientifically as dinosaurs, and none had the erect hind limb posture characteristic of true dinosaurs. Dinosaurs were the dominant terrestrial vertebrates of the Mesozoic, especially the Jurassic and Cretaceous periods. Other groups of animals were restricted in size and niches; mammals, for example, rarely exceeded the size of a domestic cat, and were generally rodent-sized carnivores of small prey.

Dinosaurs have always been an extremely varied group of animals; according to a 2006 study, over 500 non-avian dinosaur genera have been identified with certainty so far, and the total number of genera preserved in the fossil record has been estimated at around 1850, nearly 75% of which remain to be discovered. An earlier study predicted that about 3,400 dinosaur genera existed, including many that would not have been preserved in the fossil record. By September 17, 2008, 1,047 different species of dinosaurs had been named.

In 2016, the estimated number of dinosaur species that existed in the Mesozoic era was estimated to be 1,543–2,468. Some are herbivorous, others carnivorous, including seed-eaters, fish-eaters, insectivores, and omnivores. While dinosaurs were ancestrally bipedal (as are all modern birds), some prehistoric species were quadrupeds, and others, such as *Anchisaurus* and *Iguanodon*, could walk just as easily on two or four legs. Cranial modifications like horns and crests are common dinosaurian traits, and some extinct species had bony armor. Although known for large size, many Mesozoic dinosaurs were human-sized or smaller, and modern birds are generally small in size. Dinosaurs today inhabit every continent, and fossils show that they had achieved global distribution by at least the early Jurassic period. Modern birds inhabit most available habitats, from terrestrial to marine, and there is evidence that some non-avian dinosaurs (such as *Microraptor*) could fly or at least glide, and others, such as spinosaurids, had semiaquatic habits.

Distinguishing anatomical features

While recent discoveries have made it more difficult to present a universally agreed-upon list of dinosaurs' distinguishing features, nearly all dinosaurs discovered so far share certain modifications to the ancestral archosaurian skeleton, or are clear descendants of older dinosaurs showing these modifications. Although some later groups of dinosaurs featured further modified versions of these traits, they are considered typical for Dinosauria; the earliest dinosaurs had them and passed them on to their descendants. Such modifications, originating in the most recent common ancestor of a certain taxonomic group, are called the synapomorphies of such a group.

A detailed assessment of archosaur interrelations by Sterling Nesbitt confirmed or found the following twelve unambiguous synapomorphies, some previously known:

- in the skull, a supratemporal fossa (excavation) is present in front of the supratemporal fenestra, the main opening in the rear skull roof
- epipophyses, obliquely backward pointing processes on the rear top corners, present in the anterior (front) neck vertebrae behind the atlas and axis, the first two neck vertebrae
- apex of deltopectoral crest (a projection on which the deltopectoral muscles attach) located at or more than 30% down the length of the humerus (upper arm bone)
- radius, a lower arm bone, shorter than 80% of humerus length
- fourth trochanter (projection where the caudofemoralis muscle attaches on the inner rear shaft) on the femur (thighbone) is a sharp flange
- fourth trochanter asymmetrical, with distal, lower, margin forming a steeper angle to the shaft

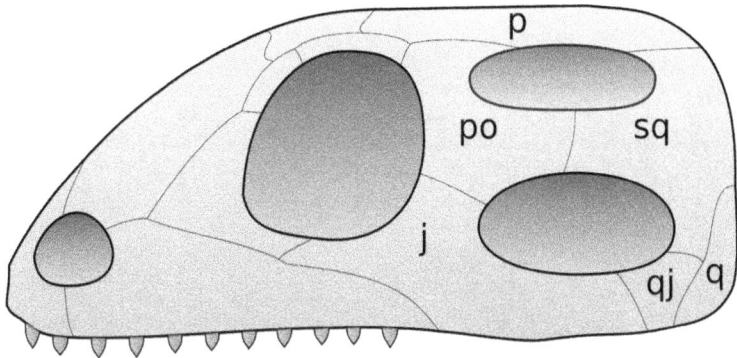

Figure 3: *Diagram of a typical diapsid skull*
j: jugal bone, po: postorbital bone, p: parietal bone, sq:
squamosal bone, q: quadrate bone, qj: quadratojugal bone

- on the astragalus and calcaneum, upper ankle bones, the proximal articular facet, the top connecting surface, for the fibula occupies less than 30% of the transverse width of the element
- exoccipitals (bones at the back of the skull) do not meet along the midline on the floor of the endocranial cavity, the inner space of the braincase
- in the pelvis, the proximal articular surfaces of the ischium with the ilium and the pubis are separated by a large concave surface (on the upper side of the ischium a part of the open hip joint is located between the contacts with the pubic bone and the ilium)
- cnemial crest on the tibia (protruding part of the top surface of the shinbone) arcs anterolaterally (curves to the front and the outer side)
- distinct proximodistally oriented (vertical) ridge present on the posterior face of the distal end of the tibia (the rear surface of the lower end of the shinbone)
- concave articular surface for the fibula of the calcaneum (the top surface of the calcaneum, where it touches the fibula, has a hollow profile)

Nesbitt found a number of further potential synapomorphies, and discounted a number of synapomorphies previously suggested. Some of these are also present in silesaurids, which Nesbitt recovered as a sister group to Dinosauria, including a large anterior trochanter, metatarsals II and IV of subequal length, reduced contact between ischium and pubis, the presence of a cnemial crest on the tibia and of an ascending process on the astragalus, and many others.

A variety of other skeletal features are shared by dinosaurs. However, because they are either common to other groups of archosaurs or were not present in all early dinosaurs, these features are not considered to be synapomorphies. For

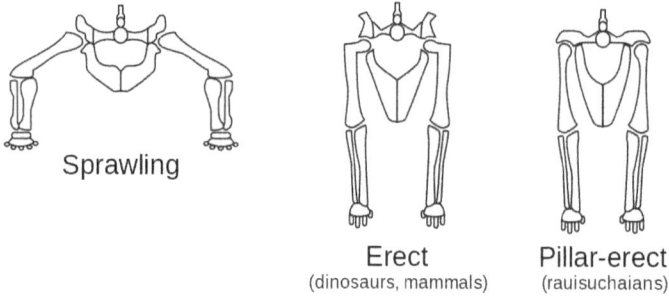

Figure 4: *Hip joints and hindlimb postures of: (left to right) typical reptiles (sprawling), dinosaurs and mammals (erect), and rauisuchians (erect)*

example, as diapsids, dinosaurs ancestrally had two pairs of temporal fenestrae (openings in the skull behind the eyes), and as members of the diapsid group Archosauria, had additional openings in the snout and lower jaw. Additionally, several characteristics once thought to be synapomorphies are now known to have appeared before dinosaurs, or were absent in the earliest dinosaurs and independently evolved by different dinosaur groups. These include an elongated scapula, or shoulder blade; a sacrum composed of three or more fused vertebrae (three are found in some other archosaurs, but only two are found in *Herrerasaurus*); and a perforate acetabulum, or hip socket, with a hole at the center of its inside surface (closed in *Saturnalia*, for example). Another difficulty of determining distinctly dinosaurian features is that early dinosaurs and other archosaurs from the late Triassic are often poorly known and were similar in many ways; these animals have sometimes been misidentified in the literature.

Dinosaurs stand with their hind limbs erect in a manner similar to most modern mammals, but distinct from most other reptiles, whose limbs sprawl out to either side. This posture is due to the development of a laterally facing recess in the pelvis (usually an open socket) and a corresponding inwardly facing distinct head on the femur. Their erect posture enabled early dinosaurs to breathe easily while moving, which likely permitted stamina and activity levels that surpassed those of "sprawling" reptiles. Erect limbs probably also helped support the evolution of large size by reducing bending stresses on limbs. Some non-dinosaurian archosaurs, including rauisuchians, also had erect limbs but achieved this by a "pillar erect" configuration of the hip joint, where instead of having a projection from the femur insert on a socket on the hip, the upper pelvic bone was rotated to form an overhanging shelf.

Evolutionary history

Origins and early evolution

Dinosaurs diverged from their archosaur ancestors during the middle to late Triassic period, roughly 20 million years after the Permian–Triassic extinction event wiped out an estimated 95% of all life on Earth. Radiometric dating of the rock formation that contained fossils from the early dinosaur genus *Eoraptor* at 231.4 million years old establishes its presence in the fossil record at this time. Paleontologists think that *Eoraptor* resembles the common ancestor of all dinosaurs; if this is true, its traits suggest that the first dinosaurs were small, bipedal predators. The discovery of primitive, dinosaur-like ornithodirans such as *Marasuchus* and *Lagerpeton* in Argentinian Middle Triassic strata supports this view; analysis of recovered fossils suggests that these animals were indeed small, bipedal predators. Dinosaurs may have appeared as early as 243 million years ago, as evidenced by remains of the genus *Nyasasaurus* from that period, though known fossils of these animals are too fragmentary to tell if they are dinosaurs or very close dinosaurian relatives.[4] Recently, it has been determined that *Staurikosaurus* from the Santa Maria Formation dates to 233.23 Ma, making it older in geologic age than *Eoraptor*.

When dinosaurs appeared, they were not the dominant terrestrial animals. The terrestrial habitats were occupied by various types of archosauromorphs and therapsids, like cynodonts and rhynchosaurs. Their main competitors were the pseudosuchia, such as aetosaurs, ornithosuchids and rauisuchians, which were more successful than the dinosaurs. Most of these other animals became extinct in the Triassic, in one of two events. First, at about 215 million years ago, a variety of basal archosauromorphs, including the protorosaurs, became extinct. This was followed by the Triassic–Jurassic extinction event (about 200 million years ago), that saw the end of most of the other groups of early archosaurs, like aetosaurs, ornithosuchids, phytosaurs, and rauisuchians. Rhynchosaurs and dicynodonts survived (at least in some areas) at least as late as early-mid Norian and early Rhaetian, respectively, and the exact date of their extinction is uncertain. These losses left behind a land fauna of crocodylomorphs, dinosaurs, mammals, pterosaurians, and turtles. The first few lines of early dinosaurs diversified through the Carnian and Norian stages of the Triassic, possibly by occupying the niches of the groups that became extinct. Also notably, there was a heightened rate of extinction during the Carnian Pluvial Event.

Figure 5: *Skeleton of Marasuchus lilloensis, a dinosaur-like ornithodiran*

Evolution and paleobiogeography

Dinosaur evolution after the Triassic follows changes in vegetation and the location of continents. In the late Triassic and early Jurassic, the continents were connected as the single landmass Pangaea, and there was a world-wide dinosaur fauna mostly composed of coelophysoid carnivores and early sauropodomorph herbivores. Gymnosperm plants (particularly conifers), a potential food source, radiated in the late Triassic. Early sauropodomorphs did not have sophisticated mechanisms for processing food in the mouth, and so must have employed other means of breaking down food farther along the digestive tract. The general homogeneity of dinosaurian faunas continued into the middle and late Jurassic, where most localities had predators consisting of ceratosaurians, spinosauroids, and carnosaurians, and herbivores consisting of stegosaurian ornithischians and large sauropods. Examples of this include the Morrison Formation of North America and Tendaguru Beds of Tanzania. Dinosaurs in China show some differences, with specialized sinraptorid theropods and unusual, long-necked sauropods like *Mamenchisaurus*. Ankylosaurians and ornithopods were also becoming more common, but prosauropods had become extinct. Conifers and pteridophytes were the most common plants. Sauropods, like the earlier prosauropods, were not oral processors, but ornithischians were evolving various means of dealing with food in the mouth, including potential cheek-like organs to keep food in the mouth, and jaw motions to grind food. Another notable evolutionary event of the Jurassic was the appearance of true birds, descended from maniraptoran coelurosaurians.

By the early Cretaceous and the ongoing breakup of Pangaea, dinosaurs were becoming strongly differentiated by landmass. The earliest part of this time

Figure 6: *The early forms Herrerasaurus (large), Eoraptor (small) and a Plateosaurus skull*

saw the spread of ankylosaurians, iguanodontians, and brachiosaurids through Europe, North America, and northern Africa. These were later supplemented or replaced in Africa by large spinosaurid and carcharodontosaurid theropods, and rebbachisaurid and titanosaurian sauropods, also found in South America. In Asia, maniraptoran coelurosaurians like dromaeosaurids, troodontids, and oviraptorosaurians became the common theropods, and ankylosaurids and early ceratopsians like *Psittacosaurus* became important herbivores. Meanwhile, Australia was home to a fauna of basal ankylosaurians, hypsilophodonts, and iguanodontians. The stegosaurians appear to have gone extinct at some point in the late early Cretaceous or early late Cretaceous. A major change in the early Cretaceous, which would be amplified in the late Cretaceous, was the evolution of flowering plants. At the same time, several groups of dinosaurian herbivores evolved more sophisticated ways to orally process food. Ceratopsians developed a method of slicing with teeth stacked on each other in batteries, and iguanodontians refined a method of grinding with tooth batteries, taken to its extreme in hadrosaurids. Some sauropods also evolved tooth batteries, best exemplified by the rebbachisaurid *Nigersaurus*.

There were three general dinosaur faunas in the late Cretaceous. In the northern continents of North America and Asia, the major theropods were tyrannosaurids and various types of smaller maniraptoran theropods, with a predominantly ornithischian herbivore assemblage of hadrosaurids, ceratopsians, ankylosaurids, and pachycephalosaurians. In the southern continents that had made up the now-splitting Gondwana, abelisaurids were the common theropods, and titanosaurian sauropods the common herbivores. Finally, in Europe, dromaeosaurids, rhabdodontid iguanodontians, nodosaurid ankylosaurians, and titanosaurian sauropods were prevalent. Flowering plants were greatly radiating, with the first grasses appearing by the end of the Cretaceous. Grinding hadrosaurids and shearing ceratopsians became extremely diverse across North America and Asia. Theropods were also radiating as herbivores or omnivores, with therizinosaurians and ornithomimosaurians becoming common.

The Cretaceous–Paleogene extinction event, which occurred approximately 66 million years ago at the end of the Cretaceous period, caused the extinction of all dinosaur groups except for the neornithine birds. Some other diapsid groups, such as crocodilians, sebecosuchians, turtles, lizards, snakes, sphenodontians, and choristoderans, also survived the event.

The surviving lineages of neornithine birds, including the ancestors of modern ratites, ducks and chickens, and a variety of waterbirds, diversified rapidly at the beginning of the Paleogene period, entering ecological niches left vacant by the extinction of Mesozoic dinosaur groups such as the arboreal enantiornithines, aquatic hesperornithines, and even the larger terrestrial theropods (in the form of *Gastornis*, eogruiids, bathornithids, ratites, geranoidids, mihirungs, and "terror birds"). It is often cited that mammals out-competed the neornithines for dominance of most terrestrial niches but many of these groups co-existed with rich mammalian faunas for most of the Cenozoic.[5] Terror birds and bathornithids occupied carnivorous guilds alongside predatory mammals,[6] and ratites are still fairly successful as mid-sized herbivores; eogruiids similarly lasted from the Eocene to Pliocene, only becoming extinct very recently after over 20 million years of co-existence with many mammal groups.[7]

Classification

Dinosaurs belong to a group known as archosaurs, which also includes modern crocodilians. Within the archosaur group, dinosaurs are differentiated most noticeably by their gait. Dinosaur legs extend directly beneath the body, whereas the legs of lizards and crocodilians sprawl out to either side.

Collectively, dinosaurs as a clade are divided into two primary branches, Saurischia and Ornithischia. Saurischia includes those taxa sharing a more recent common ancestor with birds than with Ornithischia, while Ornithischia includes all taxa sharing a more recent common ancestor with *Triceratops* than with Saurischia. Anatomically, these two groups can be distinguished most noticeably by their pelvic structure. Early saurischians—"lizard-hipped", from the Greek *sauros* (σαῦρος) meaning "lizard" and *ischion* (ἰσχίον) meaning "hip joint"—retained the hip structure of their ancestors, with a pubis bone directed cranially, or forward. This basic form was modified by rotating the pubis backward to varying degrees in several groups (*Herrerasaurus*, therizinosauroids, dromaeosaurids, and birds). Saurischia includes the theropods (exclusively bipedal and with a wide variety of diets) and sauropodomorphs (long-necked herbivores which include advanced, quadrupedal groups).

By contrast, ornithischians—"bird-hipped", from the Greek *ornitheios* (ὀρνίθειος) meaning "of a bird" and *ischion* (ἰσχίον) meaning "hip joint"—had a pelvis that superficially resembled a bird's pelvis: the pubic bone was oriented caudally (rear-pointing). Unlike birds, the ornithischian pubis also usually had an additional forward-pointing process. Ornithischia includes a variety of species which were primarily herbivores. (**NB:** the terms "lizard hip" and "bird hip" are misnomers – birds evolved from dinosaurs with "lizard hips".)

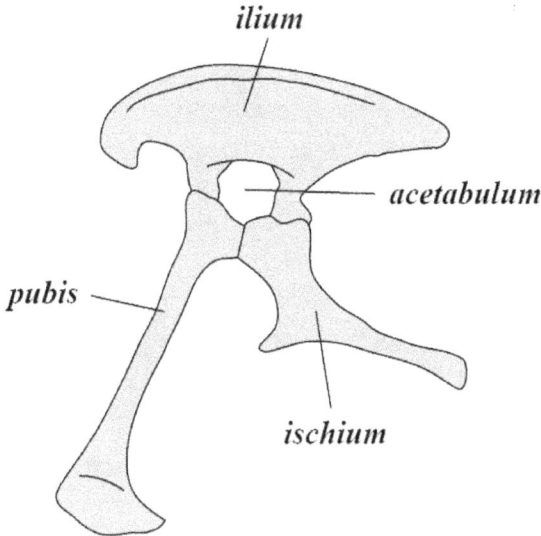

Figure 7: *Saurischian pelvis structure (left side)*

Figure 8: *Tyrannosaurus pelvis (showing saurischian structure – left side)*

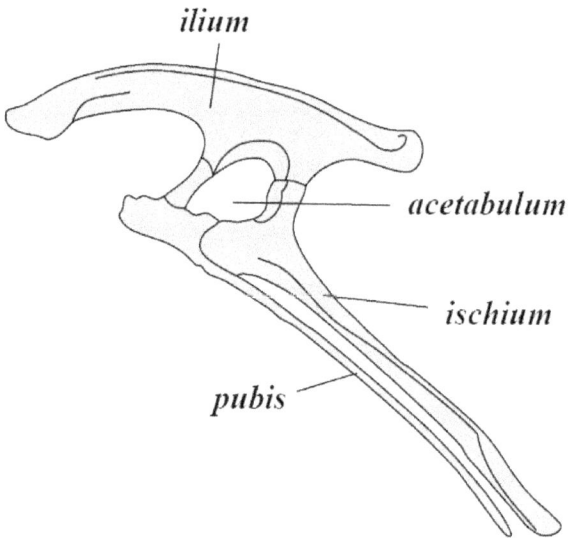

Figure 9: *Ornithischian pelvis structure (left side)*

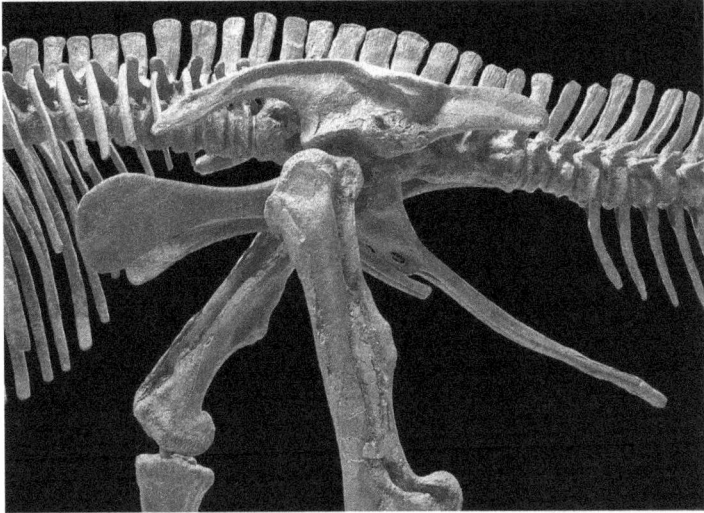

Figure 10: *Edmontosaurus pelvis (showing ornithischian structure – left side)*

Taxonomy

The following is a simplified classification of dinosaur groups based on their evolutionary relationships, and organized based on the list of Mesozoic dinosaur species provided by Holtz (2007). A more detailed version can be found at Dinosaur classification. The dagger (†) is used to signify groups with no living members.

- **Dinosauria**
    - **Saurischia** ("lizard-hipped"; includes Theropoda and Sauropodomorpha)
        - **Theropoda** (all bipedal; most were carnivorous)

            - †Herrerasauria (early bipedal carnivores)
            - †Coelophysoidea (small, early theropods; includes *Coelophysis* and close relatives)
            - †Dilophosauridae (early crested and carnivorous theropods)
            - †Ceratosauria (generally elaborately horned, the dominant southern carnivores of the Cretaceous)
            - Tetanurae ("stiff tails"; includes most theropods)

                - †Megalosauroidea (early group of large carnivores including the semiaquatic spinosaurids)

Figure 11: *Artist's impression of six dromaeosaurid theropods: from left to right Microraptor, Velociraptor, Austroraptor, Dromaeosaurus, Utahraptor, and Deinonychus*

- †Carnosauria (*Allosaurus* and close relatives, like *Carcharodontosaurus*)
- Coelurosauria (feathered theropods, with a range of body sizes and niches)
  - †Compsognathidae (common early coelurosaurs with reduced forelimbs)
  - †Tyrannosauridae (*Tyrannosaurus* and close relatives; had reduced forelimbs)
  - †Ornithomimosauria ("ostrich-mimics"; mostly toothless; carnivores to possible herbivores)
  - †Alvarezsauroidea (small insectivores with reduced forelimbs each bearing one enlarged claw)
  - Maniraptora ("hand snatchers"; had long, slender arms and fingers)
    - †Therizinosauria (bipedal herbivores with large hand claws and small heads)
    - †Oviraptorosauria (mostly toothless; their diet and lifestyle are uncertain)
    - †Archaeopterygidae (small, winged theropods or primitive birds)
    - †Deinonychosauria (small- to medium-sized; bird-like, with a distinctive toe claw)
    - Avialae (modern birds and extinct relatives)
      - †Scansoriopterygidae (small primitive avialans with long third fingers)
      - †Omnivoropterygidae (large, early short-tailed avialans)

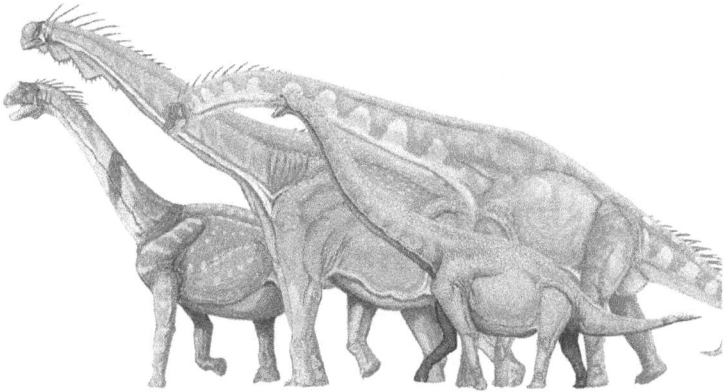

Figure 12: *Artist's impression of four macronarian sauropods: from left to right Camarasaurus, Brachiosaurus, Giraffatitan, and Euhelopus*

- †Confuciusornithidae (small toothless avialans)
- †Enantiornithes (primitive tree-dwelling, flying avialans)
- Euornithes (advanced flying birds)
  - †Yanornithiformes (toothed Cretaceous Chinese birds)
  - †Hesperornithes (specialized aquatic diving birds)
  - **Aves** (modern, beaked birds and their extinct relatives)

- †**Sauropodomorpha** (herbivores with small heads, long necks, long tails)
  - †Guaibasauridae (small, primitive, omnivorous sauropodomorphs)
  - †Plateosauridae (primitive, strictly bipedal "prosauropods")
  - †Riojasauridae (small, primitive sauropodomorphs)
  - †Massospondylidae (small, primitive sauropodomorphs)
  - †Sauropoda (very large and heavy, usually over 15 m (49 ft) long; quadrupedal)
    - †Vulcanodontidae (primitive sauropods with pillar-like limbs)

Figure 13: *Restoration of six ornithopods; far left: Camptosaurus, left: Iguanodon, center background: Shantungosaurus, center foreground: Dryosaurus, right: Corythosaurus, far right (large) Tenontosaurus.*

- †Eusauropoda ("true sauropods")
  - †Cetiosauridae ("whale reptiles")
  - †Turiasauria (European group of Jurassic and Cretaceous sauropods)
  - †Neosauropoda ("new sauropods")
    - †Diplodocoidea (skulls and tails elongated; teeth typically narrow and pencil-like)
    - †Macronaria (boxy skulls; spoon- or pencil-shaped teeth)
      - †Brachiosauridae (long-necked, long-armed macronarians)
      - †Titanosauria (diverse; stocky, with wide hips; most common in the late Cretaceous of southern continents)
- †**Ornithischia** ("bird-hipped"; diverse bipedal and quadrupedal herbivores)
  - †Heterodontosauridae (small basal ornithopod herbivores/omnivores with prominent canine-like teeth)
  - †Thyreophora (armored dinosaurs; mostly quadrupeds)
    - †**Ankylosauria** (scutes as primary armor; some had club-like tails)
    - †**Stegosauria** (spikes and plates as primary armor)

Figure 14: *Scale diagram comparing the average human to the largest known dinosaurs in five major clades: Sauropoda (Argentinosaurus huinculensis), Ornithopoda (Shantungosaurus giganteus), Theropoda (Spinosaurus aegyptiacus), Thyreophora (Stegosaurus armatus) and Marginocephalia (Triceratops prorsus)*

- †Neornithischia ("new ornithischians")
  - †**Ornithopoda** (various sizes; bipeds and quadrupeds; evolved a method of chewing using skull flexibility and numerous teeth)
  - †Marginocephalia (characterized by a cranial growth)
    - †Pachycephalosauria (bipeds with domed or knobby growth on skulls)
    - †**Ceratopsia** (quadrupeds with frills; many also had horns)

Biology

Knowledge about dinosaurs is derived from a variety of fossil and non-fossil records, including fossilized bones, feces, trackways, gastroliths, feathers, impressions of skin, internal organs and soft tissues. Many fields of study contribute to our understanding of dinosaurs, including physics (especially biomechanics), chemistry, biology, and the earth sciences (of which paleontology is a sub-discipline). Two topics of particular interest and study have been dinosaur size and behavior.[8]

Size

Current evidence suggests that dinosaur average size varied through the Triassic, early Jurassic, late Jurassic and Cretaceous periods. Predatory theropod dinosaurs, which occupied most terrestrial carnivore niches during the Mesozoic, most often fall into the 100 to 1000 kg (220 to 2200 lb) category when sorted by estimated weight into categories based on order of magnitude, whereas recent predatory carnivoran mammals peak in the 10 to 100 kg (22 to 220 lb) category. The mode of Mesozoic dinosaur body masses is between one and ten metric tonnes. This contrasts sharply with the size of Cenozoic

Figure 15: *Comparative size of Argentinosaurus to the average human*

mammals, estimated by the National Museum of Natural History as about 2 to 5 kg (4.4 to 11.0 lb).

The sauropods were the largest and heaviest dinosaurs. For much of the dinosaur era, the smallest sauropods were larger than anything else in their habitat, and the largest were an order of magnitude more massive than anything else that has since walked the Earth. Giant prehistoric mammals such as *Paraceratherium* (the largest land mammal ever) were dwarfed by the giant sauropods, and only modern whales approach or surpass them in size. There are several proposed advantages for the large size of sauropods, including protection from predation, reduction of energy use, and longevity, but it may be that the most important advantage was dietary. Large animals are more efficient at digestion than small animals, because food spends more time in their digestive systems. This also permits them to subsist on food with lower nutritive value than smaller animals. Sauropod remains are mostly found in rock formations interpreted as dry or seasonally dry, and the ability to eat large quantities of low-nutrient browse would have been advantageous in such environments.

Largest and smallest

Scientists will probably never be certain of the largest and smallest dinosaurs to have ever existed. This is because only a tiny percentage of animals ever fossilize, and most of these remain buried in the earth. Few of the specimens that are recovered are complete skeletons, and impressions of skin and other soft tissues are rare. Rebuilding a complete skeleton by comparing the size and morphology of bones to those of similar, better-known species is an inexact art, and reconstructing the muscles and other organs of the living animal is, at best, a process of educated guesswork.

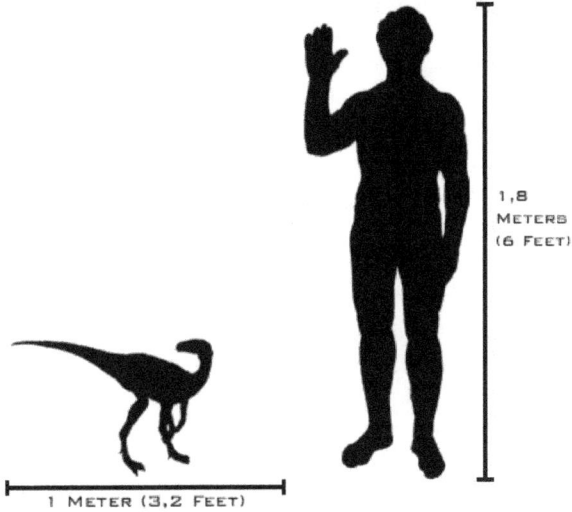

1,8
METERS
(6 FEET)

1 METER (3,2 FEET)

Figure 16: *Comparative size of Eoraptor to the average human*

The tallest and heaviest dinosaur known from good skeletons is *Giraffatitan brancai* (previously classified as a species of *Brachiosaurus*). Its remains were discovered in Tanzania between 1907 and 1912. Bones from several similar-sized individuals were incorporated into the skeleton now mounted and on display at the Museum für Naturkunde Berlin; this mount is 12 meters (39 ft) tall and 21.8–22.5 meters (72–74 ft) long, and would have belonged to an animal that weighed between 30000 and 60000 kilograms (70000 and 130000 lb). The longest complete dinosaur is the 27 meters (89 feet) long *Diplodocus*, which was discovered in Wyoming in the United States and displayed in Pittsburgh's Carnegie Natural History Museum in 1907. The longest dinosaur known from good fossil material is the *Patagotitan*: the skeleton mount in the American Museum of Natural History is 37 meters (121 ft) long. The Carmen Funes Museum has an *Argentinosaurus* reconstructed skeleton mount 39.7 metres (130 ft) long.

There were larger dinosaurs, but knowledge of them is based entirely on a small number of fragmentary fossils. Most of the largest herbivorous specimens on record were discovered in the 1970s or later, and include the massive *Argentinosaurus*, which may have weighed 80000 to 100000 kilograms (90 to 110 short tons) and reached length of 30–40 metres (98–131 ft); some of the longest were the 33.5 meters (110 ft) long *Diplodocus hallorum* (formerly *Seismosaurus*), the 33–34 meters (108–112 ft) long *Supersaurus* and

37 metres (121 ft) long *Patagotitan*; and the tallest, the 18 meters (59 ft) tall *Sauroposeidon*, which could have reached a sixth-floor window. The heaviest and longest dinosaur may have been *Amphicoelias fragillimus*, known only from a now lost partial vertebral neural arch described in 1878. Extrapolating from the illustration of this bone, the animal may have been 58 meters (190 ft) long and weighed 122400 kg (270000 lb). However, as no further evidence of sauropods of this size has been found, and the discoverer, Edward Cope, had made typographic errors before, it is likely to have been an extreme overestimation. As of 2018, *Argentinosaurus* and *Patagotitan* are considered by paleontologists as the largest dinosaurs known from reasonable remains.

The largest carnivorous dinosaur was *Spinosaurus*, reaching a length of 12.6 to 18 meters (41 to 59 ft), and weighing 7–20.9 tonnes (7.7–23 short tons). Other large carnivorous theropods included *Giganotosaurus*, *Carcharodontosaurus* and *Tyrannosaurus*. *Therizinosaurus* and *Deinocheirus* were among the tallest of the theropods. The largest Ornithischian dinosaur was probably the hadrosaurid *Shantungosaurus* which measured 16 metres (52 ft) and weighed about 13 tonnes (29,000 lb).

The smallest dinosaur known is the bee hummingbird,[9] with a length of only 5 cm (2.0 in) and mass of around 1.8 g (0.063 oz). The smallest known non-avialan dinosaurs were about the size of pigeons and were those theropods most closely related to birds. For example, *Anchiornis huxleyi* is currently the smallest non-avialan dinosaur described from an adult specimen, with an estimated weight of 110 grams and a total skeletal length of 34 cm (1.12 ft). The smallest herbivorous non-avialan dinosaurs included *Microceratus* and *Wannanosaurus*, at about 60 cm (2.0 ft) long each.

Behavior

Many modern birds are highly social, often found living in flocks. There is general agreement that some behaviors that are common in birds, as well as in crocodiles (birds' closest living relatives), were also common among extinct dinosaur groups. Interpretations of behavior in fossil species are generally based on the pose of skeletons and their habitat, computer simulations of their biomechanics, and comparisons with modern animals in similar ecological niches.

The first potential evidence for herding or flocking as a widespread behavior common to many dinosaur groups in addition to birds was the 1878 discovery of 31 *Iguanodon bernissartensis*, ornithischians that were then thought to have perished together in Bernissart, Belgium, after they fell into a deep, flooded sinkhole and drowned. Other mass-death sites have been discovered subsequently. Those, along with multiple trackways, suggest that gregarious behavior was common in many early dinosaur species. Trackways of hundreds

Figure 17: *A nesting ground of hadrosaur Maiasaura peeblesorum was discovered in 1978.*

or even thousands of herbivores indicate that duck-bills (hadrosaurids) may have moved in great herds, like the American bison or the African Springbok. Sauropod tracks document that these animals traveled in groups composed of several different species, at least in Oxfordshire, England, although there is no evidence for specific herd structures. Congregating into herds may have evolved for defense, for migratory purposes, or to provide protection for young. There is evidence that many types of slow-growing dinosaurs, including various theropods, sauropods, ankylosaurians, ornithopods, and ceratopsians, formed aggregations of immature individuals. One example is a site in Inner Mongolia that has yielded the remains of over 20 *Sinornithomimus*, from one to seven years old. This assemblage is interpreted as a social group that was trapped in mud. The interpretation of dinosaurs as gregarious has also extended to depicting carnivorous theropods as pack hunters working together to bring down large prey. However, this lifestyle is uncommon among modern birds, crocodiles, and other reptiles, and the taphonomic evidence suggesting mammal-like pack hunting in such theropods as *Deinonychus* and *Allosaurus* can also be interpreted as the results of fatal disputes between feeding animals, as is seen in many modern diapsid predators.

The crests and frills of some dinosaurs, like the marginocephalians, theropods and lambeosaurines, may have been too fragile to be used for active defense,

Figure 18: *Artist's rendering of two Centrosaurus apertus engaged in intra-specific combat*

and so they were likely used for sexual or aggressive displays, though little is known about dinosaur mating and territorialism. Head wounds from bites suggest that theropods, at least, engaged in active aggressive confrontations.

From a behavioral standpoint, one of the most valuable dinosaur fossils was discovered in the Gobi Desert in 1971. It included a *Velociraptor* attacking a *Protoceratops*, providing evidence that dinosaurs did indeed attack each other. Additional evidence for attacking live prey is the partially healed tail of an *Edmontosaurus*, a hadrosaurid dinosaur; the tail is damaged in such a way that shows the animal was bitten by a tyrannosaur but survived. Cannibalism amongst some species of dinosaurs was confirmed by tooth marks found in Madagascar in 2003, involving the theropod *Majungasaurus*.

Comparisons between the scleral rings of dinosaurs and modern birds and reptiles have been used to infer daily activity patterns of dinosaurs. Although it has been suggested that most dinosaurs were active during the day, these comparisons have shown that small predatory dinosaurs such as dromaeosaurids, *Juravenator*, and *Megapnosaurus* were likely nocturnal. Large and medium-sized herbivorous and omnivorous dinosaurs such as ceratopsians, sauropodomorphs, hadrosaurids, ornithomimosaurs may have been cathemeral, active during short intervals throughout the day, although the small ornithischian *Agilisaurus* was inferred to be diurnal.

Based on current fossil evidence from dinosaurs such as *Oryctodromeus*, some ornithischian species seem to have led a partially fossorial (burrowing) lifestyle. Many modern birds are arboreal (tree climbing), and this was also true of many Mesozoic birds, especially the enantiornithines.[10] While some

Figure 19: *Artist's impression of a striking and un-usual visual display in a Lambeosaurus magnicristatus*

early bird-like species may have already been arboreal as well (including dro-maeosaurids such as *Microraptor*) most non-avialan dinosaurs seem to have relied on land-based locomotion. A good understanding of how dinosaurs moved on the ground is key to models of dinosaur behavior; the science of biomechanics, pioneered by Robert McNeill Alexander, has provided signif-icant insight in this area. For example, studies of the forces exerted by mus-cles and gravity on dinosaurs' skeletal structure have investigated how fast di-nosaurs could run, whether diplodocids could create sonic booms via whip-like tail snapping, and whether sauropods could float.

Communication

Modern birds are known to communicate using visual and auditory signals, and the wide diversity of visual display structures among fossil dinosaur groups, such as horns, frills, crests, sails and feathers, suggests that visual communication has always been important in dinosaur biology. Reconstruc-tion of the plumage color of *Anchiornis huxleyi*, suggest the importance of color in visual communication in non-avian dinosaurs. The evolution of di-nosaur vocalization is less certain. Paleontologist Phil Senter suggests that non-avian dinosaurs relied mostly on visual displays and possibly non-vocal acoustic sounds like hissing, jaw grinding or clapping, splashing and wing beating (possible in winged maniraptoran dinosaurs). He states they were unlikely to have been capable of vocalizing since their closest relatives, crocodilians and birds, use different means to vocalize, the former via the larynx and the latter through the unique syrinx, suggesting they evolved independently and their common ancestor was mute.

The earliest remains of a syrinx, which has enough mineral content for fossilization, was found in a specimen of the duck-like *Vegavis iaai* dated 69-66 million year ago, and this organ is unlikely to have existed in non-avian dinosaurs. However, in contrast to Senter, the researchers have suggested that dinosaurs could vocalize and that the syrinx-based vocal system of birds evolved from a larynx-based one, rather than the two systems evolving independently. A 2016 study suggests that dinosaurs produced closed mouth vocalizations like cooing, which occur in both crocodilians and birds as well as other reptiles. Such vocalizations evolved independently in extant archosaurs numerous times, following increases in body size. The crests of the Lambeosaurini and nasal chambers of ankylosaurids have been suggested to function in vocal resonance, though Senter states that the presence of resonance chambers in some dinosaurs is not necessarily evidence of vocalization as modern snakes have such chambers which intensify their hisses.

Reproductive biology

All dinosaurs lay amniotic eggs with hard shells made mostly of calcium carbonate. Eggs are usually laid in a nest. Most species create somewhat elaborate nests, which can be cups, domes, plates, beds scrapes, mounds, or burrows.[11] Some species of modern bird have no nests; the cliff-nesting common guillemot lays its eggs on bare rock, and male emperor penguins keep eggs between their body and feet. Primitive birds and many non-avialan dinosaurs often lay eggs in communal nests, with males primarily incubating the eggs. While modern birds have only one functional oviduct and lay one egg at a time, more primitive birds and dinosaurs had two oviducts, like crocodiles. Some non-avialan dinosaurs, such as *Troodon*, exhibited iterative laying, where the adult might lay a pair of eggs every one or two days, and then ensured simultaneous hatching by delaying brooding until all eggs were laid.

When laying eggs, females grow a special type of bone between the hard outer bone and the marrow of their limbs. This medullary bone, which is rich in calcium, is used to make eggshells. A discovery of features in a *Tyrannosaurus rex* skeleton provided evidence of medullary bone in extinct dinosaurs and, for the first time, allowed paleontologists to establish the sex of a fossil dinosaur specimen. Further research has found medullary bone in the carnosaur *Allosaurus* and the ornithopod *Tenontosaurus*. Because the line of dinosaurs

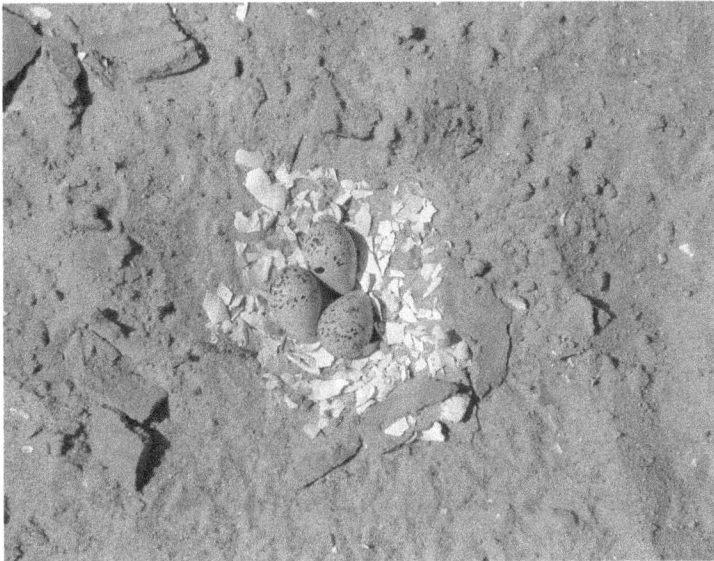

Figure 20: *Nest of a plover (Charadrius)*

that includes *Allosaurus* and *Tyrannosaurus* diverged from the line that led to *Tenontosaurus* very early in the evolution of dinosaurs, this suggests that the production of medullary tissue is a general characteristic of all dinosaurs.

Another widespread trait among modern birds (but see below in regards to fossil groups and extant megapodes) is parental care for young after hatching. Jack Horner's 1978 discovery of a *Maiasaura* ("good mother lizard") nesting ground in Montana demonstrated that parental care continued long after birth among ornithopods. A specimen of the Mongolian oviraptorid *Citipati osmolskae* was discovered in a chicken-like brooding position in 1993, which may indicate that they had begun using an insulating layer of feathers to keep the eggs warm. A dinosaur embryo (pertaining to the prosauropod *Massospondylus*) was found without teeth, indicating that some parental care was required to feed the young dinosaurs. Trackways have also confirmed parental behavior among ornithopods from the Isle of Skye in northwestern Scotland.

However, there is ample evidence of supreprecociality among many dinosaur species, particularly theropods. For instance, non-ornithuromorph birds have been abundantly demonstrated to have had slow growth rates, megapode-like egg burying behaviour and the ability to fly soon after birth.[12] Both *Tyrannosaurus rex* and *Troodon formosus* display juveniles with clear supreprecociality and likely occupying different ecological niches than the adults.[13] Superprecociality has been inferred for sauropods.[14]

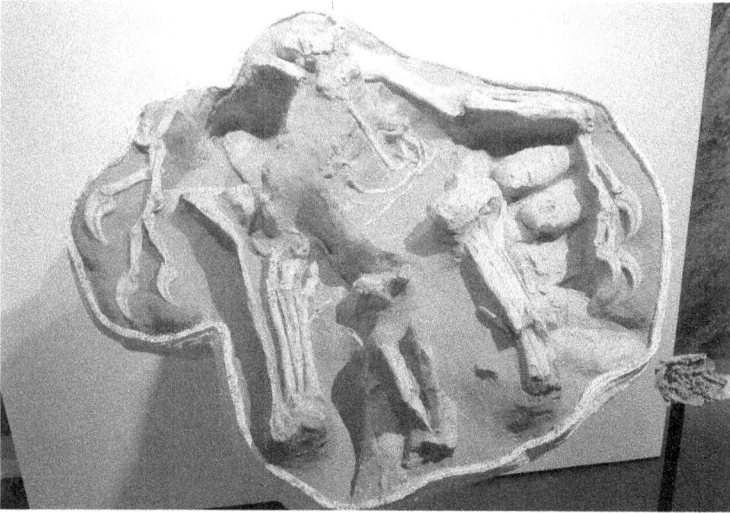

Figure 21: *Fossil interpreted as a nesting oviraptorid Citipati at the American Museum of Natural History. Smaller fossil far right showing inside one of the eggs.*

Physiology

Because both modern crocodilians and birds have four-chambered hearts (albeit modified in crocodilians), it is likely that this is a trait shared by all archosaurs, including all dinosaurs. While all modern birds have high metabolisms and are "warm blooded" (endothermic), a vigorous debate has been ongoing since the 1960s regarding how far back in the dinosaur lineage this trait extends. Scientists disagree as to whether non-avian dinosaurs were endothermic, ectothermic, or some combination of both.

After non-avian dinosaurs were discovered, paleontologists first posited that they were ectothermic. This supposed "cold-bloodedness" was used to imply that the ancient dinosaurs were relatively slow, sluggish organisms, even though many modern reptiles are fast and light-footed despite relying on external sources of heat to regulate their body temperature. The idea of dinosaurs as ectothermic and sluggish remained a prevalent view until Robert T. "Bob" Bakker, an early proponent of dinosaur endothermy, published an influential paper on the topic in 1968.

Modern evidence indicates that even non-avian dinosaurs and birds thrived in cooler temperate climates, and that at least some early species must have regulated their body temperature by internal biological means (aided by the animals' bulk in large species and feathers or other body coverings in smaller

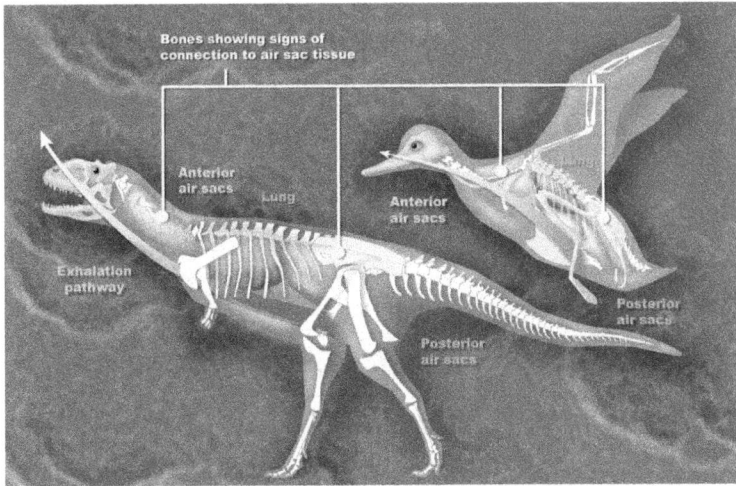

Figure 22: *Comparison between the air sacs of an abelisaur and a bird*

species). Evidence of endothermy in Mesozoic dinosaurs includes the discovery of polar dinosaurs in Australia and Antarctica as well as analysis of blood-vessel structures within fossil bones that are typical of endotherms. Scientific debate continues regarding the specific ways in which dinosaur temperature regulation evolved.

In saurischian dinosaurs, higher metabolisms were supported by the evolution of the avian respiratory system, characterized by an extensive system of air sacs that extended the lungs and invaded many of the bones in the skeleton, making them hollow. Early avian-style respiratory systems with air sacs may have been capable of sustaining higher activity levels than those of mammals of similar size and build. In addition to providing a very efficient supply of oxygen, the rapid airflow would have been an effective cooling mechanism, which is essential for animals that are active but too large to get rid of all the excess heat through their skin.

Like other reptiles, dinosaurs are primarily uricotelic, that is, their kidneys extract nitrogenous wastes from their bloodstream and excrete it as uric acid instead of urea or ammonia via the ureters into the intestine. In most living species, uric acid is excreted along with feces as a semisolid waste. However, at least some modern birds (such as hummingbirds) can be facultatively ammonotelic, excreting most of the nitrogenous wastes as ammonia. They also excrete creatine, rather than creatinine like mammals. This material, as well as the output of the intestines, emerges from the cloaca. In addition, many species regurgitate pellets, and fossil pellets that may have come from dinosaurs are known from as long ago as the Cretaceous period.

Origin of birds

The possibility that dinosaurs were the ancestors of birds was first suggested in 1868 by Thomas Henry Huxley. After the work of Gerhard Heilmann in the early 20th century, the theory of birds as dinosaur descendants was abandoned in favor of the idea of their being descendants of generalized thecodonts, with the key piece of evidence being the supposed lack of clavicles in dinosaurs. However, as later discoveries showed, clavicles (or a single fused wishbone, which derived from separate clavicles) were not actually absent; they had been found as early as 1924 in *Oviraptor*, but misidentified as an interclavicle. In the 1970s, John Ostrom revived the dinosaur–bird theory, which gained momentum in the coming decades with the advent of cladistic analysis, and a great increase in the discovery of small theropods and early birds. Of particular note have been the fossils of the Yixian Formation, where a variety of theropods and early birds have been found, often with feathers of some type. Birds share over a hundred distinct anatomical features with theropod dinosaurs, which are now generally accepted to have been their closest ancient relatives. They are most closely allied with maniraptoran coelurosaurs. A minority of scientists, most notably Alan Feduccia and Larry Martin, have proposed other evolutionary paths, including revised versions of Heilmann's basal archosaur proposal, or that maniraptoran theropods are the ancestors of birds but themselves are not dinosaurs, only convergent with dinosaurs.

Feathers

Feathers are one of the most recognizable characteristics of modern birds, and a trait that was shared by all other dinosaur groups. Based on the current distribution of fossil evidence, it appears that feathers were an ancestral dinosaurian trait, though one that may have been selectively lost in some species. Direct fossil evidence of feathers or feather-like structures has been discovered in a diverse array of species in many non-avian dinosaur groups, both among saurischians and ornithischians. Simple, branched, feather-like structures are known from heterodontosaurids, primitive neornithischians[15] and theropods, and primitive ceratopsians. Evidence for true, vaned feathers similar to the flight feathers of modern birds has been found only in the theropod subgroup Maniraptora, which includes oviraptorosaurs, troodontids, dromaeosaurids, and birds. Feather-like structures known as pycnofibres have also been found in pterosaurs, suggesting the possibility that feather-like filaments may have been common in the bird lineage and evolved before the

Figure 23: *Various feathered non-avian dinosaurs, including Archaeopteryx, Anchiornis, Microraptor and Zhenyuanlong*

appearance of dinosaurs themselves. Research into the genetics of American alligators has also revealed that crocodylian scutes do possess feather-keratins during embryonic development, but these keratins are not expressed by the animals before hatching.

Archaeopteryx was the first fossil found that revealed a potential connection between dinosaurs and birds. It is considered a transitional fossil, in that it displays features of both groups. Brought to light just two years after Darwin's seminal *The Origin of Species*, its discovery spurred the nascent debate between proponents of evolutionary biology and creationism. This early bird is so dinosaur-like that, without a clear impression of feathers in the surrounding rock, at least one specimen was mistaken for *Compsognathus*. Since the 1990s, a number of additional feathered dinosaurs have been found, providing even stronger evidence of the close relationship between dinosaurs and modern birds. Most of these specimens were unearthed in the lagerstätte of the Yixian Formation, Liaoning, northeastern China, which was part of an island continent during the Cretaceous. Though feathers have been found in only a few locations, it is possible that non-avian dinosaurs elsewhere in the world were also feathered. The lack of widespread fossil evidence for feathered non-avian dinosaurs may be because delicate features like skin and feathers are not often preserved by fossilization and thus are absent from the fossil record.

The description of feathered dinosaurs has not been without controversy; perhaps the most vocal critics have been Alan Feduccia and Theagarten Lingham-Soliar, who have proposed that some purported feather-like fossils are the result of the decomposition of collagenous fiber that underlaid the dinosaurs' skin, and that maniraptoran dinosaurs with vaned feathers were not actually dinosaurs, but convergent with dinosaurs. However, their views have for the most part not been accepted by other researchers, to the point that the scientific nature of Feduccia's proposals has been questioned.

In 2016, it was reported that a dinosaur tail with feathers had been found enclosed in amber. The fossil is about 99 million years old.

Skeleton

Because feathers are often associated with birds, feathered dinosaurs are often touted as the missing link between birds and dinosaurs. However, the multiple skeletal features also shared by the two groups represent another important line of evidence for paleontologists. Areas of the skeleton with important similarities include the neck, pubis, wrist (semi-lunate carpal), arm and pectoral girdle, furcula (wishbone), and breast bone. Comparison of bird and dinosaur skeletons through cladistic analysis strengthens the case for the link.[16]

Soft anatomy

Large meat-eating dinosaurs had a complex system of air sacs similar to those found in modern birds, according to a 2005 investigation led by Patrick M. O'Connor. The lungs of theropod dinosaurs (carnivores that walked on two legs and had bird-like feet) likely pumped air into hollow sacs in their skeletons, as is the case in birds. "What was once formally considered unique to birds was present in some form in the ancestors of birds", O'Connor said. In 2008, scientists described *Aerosteon riocoloradensis*, the skeleton of which supplies the strongest evidence to date of a dinosaur with a bird-like breathing system. CT-scanning of *Aerosteon*'s fossil bones revealed evidence for the existence of air sacs within the animal's body cavity.

Behavioral evidence

Fossils of the troodonts *Mei* and *Sinornithoides* demonstrate that some dinosaurs slept with their heads tucked under their arms. This behavior, which may have helped to keep the head warm, is also characteristic of modern birds. Several deinonychosaur and oviraptorosaur specimens have also been found preserved on top of their nests, likely brooding in a bird-like manner. The ratio between egg volume and body mass of adults among these dinosaurs

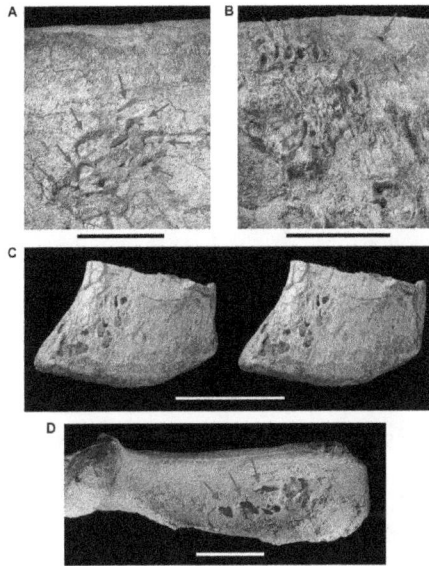

Figure 24: *Pneumatopores on the left ilium of Aerosteon riocoloradensis*

suggest that the eggs were primarily brooded by the male, and that the young were highly precocial, similar to many modern ground-dwelling birds.

Some dinosaurs are known to have used gizzard stones like modern birds. These stones are swallowed by animals to aid digestion and break down food and hard fibers once they enter the stomach. When found in association with fossils, gizzard stones are called gastroliths.

Extinction of major groups

The discovery that birds are a type of dinosaur showed that dinosaurs in general are not, in fact, extinct as is commonly stated.[17] However, all non-avian dinosaurs, estimated to have been 628-1078 species,[18] as well as many groups of birds did suddenly become extinct approximately 66 million years ago. It has been suggested that because small mammals, squamata and birds occupied the ecological niches suited for small body size, non-avian dinosaurs never evolved a diverse fauna of small-bodied species, which led to their downfall when large-bodied terrestrial tetrapods were hit by the mass extinction event. Many other groups of animals also became extinct at this time, including ammonites (nautilus-like mollusks), mosasaurs, plesiosaurs, pterosaurs, and many groups of mammals. Significantly, the insects suffered no discernible population loss, which left them available as food for other survivors. This mass

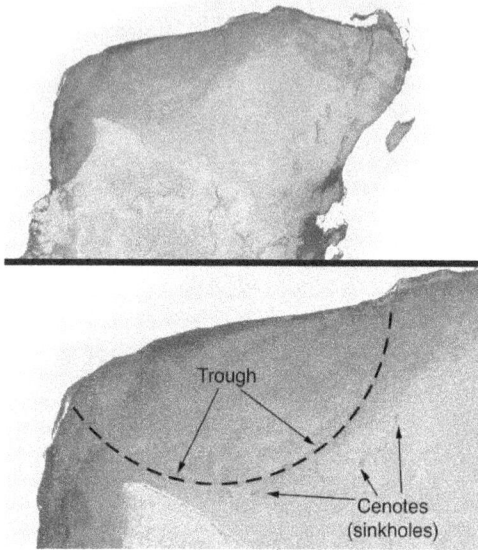

Figure 25: *The Chicxulub Crater at the tip of the Yucatán Peninsula; the impactor that formed this crater may have caused the dinosaur extinction.*

extinction is known as the Cretaceous–Paleogene extinction event. The nature of the event that caused this mass extinction has been extensively studied since the 1970s; at present, several related theories are supported by paleontologists. Though the consensus is that an impact event was the primary cause of dinosaur extinction, some scientists cite other possible causes, or support the idea that a confluence of several factors was responsible for the sudden disappearance of dinosaurs from the fossil record.[19]

Impact event

The asteroid collision theory, which was brought to wide attention in 1980 by Walter Alvarez and colleagues, links the extinction event at the end of the Cretaceous period to a bolide impact approximately 66 million years ago.[20] Alvarez *et al.* proposed that a sudden increase in iridium levels, recorded around the world in the period's rock stratum, was direct evidence of the impact. The bulk of the evidence now suggests that a bolide 5 to 15 kilometers (3.1 to 9.3 miles) wide hit in the vicinity of the Yucatán Peninsula (in southeastern Mexico), creating the approximately 180 km (110 mi) Chicxulub Crater and triggering the mass extinction. Scientists are not certain whether dinosaurs were thriving or declining before the impact event. Some scientists propose that the meteorite impact caused a long and unnatural drop in Earth's atmospheric temperature, while others claim that it would have instead created an unusual heat wave. The consensus among scientists who support this theory is that the impact caused extinctions both directly (by heat from the meteorite impact) and also indirectly (via a worldwide cooling brought about when matter ejected from the impact crater reflected thermal radiation from the sun). Although the speed of extinction cannot be deduced from the fossil record alone, various models suggest that the extinction was extremely rapid, being down to hours rather than years.

Deccan Traps

Before 2000, arguments that the Deccan Traps flood basalts caused the extinction were usually linked to the view that the extinction was gradual, as the flood basalt events were thought to have started around 68 million years ago and lasted for over 2 million years. However, there is evidence that two thirds of the Deccan Traps were created in only 1 million years about 66 million years ago, and so these eruptions would have caused a fairly rapid extinction, possibly over a period of thousands of years, but still longer than would be expected from a single impact event.

The Deccan Traps in India could have caused extinction through several mechanisms, including the release into the air of dust and sulfuric aerosols, which might have blocked sunlight and thereby reduced photosynthesis in plants. In addition, Deccan Trap volcanism might have resulted in carbon dioxide emissions, which would have increased the greenhouse effect when the dust and aerosols cleared from the atmosphere. Before the mass extinction of the dinosaurs, the release of volcanic gases during the formation of the Deccan Traps "contributed to an apparently massive global warming. Some data point to an average rise in temperature of 8 °C (14 °F) in the last half million years before the impact [at Chicxulub]."

In the years when the Deccan Traps theory was linked to a slower extinction, Luis Alvarez (who died in 1988) replied that paleontologists were being misled by sparse data. While his assertion was not initially well-received, later intensive field studies of fossil beds lent weight to his claim. Eventually, most paleontologists began to accept the idea that the mass extinctions at the end of the Cretaceous were largely or at least partly due to a massive Earth impact. However, even Walter Alvarez has acknowledged that there were other major changes on Earth even before the impact, such as a drop in sea level and massive volcanic eruptions that produced the Indian Deccan Traps, and these may have contributed to the extinctions.

Possible Paleocene survivors

Non-avian dinosaur remains are occasionally found above the Creta-ceous–Paleogene boundary. In 2001, paleontologists Zielinski and Budahn reported the discovery of a single hadrosaur leg-bone fossil in the San Juan Basin, New Mexico, and described it as evidence of Paleocene dinosaurs. The formation in which the bone was discovered has been dated to the early Pa-leocene epoch, approximately 64.5 million years ago. If the bone was not re-deposited into that stratum by weathering action, it would provide evi-dence that some dinosaur populations may have survived at least a half million years into the Cenozoic Era. Other evidence includes the finding of dinosaur remains in the Hell Creek Formation up to 1.3 m (51 in) above the Creta-ceous–Paleogene boundary, representing 40000 years of elapsed time. Similar reports have come from other parts of the world, including China. Many sci-entists, however, dismissed the supposed Paleocene dinosaurs as re-worked, that is, washed out of their original locations and then re-buried in much later sediments. Direct dating of the bones themselves has supported the later date, with U–Pb dating methods resulting in a precise age of 64.8 ± 0.9 million years ago. If correct, the presence of a handful of dinosaurs in the early Paleocene would not change the underlying facts of the extinction.

History of study

Dinosaur fossils have been known for millennia, although their true nature was not recognized. The Chinese, whose modern word for dinosaur is kǒnglóng (恐龍, or "terrible dragon"), considered them to be dragon bones and documented them as such. For example, Hua Yang Guo Zhi, a book written by Chang Qu during the Western Jin Dynasty (265–316), reported the discovery of dragon bones at Wucheng in Sichuan Province. Villagers in central China have long unearthed fossilized "dragon bones" for use in traditional medicines, a practice that continues today. In Europe, dinosaur fossils were generally believed to be the remains of giants and other biblical creatures.[21]

Scholarly descriptions of what would now be recognized as dinosaur bones first appeared in the late 17th century in England. Part of a bone, now known to have been the femur of a Megalosaurus, was recovered from a limestone quarry at Cornwell near Chipping Norton, Oxfordshire, in 1676. The fragment was sent to Robert Plot, Professor of Chemistry at the University of Oxford and first curator of the Ashmolean Museum, who published a description in his Natural History of Oxfordshire in 1677. He correctly identified the bone as the lower extremity of the femur of a large animal, and recognized that it was too large to belong to any known species. He therefore concluded it to be the thigh bone of a giant human similar to those mentioned in the Bible. In

Figure 26: *William Buckland*

1699, Edward Lhuyd, a friend of Sir Isaac Newton, was responsible for the first published scientific treatment of what would now be recognized as a dinosaur when he described and named a sauropod tooth, "Rutellum implicatum", that had been found in Caswell, near Witney, Oxfordshire.

Between 1815 and 1824, the Rev William Buckland, a professor of geology at Oxford, collected more fossilized bones of *Megalosaurus* and became the first person to describe a dinosaur in a scientific journal. The second dinosaur genus to be identified, *Iguanodon*, was discovered in 1822 by Mary Ann Mantell – the wife of English geologist Gideon Mantell. Gideon Mantell recognized similarities between his fossils and the bones of modern iguanas. He published his findings in 1825.

The study of these "great fossil lizards" soon became of great interest to European and American scientists, and in 1842 the English paleontologist Richard Owen coined the term "dinosaur". He recognized that the remains that had been found so far, *Iguanodon*, *Megalosaurus* and *Hylaeosaurus*, shared a number of distinctive features, and so decided to present them as a distinct taxonomic group. With the backing of Prince Albert, the husband of Queen Victoria, Owen established the Natural History Museum, London, to display the national collection of dinosaur fossils and other biological and geological exhibits.[22]

In 1858, William Parker Foulke discovered the first known American dinosaur, in marl pits in the small town of Haddonfield, New Jersey. (Although fossils had been found before, their nature had not been correctly discerned.) The creature was named *Hadrosaurus foulkii*. It was an extremely important find: *Hadrosaurus* was one of the first nearly complete dinosaur skeletons found

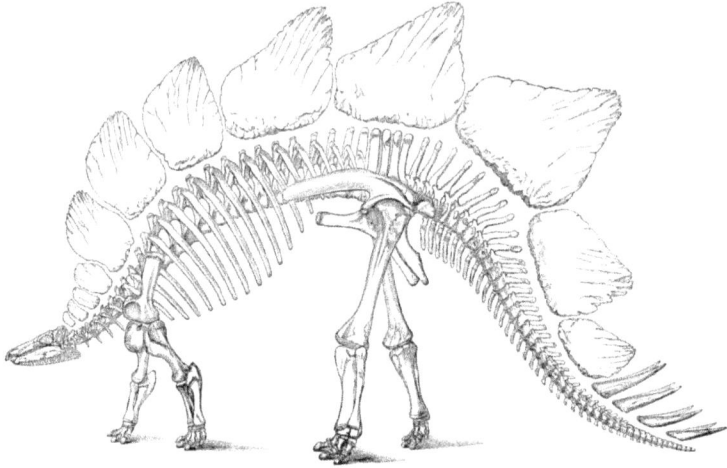

Figure 27: *Marsh's 1896 illustration of the bones of Stegosaurus, a dinosaur he described and named in 1877*

(the first was in 1834, in Maidstone, England), and it was clearly a bipedal creature. This was a revolutionary discovery as, until that point, most scientists had believed dinosaurs walked on four feet, like other lizards. Foulke's discoveries sparked a wave of dinosaur mania in the United States.

Edward Drinker Cope

Othniel Charles Marsh

Dinosaur mania was exemplified by the fierce rivalry between Edward Drinker Cope and Othniel Charles Marsh, both of whom raced to be the first to find new dinosaurs in what came to be known as the Bone Wars. The feud probably originated when Marsh publicly pointed out that Cope's reconstruction of an *Elasmosaurus* skeleton was flawed: Cope had inadvertently placed the plesiosaur's head at what should have been the animal's tail end. The fight between the two scientists lasted for over 30 years, ending in 1897 when Cope died after spending his entire fortune on the dinosaur hunt. Marsh 'won' the contest primarily because he was better funded through a relationship with the US Geological Survey. Unfortunately, many valuable dinosaur specimens were damaged or destroyed due to the pair's rough methods: for example, their diggers often used dynamite to unearth bones (a method modern paleontologists would find appalling). Despite their unrefined methods, the contributions of Cope and Marsh to paleontology were vast: Marsh unearthed 86 new species of dinosaur and Cope discovered 56, a total of 142 new species. Cope's collection is now at the American Museum of Natural History in New York, while Marsh's is on display at the Peabody Museum of Natural History at Yale University.

After 1897, the search for dinosaur fossils extended to every continent, including Antarctica. The first Antarctic dinosaur to be discovered, the ankylosaurid *Antarctopelta oliveroi*, was found on James Ross Island in 1986, although it was 1994 before an Antarctic species, the theropod *Cryolophosaurus ellioti*, was formally named and described in a scientific journal.

Current dinosaur "hot spots" include southern South America (especially Argentina) and China. China in particular has produced many exceptional feathered dinosaur specimens due to the unique geology of its dinosaur beds, as well as an ancient arid climate particularly conducive to fossilization.

"Dinosaur renaissance"

The field of dinosaur research has enjoyed a surge in activity that began in the 1970s and is ongoing. This was triggered, in part, by John Ostrom's discovery of *Deinonychus*, an active predator that may have been warm-blooded, in marked contrast to the then-prevailing image of dinosaurs as sluggish and cold-blooded. Vertebrate paleontology has become a global science. Major new dinosaur discoveries have been made by paleontologists working in previously unexploited regions, including India, South America, Madagascar, Antarctica, and most significantly China (the amazingly well-preserved feathered dinosaurs in China have further consolidated the link between dinosaurs and their living descendants, modern birds). The widespread application of cladistics, which rigorously analyzes the relationships between biological organisms, has also proved tremendously useful in classifying dinosaurs. Cladistic analysis, among other modern techniques, helps to compensate for an often incomplete and fragmentary fossil record.[23]

Figure 28: *Paleontologist Robert T. Bakker with mounted skeleton of a tyrannosaurid (Gorgosaurus libratus)*

Timeline of notable dinosaur taxonomic descriptions

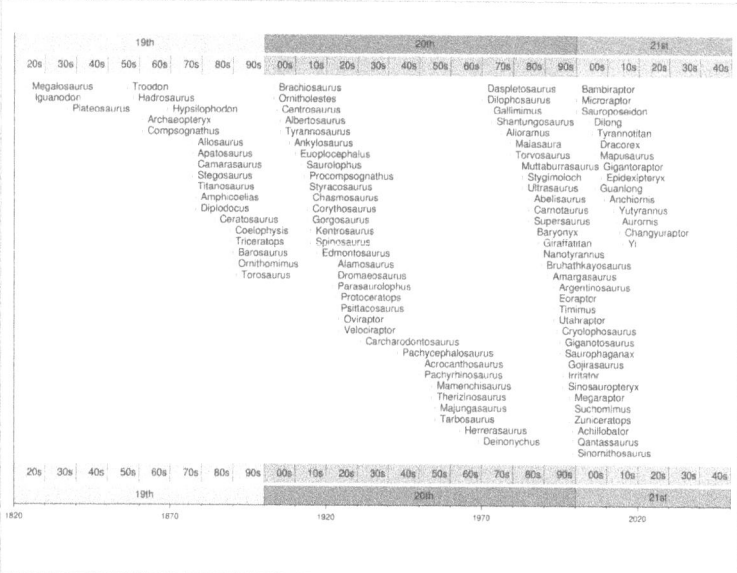

19th	20th	21st
20s 30s 40s 50s 60s 70s 80s 90s	00s 10s 20s 30s 40s 50s 60s 70s 80s 90s	00s 10s 20s 30s 40s

Megalosaurus
Iguanodon
Plateosaurus
Troodon
Hadrosaurus
Hypsilophodon
Archaeopteryx
Compsognathus
Allosaurus
Apatosaurus
Camarasaurus
Stegosaurus
Titanosaurus
Amphicoelias
Diplodocus
Ceratosaurus
Coelophysis
Triceratops
Barosaurus
Ornithomimus
Torosaurus

Brachiosaurus
Ornitholestes
Centrosaurus
Albertosaurus
Tyrannosaurus
Ankylosaurus
Euoplocephalus
Saurolophus
Procompsognathus
Styracosaurus
Corythosaurus
Chasmosaurus
Gorgosaurus
Kentrosaurus
Spinosaurus
Edmontosaurus
Alamosaurus
Dromaeosaurus
Parasaurolophus
Protoceratops
Psittacosaurus
Oviraptor
Velociraptor
Carcharodontosaurus
Pachycephalosaurus
Acrocanthosaurus
Pachyrhinosaurus
Mamenchisaurus
Therizinosaurus
Majungasaurus
Tarbosaurus
Herrerasaurus
Deinonychus

Daspletosaurus
Dilophosaurus
Gallimimus
Shantungosaurus
Alioramus
Maiasaura
Torvosaurus
Muttaburrasaurus
Stygimoloch
Ultrasauros
Abelisaurus
Carnotaurus
Supersaurus
Baryonyx
Giraffatitan
Nanotyrannus
Bruhathkayosaurus
Amargasaurus
Argentinosaurus
Eoraptor
Timimus
Utahraptor
Cryolophosaurus
Giganotosaurus
Saurophaganax
Gojirasaurus
Irritator
Sinosauropteryx
Megaraptor
Suchomimus
Zuniceratops
Achillobator
Qantassaurus
Sinornithosaurus

Bambiraptor
Microraptor
Sauroposeidon
Dilong
Tyrannotitan
Dracorex
Mapusaurus
Gigantoraptor
Epidexipteryx
Guanlong
Anchiornis
Yutyrannus
Aurornis
Changyuraptor
Yi

20s 30s 40s 50s 60s 70s 80s 90s	00s 10s 20s 30s 40s 50s 60s 70s 80s 90s	00s 10s 20s 30s 40s
19th	20th	21st

1820   1870   1920   1970   2020

Figure 29: *Scipionyx from the Natural History Museum of Milan, Italy*

Soft tissue and DNA

One of the best examples of soft-tissue impressions in a fossil dinosaur was discovered in Pietraroia, Italy. The discovery was reported in 1998, and described the specimen of a small, very young coelurosaur, *Scipionyx samniticus*. The fossil includes portions of the intestines, colon, liver, muscles, and windpipe of this immature dinosaur.

In the March 2005 issue of *Science*, the paleontologist Mary Higby Schweitzer and her team announced the discovery of flexible material resembling actual soft tissue inside a 68-million-year-old *Tyrannosaurus rex* leg bone from the Hell Creek Formation in Montana. After recovery, the tissue was rehydrated by the science team. When the fossilized bone was treated over several weeks to remove mineral content from the fossilized bone-marrow cavity (a process called demineralization), Schweitzer found evidence of intact structures such as blood vessels, bone matrix, and connective tissue (bone fibers). Scrutiny under the microscope further revealed that the putative dinosaur soft tissue had retained fine structures (microstructures) even at the cellular level. The exact nature and composition of this material, and the implications of Schweitzer's discovery, are not yet clear.

In 2009, a team including Schweitzer announced that, using even more careful methodology, they had duplicated their results by finding similar soft tissue

Figure 30: *Outdated Iguanodon statues created by Benjamin Waterhouse Hawkins for the Crystal Palace Park in 1853*

in a duck-billed dinosaur, *Brachylophosaurus canadensis*, found in the Judith River Formation of Montana. This included even more detailed tissue, down to preserved bone cells that seem even to have visible remnants of nuclei and what seem to be red blood cells. Among other materials found in the bone was collagen, as in the *Tyrannosaurus* bone. The type of collagen an animal has in its bones varies according to its DNA and, in both cases, this collagen was of the same type found in modern chickens and ostriches.

The extraction of ancient DNA from dinosaur fossils has been reported on two separate occasions; upon further inspection and peer review, however, neither of these reports could be confirmed. However, a functional peptide involved in the vision of a theoretical dinosaur has been inferred using analytical phylogenetic reconstruction methods on gene sequences of related modern species such as reptiles and birds. In addition, several proteins, including hemoglobin, have putatively been detected in dinosaur fossils.

In 2015, researchers reported finding structures similar to blood cells and collagen fibers, preserved in the bone fossils of six Cretaceous dinosaur specimens, which are approximately 75 million years old.

Figure 31: *The battles that may have occurred between Tyrannosaurus rex and Triceratops are a recurring theme in popular science and dinosaurs' depiction in culture.*

Cultural depictions

By human standards, dinosaurs were creatures of fantastic appearance and often enormous size. As such, they have captured the popular imagination and become an enduring part of human culture. Entry of the word "dinosaur" into the common vernacular reflects the animals' cultural importance: in English, "dinosaur" is commonly used to describe anything that is impractically large, obsolete, or bound for extinction.

Public enthusiasm for dinosaurs first developed in Victorian England, where in 1854, three decades after the first scientific descriptions of dinosaur remains, a menagerie of lifelike dinosaur sculptures were unveiled in London's Crystal Palace Park. The Crystal Palace dinosaurs proved so popular that a strong market in smaller replicas soon developed. In subsequent decades, dinosaur exhibits opened at parks and museums around the world, ensuring that successive generations would be introduced to the animals in an immersive and exciting way. Dinosaurs' enduring popularity, in its turn, has resulted in significant public funding for dinosaur science, and has frequently spurred new discoveries. In the United States, for example, the competition between museums for public attention led directly to the Bone Wars of the 1880s and 1890s, during which a pair of feuding paleontologists made enormous scientific contributions.

The popular preoccupation with dinosaurs has ensured their appearance in literature, film, and other media. Beginning in 1852 with a passing mention in Charles Dickens' *Bleak House*, dinosaurs have been featured in large numbers of fictional works. Jules Verne's 1864 novel *Journey to the Center of the Earth*, Sir Arthur Conan Doyle's 1912 book *The Lost World*, the iconic 1933 film *King Kong*, the 1954 *Godzilla* and its many sequels, the best-selling 1990 novel *Jurassic Park* by Michael Crichton and its 1993 film adaptation are just a few notable examples of dinosaur appearances in fiction. Authors of general-interest non-fiction works about dinosaurs, including some prominent paleontologists, have often sought to use the animals as a way to educate readers about science in general. Dinosaurs are ubiquitous in advertising; numerous companies have referenced dinosaurs in printed or televised advertisements, either in order to sell their own products or in order to characterize their rivals as slow-moving, dim-witted, or obsolete.

References

Further reading

Library resources about
Dinosaurs

- Online books[24]
- Resources in your library[25]
- Resources in other libraries[26]

- Bakker, Robert T. (1986). *The Dinosaur Heresies: New Theories Unlocking the Mystery of the Dinosaurs and Their Extinction.* New York: Morrow. ISBN 0-688-04287-2.
- Holtz, Thomas R. Jr. (2007). *Dinosaurs: The Most Complete, Up-to-Date Encyclopedia for Dinosaur Lovers of All Ages.* New York: Random House. ISBN 978-0-375-82419-7.
- Paul, Gregory S. (2000). *The Scientific American Book of Dinosaurs.* New York: St. Martin's Press. ISBN 0-312-26226-4.
- Paul, Gregory S. (2002). *Dinosaurs of the Air: The Evolution and Loss of Flight in Dinosaurs and Birds.* Baltimore: The Johns Hopkins University Press. ISBN 0-8018-6763-0.
- Randall, Lisa (2015), *Dark matter and the dinosaurs: The astounding interconnectedness of the universe*, New York: Harper Collins Publishers, ISBN 978-0-06-232847-2

- Sternberg, C. M. (1966). *Canadian Dinosaurs*, in *Geological Series*, no. 54. Second ed. [Ottawa]: National Museum of Canada. 28 p., amply ill.
- Stewart, Tabori & Chang (1997). *"The Humongous Book of Dinosaurs"*[27]. New York: Stewart, Tabori & Chang. Retrieved May 17, 2012. ISBN 1-55670-596-4 (Article: The Humongous Book of Dinosaurs)
- Zhou, Z. (2004). "The origin and early evolution of birds: discoveries, disputes, and perspectives from fossil evidence"[28] (PDF). *Naturwissenschaften*. **91** (10): 455–471. Bibcode: 2004NW.....91..455Z[29]. doi: 10.1007/s00114-004-0570-4[30]. PMID 15365634[31]. Archived from the original[32] (PDF) on 2013-05-29.

External links

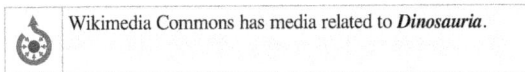

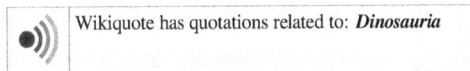

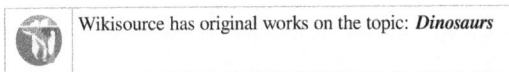

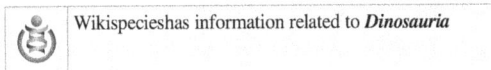

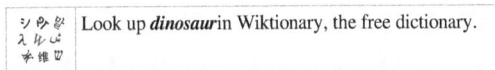

Wikimedia Commons has media related to *Dinosauria*.

Wikiquote has quotations related to: *Dinosauria*

Wikisource has original works on the topic: *Dinosaurs*

Wikispecieshas information related to *Dinosauria*

Look up *dinosaur*in Wiktionary, the free dictionary.

<indicator name="spoken-icon">))) </indicator>

General

- DinoDatabase.com | Hundreds of dinosaurs and dinosaur related topics[33]

Images

- The Science and Art of Gregory S. Paul[34] Influential paleontologist's anatomy art and paintings
- Skeletal Drawing[35] Professional restorations of numerous dinosaurs, and discussions of dinosaur anatomy.

- "Dinosaur Discovery"[36], a collection of images from early works on dinosaurs at the Linda Hall Library, in support of the exhibition, *Paper Dinosaurs, 1824–1969*[37].

Video

- BBC Nature: Dinosaur reconstructions and expert interpretations, including *Walking with Dinosaurs*[38]
- BBC Explainer – Dinosaurs – a complete history in 4 minutes, animation[39]
- Origin, evolution and extinction of the dinosaurs[40] Stephen Brusatte video lecture April 15, 2014

Popular

- Dinosaurs & other extinct creatures[41]: From the Natural History Museum, a well illustrated dinosaur directory.
- Dinosaurnews[42] Dinosaur-related headlines from around the world, including finds and discoveries, and many links.
- Dinosauria[43] From UC Berkeley Museum of Paleontology.
- LiveScience.com[44] Dinosaur pages
- Zoom Dinosaurs[45] From Enchanted Learning. Kids' site, info pages and stats, theories, history.
- Dinosaur genus list[46] contains data tables on nearly every published Mesozoic dinosaur genus as of January 2011.

Technical

- *Palaeontologia Electronica*[47] From Coquina Press. Online technical journal.

<indicator name="featured-star"> ☆ </indicator>

Evolution of dinosaurs

Evolution of dinosaurs

This article gives an outline and examples of dinosaur evolution. For a detailed list of interrelationships see Dinosaur classification.

Dinosaurs evolved within a single lineage of archosaurs 232-234 Ma (million years ago) in the Ladinian age, the latter part of the middle Triassic. Dinosauria is a well-supported clade, present in 98% of bootstraps. It is diagnosed by many features including loss of the postfrontal on the skull and an elongate deltopectoral crest on the humerus.[48]

In March 2017, scientists reported a new way of classifying the dinosaur family tree, based on newer and more evidence than available earlier. According to the new classification, the original dinosaurs, arising 200 million years ago, were small, two-footed omnivorous animals with large grasping hands. Descendants (for the non-avian dinosaurs) lasted until 66 million years ago.

Origins amongst archosaurs

The process leading up to the Dinosauromorpha and the first true dinosaurs can be followed through fossils of the early Archosaurs such as the Proterosuchidae, *Erythrosuchidae* and *Euparkeria* which have fossils dating back to 250 Ma, through mid-Triassic archosaurs such as *Ticinosuchus* 232-236 Ma. Crocodiles are also descendants of mid-Triassic archosaurs.

Dinosaurs can be defined as the last common ancestor of birds (Saurischia) and *Triceratops* (Ornithischia) and all the descendants of that ancestor. With that definition, the pterosaurs and several species of archosaurs narrowly miss out on being classified as dinosaurs. The pterosaurs are famous for flying through the Mesozoic skies on leathery wings and reaching the largest sizes of any flying animal that ever existed. Archosaur genera that also narrowly miss out on being classified as dinosaurs include *Schleromochlus* 220-225 Ma, *Lagerpeton* 230-232 Ma and *Marasuchus* 230-232 Ma.

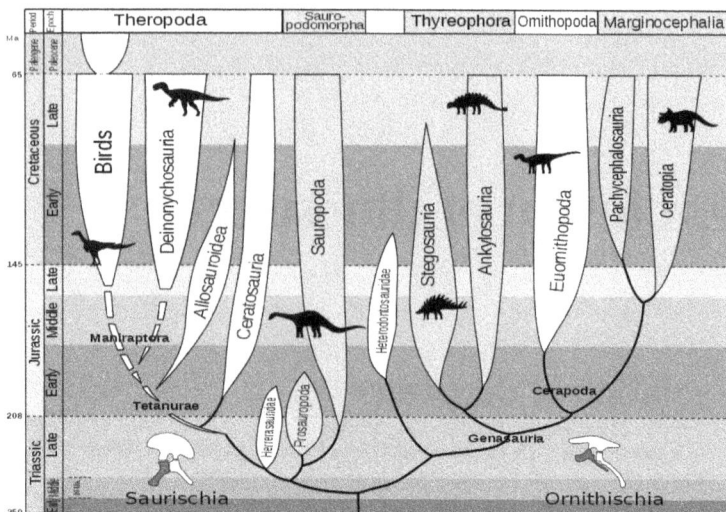

Figure 32: *Evolution of dinosaurs*

Earliest dinosaurs

The first known dinosaurs were bipedal predators that were 1-2 metres (3.3-6.5 ft) long.

Spondylosoma may or may not be a dinosaur; the fossils (all postcranial) are tentatively dated at 235-242 Ma.

The earliest confirmed dinosaur fossils include saurischian ('lizard-hipped') dinosaurs *Nyasasaurus* 243 Ma, *Saturnalia* 225-232 Ma, *Herrerasaurus* 220-230 Ma, *Staurikosaurus* possibly 225-230 Ma, *Eoraptor* 220-230 Ma and *Alwalkeria* 220-230 Ma. *Saturnalia* may be a basal saurischian or a prosauropod. The others are basal saurischians.

Among the earliest ornithischian ('bird-hipped') dinosaurs is *Pisanosaurus* 220-230 Ma. Although *Lesothosaurus* comes from 195-206 Ma, skeletal features suggest that it branched from the main Ornithischia line at least as early as *Pisanosaurus*.

A. *Eoraptor*, an early saurischian, **B** *Lesothosaurus*, a primitive ornithischian, **C** *Staurikosaurus* (Saurischia) pelvis, **D** *Lesothosaurus* pelvis

It is clear from this figure that early saurischians resembled early ornithischians, but not modern crocodiles. Saurischians are distinguished from the ornithischians by retaining the ancestral configuration of bones in the pelvis. Another difference is in the skull, the upper skull of the Ornithischia is more solid

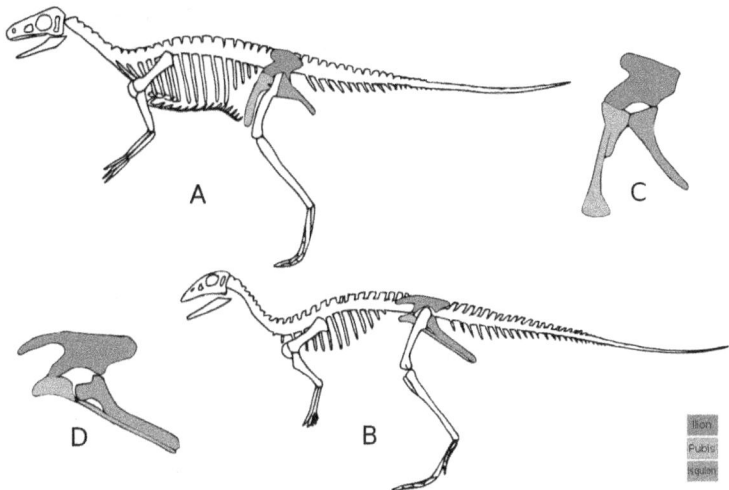

and the joint connecting the lower jaw is more flexible; both are adaptations to herbivory and both can already be seen in *Lesothosaurus*.

Saurischia

Setting aside the basal Saurischia, the rest of the Saurischia are split into the Sauropodomorpha and Theropoda. The Sauropodomorpha is split into Prosauropoda and Sauropoda. The evolutionary paths taken by the Theropoda are very complicated. *The Dinosauria* (2004), a major reference work on dinosaurs, splits the Theropoda into groups Ceratosauria, Basal Tetanurae, Tyrannosauroidea, Ornithomimosauria, Therizinosauroidea, Oviraptorosauria, Troodontidae, Dromaeosauridae and Basal Avialae in turn. Each group branches off the main trunk at a later date. See Dinosaur classification for the detailed interrelationships between these.

Sauropodomorpha

The first sauropodomorphs were prosauropods. Prosauropod fossils are known from the late Triassic to early Jurassic 227-180 Ma. They could be bipedal or quadrupedal and had developed long necks and tails and relatively small heads. They had lengths of 2.5 (8.2 ft) to 10 m (33 ft) and were primarily herbivorous. The earliest prosauropods, such as *Thecodontosaurus* from 205-220 Ma, still retained the ancestral bipedal stance and large head to body ratio.

These evolved into the sauropods which became gigantic quadrupedal herbivores, some of which reached lengths of at least 26 m (85 ft). Features defining this clade include a ratio of forelimb length to hindlimb length greater than 0.6. Most sauropods still had hindlimbs larger than forelimbs; one notable exception is *Brachiosaurus* whose long forelimbs suggest that it had evolved to feed from tall trees like a modern-day giraffe.

Sauropod fossils are found from the times of the earliest dinosaurs right up to the Cretaceous–Paleogene extinction event, from 227 to 66 Ma. Most sauropods are known from the Jurassic, to be more precise between 227 and 121 Ma.

The Cretaceous sauropods form two groups. The Diplodocoidea lived from 121 to 66 Ma. The Titanosauriformes lived from 132 to 66 Ma. The latter clade consists of series of nested subgroups, the Titanosauria, the Titanosauridae and Saltasauridae. Both the Diplodocoidea and Titanosauriformes are descended from the Neosauropoda, the earliest of which lived in about 169 Ma.

The sauropods are famous for being the largest land animals that ever lived, and for having relatively small skulls. The enlargement of prosauropod and sauropod dinosaurs into these giants and the change in skull length is illustrated in the following charts.

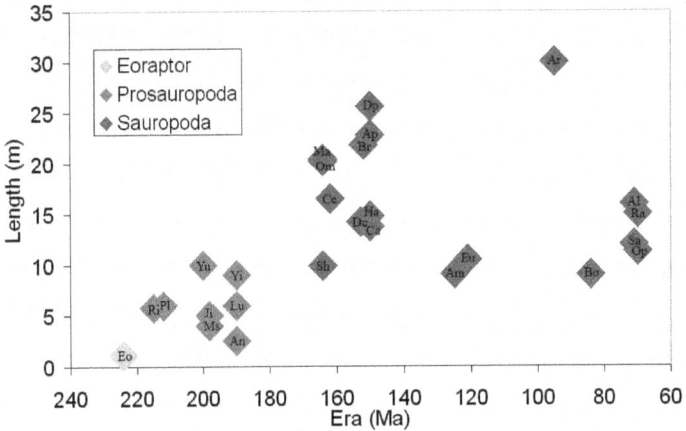

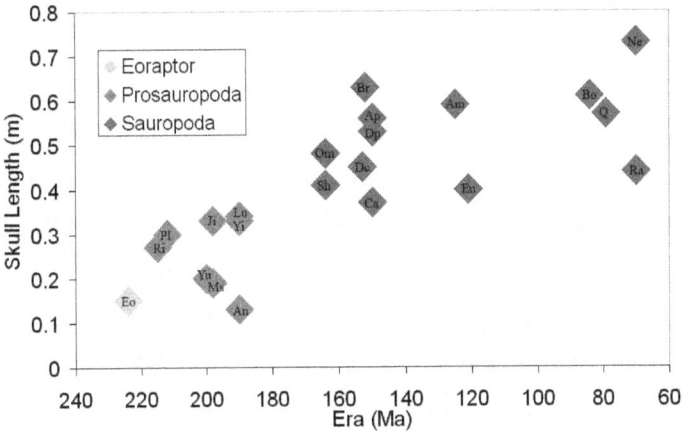

Dinosaurs used in creating these charts are (in date order): Eo *Eoraptor*; Prosauropods Ri *Riojasaurus*, Pl *Plateosaurus*, Yu *Yunnanosaurus*, Ms *Massospondylus*, Ji *Jingshanosaurus*, An *Anchisaurus*, Lu *Lufengosaurus*, Yi *Yimenosaurus*, ; and Sauropods Sh *Shunosaurus*, Om *Omeisaurus*, Mm *Mamenchisaurus*, Ce *Cetiosaurus*, Dc *Dicraeosaurus*, Br *Brachiosaurus*, Eu *Euhelopus*, Ap *Apatosaurus*, Ca *Camarasaurus*, Dp *Diplodocus*, Ha *Haplocanthosaurus*, Am *Amargasaurus*, Ar *Argentinosaurus (approx)*, Bo *Bonitasaura*, Q *Quaesitosaurus*, Al *Alamosaurus*, Sa *Saltasaurus*, Ra *Rapetosaurus*, Op *Opisthocoelicaudia*, Ne *Nemegtosaurus*.

With the exception of *Argentinosaurus* (included to fill a gap in time), these graphs show only the length of sauropods for whom near-complete fossil skeletons are known. It doesn't show other very large sauropods (see Dinosaur size#Sauropods) because these are only known from very incomplete skeletons. The ratio of skull length to body length is much higher in *Eoraptor* than in sauropods. The longest skull graphed is of *Nemegtosaurus*, which is not thought be a particularly large sauropod. The skull of *Nemegtosaurus* was found near the headless skeleton of 11 metre (36 ft) long *Opisthocoelicaudia*, and it has been suggested that they may be the same species, but see Nemegtosauridae.

The relationship between the evolution of large herbivores and large plants remains uncertain. About 50% of the plants over the time of the dinosaurs were conifers, they increased in number in the Triassic until stabilising in about 190 Ma. Cycads formed the second largest group until about 120 Ma. Ferns were present in roughly constant numbers the whole time. Flowering plants began about 120 Ma and by the end of the period had taken over from the cycads. All dinosaur herbivores appear to have been adversely affected by the extinction event at the end of the Jurassic.

Theropoda

By far the earliest fossils of Theropoda (not counting the basal saurischians) are of the Coelophysoidea, including *Coelophysis* and others, from late Triassic and early Jurassic 227-180 Ma. Cladistic analysis sometimes connects these to the group called Ceratosauria. Principal features of both include changes in the pelvic girdle and hind limb that differ between the sexes. Other ceratosauria first appear in the late Jurassic of western North America.

These are followed by the basal Tetanurae, of whom fossils have been found from the mid Jurassic to past the end of the early Cretaceous 180 Ma to 94 Ma. They have a relatively short maxillary tooth row. They did not all branch off the evolutionary line leading to coelurosaurs at the same time. Basal tetanurans include Megalosauridae, spinosaurids, a diverse clade of allosaurs, and several genera of less certain affinities, including *Compsognathus*. With the exception of *Compsognathus* they are large-bodied. Allosaurs form a distinct long-lived clade that share some cranial characters. They include the well known *Allosaurus* and *Sinraptor* among others.

The great radiation of Theropoda into many different clades of Coelurosauria must have happened in the mid to late Jurassic, because *Archaeopteryx* was around in about 152-154 Ma, and cladistic analysis has shown that many other groups of Coelurosauria branched off before that.[49] Fossil evidence from China suggests that the earliest feathers were found on the primitive Coelurosauria. The most primitive of these, e.g. on the tyrannosauroid *Dilong*, were simply hollow-cored fibres that would have been useful for insulation but useless for flying.

Occasional bones and cladistic analyses point to the Tyrannosauroidea branching off from the other Theropoda early, in the middle Jurassic, although nearly complete skeletons haven't yet appeared before *Eotyrannus* from 121-127 Ma, and the many close relatives of *Tyrannosaurus* itself don't appear before 84 Ma, near the end of the late Cretaceous.

Ornithomimosauria fossils are known from 127 to 65 Ma. The earliest branch from the main line of Ornithomimosauria is believed to be *Harpymimus*.

The Therizinosauroidea are unusual theropods in being almost all vegetarian. Fossil Therizinosauroidea are known from 127 to 65 Ma.

Maniraptorans include Oviraptorosauria, Deinonychosaurs and birds. They are characterized by an ulna with a curved shaft.

Oviraptorosaurian fossils are known from 127 to 65 Ma. They have a toothless skull that is extremely modified. The skeleton has an unusually short tail.

Deinonychosaurs, named after the enlarged sickle-shaped second digit of the foot, are closely related to birds. They have two distinct families, Troodontidae and Dromaeosauridae. Troodontid fossils are known from 127 to 65 Ma. They have a more slender build and longer limbs. The earliest named troodontid fossil known is *Sinornithoides*. Dromaeosaurid fossils are known from about 127 to 65 Ma with the exception of *Utahraptor*. The skeletal remains of *Utahraptor* are about 127-144 Ma. This is interesting because according to a recent cladistic analysis, *Utahraptor* is about as far from the ancestral Theropoda as it is possible to get, further than *Archaeopteryx*. Dromaeosaurids have a larger second digit; this family includes the well known dinosaurs *Dromaeosaurus*, *Deinonychus* and *Velociraptor*.

Ancient birds (Avialae) include both the Aves, which are defined as descendants of the common ancestor of modern birds and *Archaeopteryx*, and the more primitive *Epidendrosaurus*. Fossil birds stretch down from 154 Ma through the Cretaceous–Paleogene extinction event at 65 Ma to the present day. Scores of complete skeletons have now been found of the more recent *Confuciusornis*, which is an early representative of the Ornithurae. Ornithurans all have a bony pygostyle, to which tail feathers are anchored. For more details on the evolution of birds, see Evolution of birds.

Ornithischia

Ornithischia, as the name indicates, was coined for the birdlike pelvic girdle, although they are not the ancestors of birds.

The ornithischian skull and dentition was modified very early by a herbivorous diet.[50] *Lesothosaurus* separated early, but the skull of *Lesothosaurus* already shows such adaptations, with broad proportions, a less flexible upper jaw, and a more mobile connection for the lower jaw.

Heterodontosauridae has been shown to be the basalmost group within Ornithischia.[51] Heterodontosaurids are very small (body length < 1 m) and lived from the Late Triassic to Early Cretaceous. Apart from *Abrictosaurus* all have a short upper canine and longer lower canine. The forelimbs in known fossils are relatively long.

The major clades were already established by the early Jurassic. The ornithischians divided into armoured thyreophorans and unarmoured ornithopods and marginocephalians.

Thyreophorans

Surface body armour (scutes) is the most striking feature of the thyreophorans. *Scutellosaurus* has these but otherwise differs little from *Lesothosaurus*. It has a long tail and combined bipedal-quadrupedal posture that separates it from all later thyreophorans including Stegosauria and Ankylosauria. These two clades, although quite different in overall appearance, share many unusual features in the skull and skeleton.

Stegosaurs are easily recognised by the prominent row of plates above the spine and long spines on the tail. Most stegosaurs, but not *Stegosaurus*, also have a spine over each shoulder. These spines and plates have evolved from the earlier surface scutes. *Huayangosaurus* is the oldest and most primitive known stegosaur.

Ankylosaurs are easily recognised by their extensive body armour. The skull is heavily ossified. Early in their evolution, ankylosaurs split into the Nodosauridae and Ankylosauridae, distinguished by features of the skull.

Ornithopoda

Ornithopods fall into distinct clades - Hypsilophodontidae, and Iguanodontia.

Hypsilophodontids more closely resemble their ancestors than the heterodontosaurids do. The most distinctive features are short scapula and rod-shaped pre-pubic process. The earliest is *Agilisaurus* from the middle Jurassic of China.

Iguanodontians are a diverse but morphologically tight knit array of genera known from fossils of the late Cretaceous. Significant modifications include the evolution of tooth batteries, a ligament-bound metacarpus and a digitigrade hand posture. *Tenontosaurus* is the most basal iguanodontian. Others include *Iguanodon*, *Camptosaurus* and *Muttaburrasaurus*.

Marginocephalia

Marginocephalia are named for a shelf that projects over the back of the skull. They include the pachycephalosaurians and ceratopsians.

Pachycephalosaurs are best known for their thick upper fronts to their skull. The oldest known is *Stenopelix*, from the early Cretaceous of Europe.

Ceratopsians, famous for *Protoceratops*, *Triceratops* and *Styracosaurus* illustrate the evolution of frilled and horned skulls. The frills evolved from the shelf common to all Marginocephalia. Ceratopsians are separated into basal ceratopsians, including the parrot-beaked *Psittacosaurus*, and neoceratopsians.

Diversity of ceratopsian skulls. A) Skeleton of *Protoceratops*. B) to I) Skulls. B) & C) *Psittacosaurus* side & top. D) & E) *Protoceratops* side & top. F) & G) *Triceratops* side & top. H) & I) *Styracosaurus* side (without lower jaw) & top.

The evolution of ceratopsid dinosaurs shares characteristics with the evolution of some mammal groups, both were "geologically brief" events precipitating the simultaneous evolution of large body size, derived feeding structures, and "varied hornlike organs."

The sequence of ceratopsian evolution in the Cretaceous is roughly from *Psittacosaurus* (121 -99 Ma) to *Protoceratops* (83 Ma) to (*Triceratops* 67 Ma and

Styracosaurus 72 Ma). In side view the skull of *Psittacosaurus* bears very little resemblance to that of *Styracosaurus* but in top view a similar pentagonal arrangement can be seen.

Fossil record

The first few lines of primitive dinosaurs diversified rapidly through the Triassic period; dinosaur species quickly evolved the specialised features and range of sizes needed to exploit nearly every terrestrial ecological niche. During the period of dinosaur predominance, which encompassed the ensuing Jurassic and Cretaceous periods, nearly every known land animal larger than 1 meter in length was a dinosaur.

One measure of the quality of the fossil record is obtained by comparing the date of first appearance with the order of branching of a cladogram based on the shape of fossil elements. Close correspondence exists for ornithiscians, saurischians and subgroups. The cladogram link between coelophysids and ceratosaurs is an exception, it would place the origin of coelophysids much too late. The simplest explanation is convergent evolution - ceratosaur bones evolved independently into a shape that resembles that of the earlier coelophysids. The other possibility is that ceratosaurs evolved much earlier than the fossil record suggests.

Most dinosaur fossils have been found in the Norian-Sinemurian, Kimmeridgian-Tithonian, and Campanian-Maastrichtian periods. Continuity of lineages across the intervening gaps shows that those gaps are artifacts of preservation rather than any reduction in diversity or abundance.

In many instances, cladistic analysis shows that ancestral lineages of varying durations fall in those gaps. The length of missing ancestral lineages in 1997 range from 25 Ma (*Lesothosaurus*, Genasauria, Hadrosauroidea, Sauropoda, Neoceratopsia, Coelurosauria) to 85 Ma (Carcharodontosauridae). Because the dinosaurian radiation began at small body size, the unrecorded early history may be due to less reliable fossilization of smaller species. However, some missing lineages, notably of Carcharodontosauridae and Abelisauridae, require alternative explanations because the missing range extends across stages rich in fossil materials.

Evolutionary trends

Body size

Body size is important because of its correlation with metabolism, diet, life history, geographic range and extinction rate. The modal body mass of dinosaurs lies between 1 and 10 tons throughout the Mesozoic and across all major continental regions. There was a trend towards increasing body size within many dinosaur clades, including the Thyreophora, Ornithopoda, Pachycephalosauria, Ceratopsia, Sauropomorpha, and basal Theropoda. Marked decreases in body size have also occurred in some lineages, but are more sporadic. The best known example is the decrease in body size leading up to the first birds; *Archaeopteryx* was below 10 kg in weight, and later birds *Confuciusornis* and *Sinornis* are starling- to pigeon-sized. This occurred for easier flight.

Mobility

The ancestral dinosaur was a biped. The evolution of a quadrupedal posture occurred four times, among the ancestors of Euornithopoda, Thyreophora, Ceratopsia and Sauropodomorpha. In all four cases this was associated with an increase in body size, and in all four cases the trend is unidirectional without reversal.

Dinosaurs exhibit a pattern of the reduction and loss of fingers on the lateral side of the hand (digits III, IV and V). The primitive function of the dinosaur hand is grasping with a partially opposable thumb, rather than weight-bearing. The reduction of digits is one of the defining features of tyrannosaurids, only having two functional digits on very short forelimbs.

Effect of food sources

The ancestral dinosaur was a carnivore. Herbivory among dinosaurs arose three times, at the origin of the ornithischian, sauropodomorph, and therizinosaurid clades. Individual therizinosaurids are herbivorous or omnivorous. Herbivory among the ornithischians and sauropodomorphs was never reversed.

The potential co-evolution of plants and herbivorous dinosaurs has been subject to extensive speculation. The appearance of prosauropods in the late Triassic has been tentatively linked either to the demise or diversification of types of flora at that time. The rise of ceratopsids and iguanodont and hadrosaurid ornithopods in the Cretaceous has been tentatively linked to the angiosperm radiation. Unfortunately, there are still no hard data on dietary preferences of herbivorous dinosaurs, apart from data on chewing technique and gastroliths.

Biogeography

Dinosaurian faunas, which were relatively uniform in character when Pangaea began to break up, became markedly differentiated by the close of the Cretaceous. Biogeography is based on the splitting of an ancestral species by the emplacement of a geographic barrier. Interpretation is limited by a lack of fossil evidence for eastern North America, Madagascar, India, Antarctica and Australia. No unequivocal proof of the biogeographical action on dinosaur species has been obtained, but some authors have outlined centres of origin for many dinosaur groups, multiple dispersal routes, and intervals of geographic isolation.

Dinosaurs that have been given as evidence of biogeography include abelisaurid theropods from South America and possibly elsewhere on Gondwana.

Relationships between dinosaurs show abundant evidence of dispersal from one region of the globe to another. Tetanuran theropods travelled widely through western North America, Asia, South America, Africa and Antarctica. Pachycephalosaurs and ceratopsians show clear evidence of multiple bidirectional dispersion events across Beringa.

Extinction

The Cretaceous–Paleogene extinction event, which occurred 66 million years ago at the end of the Cretaceous period, caused the extinction of all dinosaurs except for the line that had already given rise to the first birds.

References

- Sampson, S. D., 2001, Speculations on the socioecology of Ceratopsid dinosaurs (Orinthischia: Neoceratopsia): In: Mesozoic Vertebrate Life, edited by Tanke, D. H., and Carpenter, K., Indiana University Press, pp. 263-276.
- Paul C. Sereno (1999) *The evolution of dinosaurs*, Science, Vol 284, pp. 2137–2146 http://www.sciencemag.org/cgi/content/abstract/284/5423/2137

Classification

Dinosaur classification

Dinosaur classification began in 1842 when Sir Richard Owen placed *Iguanodon*, *Megalosaurus*, and *Hylaeosaurus* in "a distinct tribe or suborder of Saurian Reptiles, for which I would propose the name of Dinosauria."[52] In 1887 and 1888 Harry Seeley divided dinosaurs into the two orders Saurischia and Ornithischia, based on their hip structure.[53] These divisions have proved remarkably enduring, even through several seismic changes in the taxonomy of dinosaurs.

The largest change was prompted by entomologist Willi Hennig's work in the 1950s, which evolved into modern cladistics. For specimens known only from fossils, the rigorous analysis of characters to determine evolutionary relationships between different groups of animals (*clades*) proved incredibly useful. When computer-based analysis using cladistics came into its own in the 1990s, paleontologists became among the first zoologists to almost wholeheartedly adopt the system. Progressive scrutiny and work upon dinosaurian interrelationships, with the aid of new discoveries that have shed light on previously uncertain relationships between taxa, have begun to yield a stabilizing classification since the mid-2000s. While cladistics is the predominant classificatory system among paleontology professionals, the Linnean system is still in use, especially in works intended for popular distribution.

Benton classification

As most dinosaur paleontologists have advocated a shift away from traditional, ranked Linnaean taxonomy in favor of rankless phylogenetic systems, few ranked taxonomies of dinosaurs have been published since the 1980s. The following schema is among the most recent, from the third edition of *Vertebrate Palaeontology*,[54] a respected undergraduate textbook. While it is structured so as to reflect evolutionary relationships (similar to a cladogram), it also retains

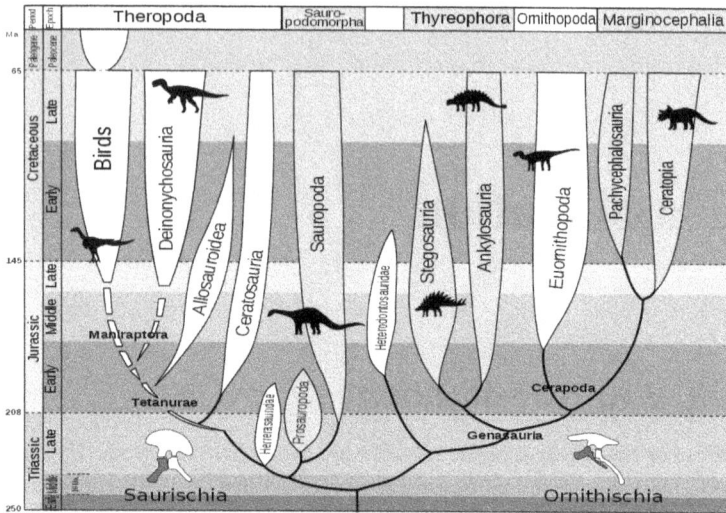

Figure 33: *Classification of dinosaurs*

the traditional ranks used in Linnaean taxonomy. The classification has been updated from the second edition in 2000 to reflect new research, but remains fundamentally conservative.

Michael Benton classifies all dinosaurs within the Series Amniota, Class Sauropsida, Subclass Diapsida, Infraclass Archosauromorpha, Division Archosauria, Subdivision Avemetatarsalia, Infradivision Ornithodira, and Superorder Dinosauria. Dinosauria is then divided into the two traditional orders, Saurischia and Ornithischia. The dagger (†) is used to indicate taxa with no living members.

Order Saurischia

- **Suborder Theropoda**
  - †Infraorder Herrerasauria
  - †Infraorder Coelophysoidea
  - †Infraorder Ceratosauria+
    - †Division Neoceratosauria+
      - †Subdivision Abelisauroidea
        - †Family Abelisauridae
        - †Family Noasauridae
      - †Subdivision Ceratosauridae
  - Infraorder Tetanurae
    - †Division Megalosauria

- †Subdivision Spinosauroidea
  - †Family Megalosauridae
  - †Family Spinosauridae
- †Division Carnosauria
  - †Subdivision Allosauroidea
    - †Family Allosauridae
    - †Family Carcharodontosauridae
    - †Family Neovenatoridae
    - †Family Metriacanthosauridae
- Division Coelurosauria
  - †Family Coeluridae
  - Subdivision Maniraptoriformes
    - †Family Tyrannosauridae
    - †Family Ornithomimidae
    - Infradivision Maniraptora
      - †Family Alvarezsauridae
      - †Family Therizinosauridae
      - †Cohort Deinonychosauria
        - †Family Troodontidae
        - †Family Dromaeosauridae
      - Class Aves
- **†Suborder Sauropodomorpha**
  - †*Thecodontosaurus*
  - †Family Plateosauridae
  - †*Riojasaurus*
  - †Family Massospondylidae
  - †Infraorder Sauropoda
    - †Family Vulcanodontidae
    - †Family Omeisauridae
    - †Division Neosauropoda
      - †Family Cetiosauridae
      - †Family Diplodocidae
      - †Subdivision Macronaria
        - †Family Camarasauridae
        - †Infradivision Titanosauriformes
          - †Family Brachiosauridae
          - †Cohort Somphospondyli
            - †Family Euhelopodidae
            - †Family Titanosauridae

†Order Ornithischia

- †Family Pisanosauridae
- †Family Fabrosauridae
- **†Suborder Thyreophora**
  - †Family Scelidosauridae
  - †Infraorder Stegosauria
  - †Infraorder Ankylosauria
    - †Family Nodosauridae
    - †Family Ankylosauridae
- **†Suborder Cerapoda**
  - †Infraorder Pachycephalosauria
  - †Infraorder Ceratopsia
    - †Family Psittacosauridae
    - †Family Protoceratopsidae
    - †Family Ceratopsidae
  - †Infraorder Ornithopoda
    - †Family Heterodontosauridae
    - †Family Hypsilophodontidae
    - †Family Iguanodontidae *
    - †Family Hadrosauridae

Weishampel/Dodson/Osmólska classification

The following is based on the second edition of *The Dinosauria*,[55] a compilation of articles by experts in the field that provided the most comprehensive coverage of Dinosauria available when it was first published in 1990. The second edition updates and revises that work.

The cladogram and phylogenetic definitions below reflect the current understanding of evolutionary relationships. The taxa and symbols in parentheses after a given taxa define these relationships. The plus symbol ("+") between taxa indicates the given taxa is a node-based clade, defined as comprising all descendants of the last common ancestor of the "added" taxa. The greater-than symbol (">") indicates the given taxon is a stem-based taxon, comprising all organisms sharing a common ancestor that is not also an ancestor of the "lesser" taxon.

Saurischia

(*Tyrannosaurus/Allosaurus* > *Triceratops/Stegosaurus*)

- Herrerasauria (*Herrerasaurus* > *Liliensternus*, *Plateosaurus*)
  - Herrerasauridae (*Herrerasaurus* + *Staurikosaurus*)

- *? Eoraptor lunensis*
- **Sauropodomorpha** (*Saltasaurus* > Theropoda)
  - *? Saturnalia tupiniquim*
  - ? Thecodontosauridae
  - Prosauropoda (*Plateosaurus* > Sauropoda)
    - ? Thecodontosauridae
    - ? Anchisauria (*Anchisaurus* + *Melanorosaurus*)
      - ? Anchisauridae (*Anchisaurus* > Melanorosaurus*)
      - ? Melanorosauridae (*Melanorosaurus* > *Anchisaurus*)
    - Plateosauria (*Jingshanosaurus* + *Plateosaurus*)
      - Massospondylidae
      - Yunnanosauridae
      - Plateosauridae (*Plateosaurus* > *Yunnanosaurus*, *Massospondylus*)
  - Sauropoda (*Saltasaurus* > *Plateosaurus*)
    - ? Anchisauridae
    - ? Melanorosauridae
    - Blikanasauridae
    - Vulcanodontidae
    - Eusauropoda (*Shunosaurus* + *Saltasaurus*)
      - ? Euhelopodidae
      - Mamenchisauridae
      - Cetiosauridae (*Cetiosaurus* > *Saltasaurus*)
      - Neosauropoda (*Diplodocus* + *Saltasaurus*)
        - Diplodocoidea (*Diplodocus* > *Saltasaurus*)
          - Rebbachisauridae (*Rebbachisaurus* > *Diplodocus*)
          - Flagellicaudata
            - Dicraeosauridae (*Dicraeosaurus* > *Diplodocus*)
            - Diplodocidae (*Diplodocus* > *Dicraeosaurus*)
        - Macronaria (*Saltasaurus* > *Diplodocus*)
          - *? Jobaria tiguidensis*
          - Camarasauromorpha (*Camarasaurus* + *Saltasaurus*)
            - Camarasauridae
            - Titanosauriformes (*Brachiosaurus* + *Saltasaurus*)
              - Brachiosauridae (*Brachiosaurus* > *Saltasaurus*)
              - Titanosauria (*Saltasaurus* > *Brachiosaurus*)
                - Andesauridae
                - Lithostrotia (*Malawisaurus* + *Saltasaurus*)
                  - *Isisaurus colberti*
                  - *Paralititan stromeri*
                  - Nemegtosauridae
                  - Saltasauridae (*Opisthocoelicaudia* + *Saltasaurus*)

- **Theropoda** (*Passer domesticus* > *Cetiosaurus oxoniensis*)
  - ? *Eoraptor lunensis*
  - ? Herrerasauridae
  - Ceratosauria (*Ceratosaurus nasicornis* > Aves)
    - ? Coelophysoidea (*Coelophysis* > *Ceratosaurus*)
      - ? *Dilophosaurus wetherilli*
      - Coelophysidae (*Coelophysis* + *Megapnosaurus*)
    - ? Neoceratosauria (*Ceratosaurus* > *Coelophysis*)
      - Ceratosauridae
      - Abelisauroidea (*Carnotaurus sastrei* > *C. nasicornis*)
        - Abelisauria (*Noasaurus* + *Carnotaurus*)
        - Noasauridae
        - Abelisauridae (*Abelisaurus comahuensis* + *C. sastrei*)
          - Carnotaurinae (*Carnotaurus* > *Abelisaurus*)
          - Abelisaurinae (*Abelisaurus* > *Carnotaurus*)
  - Tetanurae (*P. domesticus* > *C. nasicornis*)
    - ? Spinosauroidea (*Spinosaurus aegyptiacus* > *P. domesticus*)
      - Megalosauridae (*Megalosaurus bucklandii* > *P. domesticus*, *S. aegyptiacus*, *Allosaurus fragilis*)
        - Megalosaurinae (*M. bucklandii* > *Eustreptospondylus oxoniensis*)
        - Eustreptospondylinae (*E. oxoniensis* > *M. bucklandii*)
      - Spinosauridae (*S. aegyptiacus* > *P. domesticus*, *M. bucklandii*, *A. fragilis*)
        - Baryonychinae (*Baryonyx walkeri* > *S. aegyptiacus*)
        - Spinosaurinae (*S. aegyptiacus* > *B. walkeri*)
    - Avetheropoda (*A. fragilis* + *P. domesticus*)
      - Carnosauria (*A. fragilis* > Aves)
        - ? Spinosauroidea
        - *Monolophosaurus jiangi*
        - Allosauroidea (*A. fragilis* + *Sinraptor dongi*)
          - Allosauridae (*A. fragilis* > *S. dongi*, *Carcharodontosaurus saharicus*)
          - Sinraptoridae (*S. dongi* > *A. fragilis*, *C. saharicus*)
          - Carcharodontosauridae (*C. saharicus* > *A. fragilis*, *S. dongi*)
      - Coelurosauria (*P. domesticus* > *A. fragilis*)
        - Compsognathidae (*Compsognathus longipes* > *P. domesticus*)
        - *Proceratosaurus bradleyi*
        - *Ornitholestes hermanni*
        - Tyrannoraptora (*Tyrannosaurus rex* + *P. domesticus*)
          - *Coelurus fragilis*

- Tyrannosauroidea (*T. rex* > *Ornithomimus velox*, *Deinonychus antirrhopus*, *A. fragilis*)
  - Dryptosauridae
  - Tyrannosauridae (*T. rex* + *Tarbosaurus bataar* + *Daspletosaurus torosus* + *Albertosaurus sarcophagus* + *Gorgosaurus libratus*)
    - Tyrannosaurinae (*T. rex* > *A. sarcophagus*)
    - Albertosaurinae (*A. sarcophagus* > *T. rex*)
- Maniraptoriformes (*O. velox* + *P. domesticus*)
  - Ornithomimosauria (*Ornithomimus edmontonicus* + *Pelecanimimus polyodon*)
    - Harpymimidae
    - Garudimimidae
    - Ornithomimidae
  - Maniraptora (*P. domesticus* > *O. velox*)
    - Oviraptorosauria (*Oviraptor philoceratops* > *P. domesticus*)
      - Caenagnathoidea (*O. philoceratops* + *Caenagnathus collinsi*)
        - Caenagnathidae (*C. collinsi* > *O. philoceratops*)
        - Oviraptoridae (*O. philoceratops* > *C. collinsi*)
          - Oviraptorinae (*O. philoceratops* + *Citipati osmolskae*)
    - Therizinosauroidea (*Therizinosaurus* + *Beipiaosaurus*)
      - Alxasauridae
      - Therizinosauridae
    - Paraves (*P. domesticus* > *O. philoceratops*)
      - Eumaniraptora (*P. domesticus* + *D. antirrhopus*)
        - Deinonychosauria (*D. antirrhopus* > *P. domesticus* or *Dromaeosaurus albertensis* + *Troodon formosus*)
          - Troodontidae (*T. formosus* > *Velociraptor mongoliensis*)
          - Dromaeosauridae (*Microraptor zhaoianus* + *Sinornithosaurus millenii* + *V. mongoliensis*)
        - Avialae (*Archaeopteryx* + Neornithes)

Ornithischia

(*Iguanodon*/*Triceratops* > *Cetiosaurus*/*Tyrannosaurus*)

- *? Lesothosaurus diagnosticus*
- *?* Heterodontosauridae
- Genasauria (*Ankylosaurus* + *Triceratops*)
- **Thyreophora** (*Ankylosaurus* > *Triceratops*)
  - Scelidosauridae
  - Eurypoda (*Ankylosaurus* + *Stegosaurus*)
  - Stegosauria (*Stegosaurus* > *Ankylosaurus*)
    - Huayangosauridae (*Huayangosaurus* > *Stegosaurus*)
    - Stegosauridae (*Stegosaurus* > *Huayangosaurus*)
      - *Dacentrurus armatus*
      - Stegosaurinae (*Stegosaurus* > *Dacentrurus*)
  - Ankylosauria (*Ankylosaurus* > *Stegosaurus*)
    - Ankylosauridae (*Ankylosaurus* > *Panoplosaurus*)
      - *Gastonia burgei*
      - *Shamosaurus scutatus*
      - Ankylosaurinae (*Ankylosaurus* > *Shamosaurus*)
    - Nodosauridae (*Panoplosaurus* > *Ankylosaurus*)
- **Cerapoda** (*Triceratops* > *Ankylosaurus*)
- Ornithopoda (*Edmontosaurus* > *Triceratops*)
  - *?* Lesothosaurus diagnosticus
  - *?* Heterodontosauridae
  - Euornithopoda
    - *Hypsilophodon foxii*
    - *Thescelosaurus neglectus*
    - Iguanodontia (*Edmontosaurus* > *Thescelosaurus*)
      - *Tenontosaurus tilletti*
      - Rhabdodontidae
      - Dryomorpha
        - Dryosauridae
        - Ankylopollexia
          - Camptosauridae
          - Styracosterna
            - *Lurdusaurus arenatus*
            - Iguanodontoidea (=Hadrosauriformes)
              - Iguanodontidae
              - Hadrosauridae (*Telmatosaurus* + *Parasaurolophus*)
                - *Telmatosaurus transsylvanicus*
                - Euhadrosauria

- Lambeosaurinae
- Saurolophinae (=Hadrosaurinae)
- Marginocephalia
  - Pachycephalosauria (*Pachycephalosaurus wyomingensis* > *Triceratops horridus*)
    - Goyocephala (*Goyocephale* + *Pachycephalosaurus*)
      - Homalocephaloidea (*Homalocephale* + Pachycephalosaurus)
        - Homalocephalidae
        - Pachycephalosauridae
  - Ceratopsia (*Triceratops* > *Pachycephalosaurus*)
    - Psittacosauridae
    - Neoceratopsia
      - Coronosauria
        - Protoceratopsidae
        - Bagaceratopidae
        - Ceratopsoidea
          - Leptoceratopsidae
          - Ceratopsomorpha
            - Ceratopsidae
              - Centrosaurinae
              - Chasmosaurinae

Baron/Norman/Barrett classification

In 2017 Matthew G. Baron and his colleagues published a new analysis proposing to put Theropoda (except Herrerasauridae) and Ornithischia within a new group called Ornithoscelida (a name originally coined by Thomas Henry Huxley in 1870), redefining Saurischia to cover Sauropodomorpha and Herrerasauridae. Amongst other things this would require hypercarnivory to have evolved independently for Theropoda and Herrerasauridae. This scheme is currently debated among palaeontologists, with recent studies finding little difference between the traditional and newly proposed models.

- **Dinosauria**
  - Ornithoscelida
    - Ornithischia
    - Theropoda
  - Saurischia
    - Sauropodomorpha
    - Herrerasauridae

References

• Benton, Michael J. (2004). *Vertebrate Palaeontology, Third Edition.* Blackwell Publishing. p. 472 pp. ISBN 9780632056378.

• Owen, Richard (1842). "Report on British Fossil Reptiles: Part II". *Report of the British Association for the Advancement of Science.* **11**: 60–204.

• Seeley, Harry Govier (1888). "On the classification of the Fossil Animals commonly named Dinosauria". *Proceedings of the Royal Society of London.* **43** (258-265): 165–171. Bibcode: 1887RSPS...43..165S[56]. doi: 10.1098/rspl.1887.0117[57]..

• Weishampel, David B. (2004). Dodson, Peter; Osmólska, Halszka, eds. *The Dinosauria, Second Edition.* University of California Press. p. 861 pp. ISBN 0-520-24209-2.

Dinosaur size

Dinosaur size

Size has been one of the most interesting aspects of **dinosaur** science to the general public and to scientists. Dinosaurs show some of the most extreme variations in size of any land animal group, ranging from the tiny hummingbirds, which can weigh as little as three grams, to the extinct titanosaurs, which could weigh as much as 70 tonnes (69 long tons; 77 short tons).

Scientists will probably never be certain of the largest and smallest dinosaurs to have ever existed. This is because only a tiny percentage of animals ever fossilize, and most of these remain buried in the earth. Few of the specimens that are recovered are complete skeletons, and impressions of skin and other soft tissues are rare. Rebuilding a complete skeleton by comparing the size and morphology of bones to those of similar, better-known species is an inexact art, and reconstructing the muscles and other organs of the living animal is, at best, a process of educated guesswork. Weight estimates for dinosaurs are much more variable than length estimates, because estimating length for extinct animals is much more easily done from a skeleton than estimating weight. Estimating weight is most easily done with the laser scan skeleton technique that puts a "virtual" skin over it, but even this is only an estimate.[58]

Current evidence suggests that dinosaur average size varied through the Triassic, early Jurassic, late Jurassic and Cretaceous periods. Predatory theropod dinosaurs, which occupied most terrestrial carnivore niches during the Mesozoic, most often fall into the 100- to 1,000-kilogram (220 to 2,200 lb) category when sorted by estimated weight into categories based on order of magnitude, whereas recent predatory carnivoran mammals peak in the 10- to 100-kilogram (22 to 220 lb) category. The mode of Mesozoic dinosaur body masses is between one and ten metric tonnes. This contrasts sharply with the size of Cenozoic mammals, estimated by the National Museum of Natural History as about 2 to 5 kg (4.4 to 11.0 lb).

Figure 34: *Reconstructed skeleton of the titanosaur Argenti-nosaurus huinculensis, often considered the largest-known dinosaur.*

Record sizes

The sauropods were the largest and heaviest dinosaurs. For much of the di-nosaur era, the smallest sauropods were larger than anything else in their habi-tat, and the largest were an order of magnitude more massive than anything else that has since walked the Earth. Giant prehistoric mammals such as *Parac-eratherium* and *Palaeoloxodon* (the largest land mammals ever) were dwarfed by the giant sauropods, and only modern whales surpass them in size. There are several proposed advantages for the large size of sauropods, including pro-tection from predation, reduction of energy use, and longevity, but it may be that the most important advantage was dietary. Large animals are more effi-cient at digestion than small animals, because food spends more time in their digestive systems. This also permits them to subsist on food with lower nutri-tive value than smaller animals. Sauropod remains are mostly found in rock formations interpreted as dry or seasonally dry, and the ability to eat large quantities of low-nutrient browse would have been advantageous in such en-vironments.[59]

One of the tallest and heaviest dinosaurs known from good skeletons is *Gi-raffatitan brancai* (previously classified as a species of *Brachiosaurus*). Its re-mains were discovered in Tanzania between 1907 and 1912. Bones from sev-eral similar-sized individuals were incorporated into the skeleton now mounted

Figure 35: *Skeleton of Giganotosaurus, one of the largest theropods known.*

Figure 36: *Scale diagram comparing a human and
the largest-known dinosaurs of five major clades*

and on display at the Museum für Naturkunde Berlin; this mount is 12 metres (39 ft) tall and 21.8–22.5 metres (72–74 ft) long, and would have belonged to an animal that weighed between 30,000 to 60,000 kilograms (66,000 to 132,000 lb). One of the longest complete dinosaurs is the 27-metre-long (89 ft) *Diplodocus*, which was discovered in Wyoming in the United States and displayed in Pittsburgh's Carnegie Natural History Museum in 1907.

There were larger dinosaurs, but knowledge of them is based entirely on a small number of fragmentary fossils. Most of the largest herbivorous specimens on record were discovered in the 1970s or later, and include the massive titanosaur *Argentinosaurus huinculensis*, which is the largest dinosaur known from uncontroversial evidence, estimated to have been 96.4 metric tons (106.3

short tons) and 39.7 m (130 ft) long. Some of the longest sauropods were those with exceptionally long, whip-like tails, such as the 33.5-metre-long (110 ft) *Diplodocus hallorum* (formerly *Seismosaurus*) and the 33- to 34-metre-long (108–112 ft) *Supersaurus*. The tallest was the 18-metre-tall (59 ft) *Sauroposeidon*.

In 2014, the fossilized remains of a previously unknown species of sauropod were discovered in Argentina. The titanosaur, named *Patagotitan*, would have been around 40m long and weighed around 77 tonnes, larger than any other previously found sauropod. The specimens found were remarkably complete, significantly more so than previous titanosaurs. Research as of 2017 estimated *Patagotitan mayorum* to have been 37 m (121 ft) long[60]

Tyrannosaurus was for many decades the largest theropod and best-known to the general public. Since its discovery, however, a number of other giant carnivorous dinosaurs have been described, including *Spinosaurus*, *Carcharodontosaurus*, and *Giganotosaurus*. These large theropod dinosaurs rivaled or even exceeded Tyrannosaurus in size, though more recent studies show some indication that Tyrannosaurus, although shorter, was the heavier predator. Wikipedia:Citation needed There is still no clear explanation for exactly why these animals grew so much larger than the land predators that came before and after them.

The largest extant theropod is the common ostrich, up to 2.74 metres (9 ft 0 in) tall and weighs between 63.5 and 145.15 kilograms (140.0 and 320.0 lb).[61]

The smallest non-avialan theropod known from adult specimens may be *Anchiornis huxleyi*, at 110 grams (3.9 ounces) in weight and 34 centimetres (13 in) in length.[62] However, some studies suggest that *Anchiornis* was actually an avialan. The smallest dinosaur known from adult specimens which is definitely not an avialan is *Parvicursor remotus*, at 162 grams (5.7 oz) and measuring 39 centimetres (15 in) long.[63] When modern birds are included, the bee hummingbird *Mellisuga helenae* is smallest at 1.9 g (0.067 oz) and 5.5 cm (2.2 in) long.[64]

Recent theories propose that theropod body size shrank continuously over the past 50 million years, from an average of 163 kilograms (359 lb) down to 0.8 kg (1.8 lb), as they eventually evolved into modern birds. This is based on evidence that theropods were the only dinosaurs to get continuously smaller, and that their skeletons changed four times faster than those of other dinosaur species.

Figure 37: *Size comparison of selected giant sauropod dinosaurs*

Sauropodomorphs

Sauropodomorph size is difficult to estimate given their usually fragmentary state of preservation. Sauropods are often preserved without their tails, so the margin of error in overall length estimates is high. Mass is calculated using the cube of the length, so for species in which the length is particularly uncertain, the weight is even more so. Estimates that are particularly uncertain (due to very fragmentary or lost material) are preceded by a question mark. Each number represents the highest estimate of a given research paper. One large sauropod, *Amphicoelias fragillimus*, was based on particularly scant remains that have been lost since their description by paleontologists in 1878. Analysis of the illustrations included in the original report suggested that *A. fragillimus* may have been the largest land animal of all time, weighing up to 100–150 t (110–170 short tons) and measuring between 40–60 m (130–200 ft) long. However, later analysis of the surviving evidence, and the biological plausibility of such a large land animal, suggested that the enormous size of this animal was an over-estimate due partly to typographical errors in the original report.

Generally, the giant sauropods can be divided into two categories: the shorter but stockier and more massive forms (mainly titanosaurs and some brachiosaurids), and the longer but slenderer and more light-weight forms (mainly diplodocids).

Because different methods of estimation sometimes give conflicting results, mass estimates for sauropods can vary widely causing disagreement among scientists over the accurate number. For example, the titanosaur *Dreadnoughtus* was originally estimated to weigh 59.3 tonnes by the allometric scaling of limb-bone proportions, whereas more recent estimates, based on three-dimensional reconstructions, yield a much smaller figure of 22.1–38.2 tonnes.

Heaviest sauropodomorphs

1. *Argentinosaurus huinculensis*: 50–96.4 t (55.1–106.3 short tons)
2. *"Antarctosaurus" giganteus*: 39.5–80 t (43.5–88.2 short tons)
3. *Notocolossus gonzalezparejasi*: 44.9–75.9 t (49.5–83.7 short tons)
4. *Mamenchisaurus sinocanadorum*: 75 t (83 short tons)
5. *Apatosaurus ajax*: 32.7–72.6 t (36.0–80.0 short tons)[65]
6. *Patagotitan mayorum*: 69 t (76 short tons)[66]
7. *Sauroposeidon proteles*: 40–60 t (44–66 short tons)
8. *Dreadnoughtus schrani*: 22.1–59.3 t (24.4–65.4 short tons)
9. *Paralititan stromeri*: 20–59 t (22–65 short tons)
10. Unnamed (MPM-PV-39): 58 t (64 short tons)[67]

Longest sauropodomorphs

1. *Amphicoelias fragillimus*:58–60 m (190–197 ft)<
2. *Argentinosaurus huinculensis*: 25–39.7 m (82–130 ft)
3. *Turiasaurus riodevensis*: 30–39 m (98–128 ft)
4. *Patagotitan mayorum*: 33.5–37 m (110–121 ft)[68]
5. *Supersaurus vivianae*: 32.5–35 m (107–115 ft)
6. *Diplodocus hallorum*: 30–35 m (98–115 ft)
7. *Mamenchisaurus sinocanadorum*: 26–35 m (85–115 ft)
8. *Sauroposeidon proteles*: 27–34 m (89–112 ft)
9. *"Antarctosaurus" giganteus*: 23–33 m (75–108 ft)
10. *Xinjiangtitan shanshanesis*: 30–32 m (98–105 ft)
11. *Ruyangosaurus giganteus*: 30 m (98 ft)

Shortest sauropods

1. *Ohmdenosaurus liasicus*: 4 m (13 ft)
2. *Blikanasaurus cromptoni*: 4–5 m (13–16 ft)
3. *Lirainosaurus astibiae*: 4–7 m (13–23 ft)[69]
4. *Magyarosaurus dacus*: 5.3–6 m (17–20 ft)
5. *Europasaurus holgeri*: 5.7–6.2 m (19–20 ft)
6. *Vulcanodon karibaensis*: 6.5–11 m (21–36 ft)
7. *Isanosaurus attavipachi*: 6.5–17 m (21–56 ft)
8. *Saltasaurus loricatus*: 7–12.8 m (23–42 ft)
9. *Neuquensaurus australis*: 7–15 m (23–49 ft)[70]
10. *Antetonitrus ingenipes*: 8–12.2 m (26–40 ft)

Lightest sauropods

1. *Blikanasaurus cromptoni*: 0.25 t (0.28 short tons)
2. *Astrodon johnstoni*: 0.5 t (0.55 short tons)
3. *Europasaurus holgeri*: 0.75–1 t (0.83–1.10 short tons)
4. *Magyarosaurus dacus*: 0.75–1.1 t (0.83–1.21 short tons)
5. *Bonatitan reigi*: 1 t (1.1 short tons)
6. *Lirainosaurus astibiae*: 1–4 t (1.1–4.4 short tons)
7. *Lapparentosaurus madagascariensis*: 1.4 t (1.5 short tons)
8. *Antetonitrus ingenipes*: 1.5–5.6 t (1.7–6.2 short tons)
9. *Lessemsaurus sauropoides*: 1.8 t (2.0 short tons)
10. *Neuquensaurus australis*: 1.8 t (2.0 short tons)

Lightest non-sauropod sauropodomorphs

1. *Eoraptor lunensis*: 2–17.3 kg (4.4–38.1 lb)
2. *Pampadromaeus barberenai*: 8.5 kg (19 lb)
3. *Saturnalia tupiniquim*: 10–10.6 kg (22–23 lb)
4. *Chromogisaurus novasi*: 13.1 kg (29 lb)
5. *Asylosaurus yalensis*: 25 kg (55 lb)
6. *Guaibasaurus candelariensis*: 25–30.3 kg (55–67 lb)
7. *Adeopapposaurus mognai*: 43.9–70 kg (97–154 lb)
8. *Coloradisaurus brevis*: 70 kg (150 lb)
9. *Anchisaurus polyzelus*: 70–137.6 kg (154–303 lb)
10. *Sarahsaurus aurifontanalis*: 100.2 kg (221 lb)

Shortest non-sauropod sauropodomorphs

1. *Agnosphitys cromhallensis*: 70 cm (2.3 ft)
2. *Eoraptor lunensis*: 1–1.7 m (3.3–5.6 ft)
3. *Pampadromaeus barberenai*: 1.5 m (4.9 ft)
4. *Saturnalia tupiniquim*: 1.5 m (4.9 ft)
5. *Chromogisaurus novasi*: 1.5 m (4.9 ft)
6. *Guaibasaurus candelariensis*: 2 m (6.6 ft)
7. *Asylosaurus yalensis*: 2–2.1 m (6.6–6.9 ft)
8. *Leyesaurus marayensis*: 2.1 m (6.9 ft)?
9. *Adeopapposaurus mognai*: 2.1–3 m (6.9–9.8 ft)
10. *Unaysaurus tolentinoi*: 2.5 m (8.2 ft)

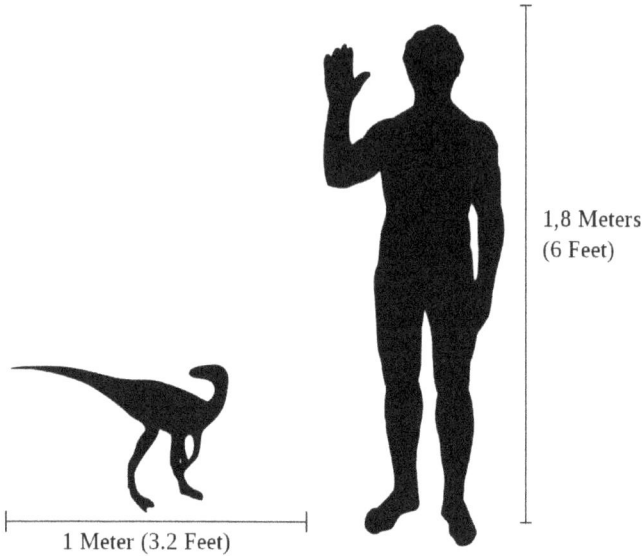

1,8 Meters
(6 Feet)

1 Meter (3.2 Feet)

Figure 38: *Eoraptor compared in size to a human.*

Theropods

Sizes are given with a range, where possible, of estimates that have not been
contradicted by more recent studies. In cases where a range of currently accepted estimates exist, sources are given for the sources with the lowest and
highest estimates, respectively, and only the highest values are given if these
individual sources give a range of estimates. Some other giant theropods are
also known; for example, a theropod trackmaker in Morocco that was perhaps
between 10 and 19 metres (33 and 62 ft) long, but the information is too scarce
to make precise size estimates.[71]

Heaviest theropods

1. *Spinosaurus aegyptiacus*: 6–20.9 t (6.6–23.0 short tons)
2. *Tyrannosaurus rex*: 4.5–18.5 t (5.0–20.4 short tons)
3. *Carcharodontosaurus saharicus*: 3–15.1 t (3.3–16.6 short tons)
4. *Giganotosaurus carolinii*: 6–13.8 t (6.6–15.2 short tons)
5. *Acrocanthosaurus atokensis*: 2.4–7.3 t (2.6–8.0 short tons)
6. *Oxalaia quilombensis*: 5–7 t (5.5–7.7 short tons)
7. *Tyrannotitan chubutensis*: 4.9–7 t (5.4–7.7 short tons)
8. *Deinocheirus mirificus*: 5–6.4 t (5.5–7.1 short tons)
9. *Chilantaisaurus tashuikouensis*: 2.5–6 t (2.8–6.6 short tons)

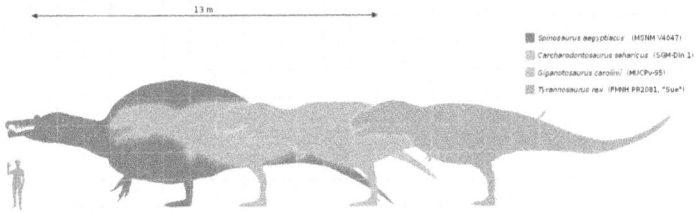

Figure 39: *Size comparison of selected giant theropod dinosaurs*

10. *Suchomimus tenerensis*: 2.5–5.2 t (2.8–5.7 short tons)

Longest theropods

1. *Spinosaurus aegyptiacus*: 15 m (49 ft)[72]
2. *Giganotosaurus carolinii*: 12.2–14 m (40–46 ft)
3. *Oxalaia quilombensis*: 11–14 m (36–46 ft)
4. *Saurophaganax maximus*: 10.5–14 m (34–46 ft)
5. *Carcharodontosaurus saharicus*: 12–13.3 m (39–44 ft)
6. *Tyrannotitan chubutensis*: 12.2–13 m (40–43 ft)
7. *Chilantaisaurus tashuikouensis*: 11–13 m (36–43 ft)?
8. *Allosaurus fragilis*: 8.5–13 m (28–43 ft)
9. *Mapusaurus roseae*: 10.2–12.6 m (33–41 ft)
10. *Tyrannosaurus rex* : 12–12.5 m (39–41 ft)

Lightest theropods

1. *Mellisuga helenae*: 2 g (0.071 oz)
2. *Mellisuga minima*: 2–2.4 g (0.071–0.085 oz)
3. *Selasphorus rufus*: 2–5 g (0.071–0.176 oz)
4. *Lophornis magnificus*: 2.1 g (0.074 oz)[73,74]
5. *Atthis heloisa*: 2.2 g (0.078 oz)
6. *Lophornis brachylophus*: 2.7 g (0.095 oz)[75]
7. *Calypte costae*: 3.38–4.43 g (0.119–0.156 oz)[76]
8. *Calypte anna*: 3.85–5.33 g (0.136–0.188 oz)
9. *Gerygone albofrontata*: 5.5–10 g (0.19–0.35 oz)
10. *Coereba flaveola*: 5.5–19 g (0.19–0.67 oz)

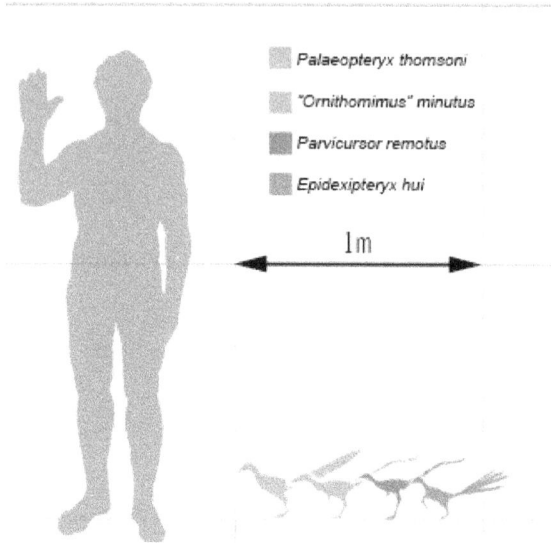

Figure 40: *Size comparison of the smallest non-avialan theropods*

Shortest theropods

1. *Mellisuga helenae*: 5–6 cm (2.0–2.4 in)[77]
2. *Mellisuga minima*: 6 cm (2.4 in)
3. *Lophornis magnificus*: 6.5–7 cm (2.6–2.8 in)
4. *Dicaeum ignipectus*: 7 cm (2.8 in)-
5. *Chaetocercus heliodor*: 7 cm (2.8 in)
6. *Myrmia micrura*: 7 cm (2.8 in)
7. *Lophornis brachylophus*: 7–7.5 cm (2.8–3.0 in)
8. *Atthis heloisa*: 7–7.5 cm (2.8–3.0 in)[78]
9. *Selasphorus rufus*: 7–9 cm (2.8–3.5 in)[79]
10. *Regulus regulus*: 8.5–9.5 cm (3.3–3.7 in)

Shortest non-avialan theropods

1. Unnamed (BEXHM: 2008.14.1): 16–50 cm (6.3–19.7 in)[80]
2. *Epidexipteryx hui*: 25–30 cm (9.8–11.8 in)
3. *"Ornithomimus" minutus*: 30 cm (12 in)
4. *Palaeopteryx thompsoni*: 30 cm (12 in)?
5. *Parvicursor remotus*: 30–39 cm (12–15 in)
6. *Nqwebasaurus thwazi*: 30–100 cm (12–39 in)
7. *Mei long*: 45–70 cm (18–28 in)

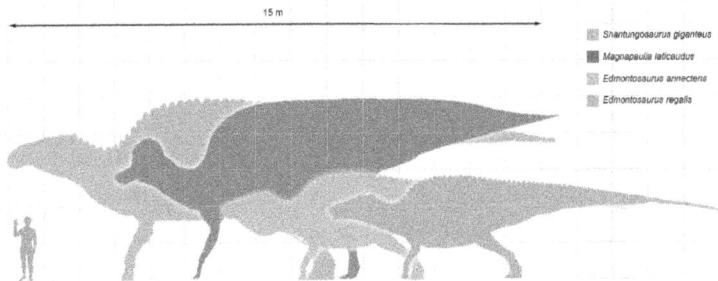

Figure 41: *Size comparison of selected giant ornithopod dinosaurs*

8. *Xixianykus zhangi*: 50 cm (20 in)
9. *Jinfengopteryx elegans*: 50–55 cm (20–22 in)
10. *Linhenykus monodactylus*: 50–60 cm (20–24 in)

Lightest non-avialan theropods

1. *Parvicursor remotus*: 137–200 g (4.8–7.1 oz)
2. *Epidexipteryx hui*: 164–391 g (5.8–13.8 oz)
3. *Compsognathus longipes*: 0.26–9 kg (0.57–19.84 lb)
4. *Ceratonykus oculatus*: 0.3–1 kg (0.66–2.20 lb)
5. *Zhongjianosaurus yangi*: 0.31 kg (0.68 lb)
6. *Ligabueino andesi*: 0.35–0.5 kg (0.77–1.10 lb)
7. *Yi qi*: 0.38 kg (0.84 lb)
8. *Microraptor zhaoianus*: 0.4–0.6 kg (0.88–1.32 lb)
9. *Mahakala omnogovae*: 0.4–0.79 kg (0.88–1.74 lb)[81]
10. *Mei long*: 0.4–0.85 kg (0.88–1.87 lb)

Ornithopods

Longest ornithopods

1. *Shantungosaurus giganteus*: 14.7–18.7 m (48–61 ft)
2. *Edmontosaurus annectens*: 12–15.2 m (39–50 ft)[82,83]
3. *Hypsibema crassicauda*: 15 m (49 ft)?
4. *Hypsibema missouriensis (Parrosaurus)*: 15 m (49 ft)?
5. *Iguanodon bernissartensis*: 10–13 m (33–43 ft)
6. *Charonosaurus jiayinensis*: 10–13 m (33–43 ft)
7. *Edmontosaurus regalis*: 9–13 m (30–43 ft)
8. *Magnapaulia laticaudus*: 12.5 m (41 ft)

9. *Saurolophus angustirostris*: 12 m (39 ft)
10. *Ornithotarsus immanis*: 12 m (39 ft)?

Heaviest ornithopods

1. *Shantungosaurus giganteus*: 9.9–22.5 t (10.9–24.8 short tons)
2. *Iguanodon seeleyi*: 15.3 t (16.9 short tons)
3. *Edmontosaurus annectens*: 3–13.2 t (3.3–14.6 short tons)[84]
4. *Iguanodon bernissartensis*: 3.08–8.3 t (3.40–9.15 short tons)
5. *Edmontosaurus regalis*: 4–7.6 t (4.4–8.4 short tons)
6. *Brachylophosaurus canadensis*: 4.5–7 t (5.0–7.7 short tons)
7. *Saurolophus osborni*: 1.9–6.6 t (2.1–7.3 short tons)
8. *Lanzhousaurus magnidens*: 6 t (6.6 short tons)
9. *Parasaurolophus walkeri*: 2.5–5.1 t (2.8–5.6 short tons)[85]
10. *Charonosaurus jiayinensis*: 5 t (5.5 short tons)

Shortest ornithopods

1. *Gasparinisaura cincosaltensis*: 0.65–1.7 m (2.1–5.6 ft)
2. *Leaellynasaura amicagraphica*: 0.9–3 m (3.0–9.8 ft)
3. *Valdosaurus canaliculatus*: 1.3 m (4.3 ft)
4. *Notohypsilophodon comodorensis*: 1.3 m (4.3 ft)
5. *Fulgurotherium australe*: 1.3–2 m (4.3–6.6 ft)
6. *Siluosaurus zhangqiani*: 1.4 m (4.6 ft)
7. *Qantassaurus intrepidus*: 1.4–2 m (4.6–6.6 ft)
8. *Changchunsaurus parvus*: 1.5 m (4.9 ft)
9. *Thescelosaurus* sp.: 1.5 m (4.9 ft)
10. *Yandusaurus hongheensis*: 1.5–3.8 m (4.9–12.5 ft)

Lightest ornithopods

1. *Gasparinisaura cincosaltensis*: 1–13 kg (2.2–28.7 lb)[86]
2. *Yueosaurus tiantaiensis*: 3.9 kg (8.6 lb)
3. *Fulgurotherium australe*: 6 kg (13 lb)
4. *Notohypsilophodon comodorensis*: 6 kg (13 lb)
5. *Yandusaurus hongheensis*: 6.6–7.5 kg (15–17 lb)
6. *Hypsilophodon foxii*: 7–21 kg (15–46 lb)
7. *Thescelosaurus* sp.: 7.9–86 kg (17–190 lb)
8. *Valdosaurus canaliculatus*: 10 kg (22 lb)
9. *Haya griva*: 11 kg (24 lb)
10. *Agilisaurus louderbacki*: 12 kg (26 lb)

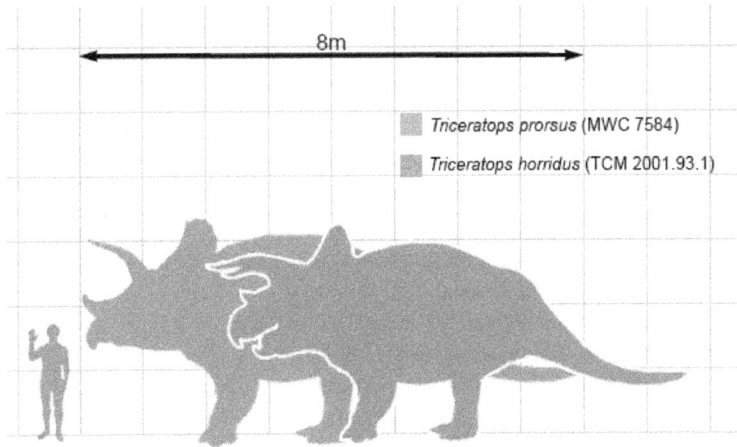

Figure 42: *Size of Triceratops prorsus (orange) and T. horridus (green) compared to a human.*

Ceratopsians

Longest ceratopsians

1. *Eotriceratops xerinsularis*: 8.5 m (28 ft)
2. *Triceratops horridus*: 8 m (26 ft)
3. *Triceratops prorsus*: 8 m (26 ft)
4. *Torosaurus latus*: 8 m (26 ft)
5. *Ojoceratops fowleri*: 8 m (26 ft)
6. *Titanoceratops ouranos*: 6.5–6.8 m (21–22 ft)
7. *Pachyrhinosaurus canadensis*: 6 m (20 ft)
8. *Achelousaurus horneri*: 6 m (20 ft)
9. *Albertaceratops nesmoi*: 5.8 m (19 ft)
10. *Pentaceratops sternbergii*: 5.5 m (18 ft)

Heaviest ceratopsians

1. *Triceratops horridus*: 9–13.5 t (9.9–14.9 short tons)
2. *Triceratops prorsus*: 9–10.9 t (9.9–12.0 short tons)
3. *Titanoceratops ouranos*: 4.5–10.8 t (5.0–11.9 short tons)
4. *Eotriceratops xerinsularis*: 10 t (11 short tons)
5. *Pachyrhinosaurus canadensis*: 3–4.4 t (3.3–4.9 short tons)
6. *Styracosaurus albertensis*: 1.8–4.2 t (2.0–4.6 short tons)
7. *Albertaceratops nesmoi*: 3.5 t (3.9 short tons)
8. *Chasmosaurus russelli*: 1.5–3.5 t (1.7–3.9 short tons)

9. *Chasmosaurus belli*: 2–3.1 t (2.2–3.4 short tons)
10. *Pentaceratops sternbergii*: 2.5 t (2.8 short tons)

Shortest ceratopsians

1. *Yamaceratops dorngobiensis*: 50 cm (1.6 ft)
2. *Liaoceratops yanzigouensis*: 50 cm (1.6 ft)
3. *Archaeoceratops yujingziensis*: 55 cm (1.80 ft)
4. *Microceratus gobiensis*: 60 cm (2.0 ft)
5. *Bagaceratops rozhdestvenskyi*: 80 cm (2.6 ft)
6. *Archaeoceratops oshimai*: 80–90 cm (2.6–3.0 ft)
7. *Psittacosaurus lujiatunensis*: 90 cm (3.0 ft)
8. *Micropachycephalosaurus hongtuyanensis*: 100 cm (3.3 ft)
9. *Chaoyangsaurus youngi*: 100 cm (3.3 ft)
10. *Xuanhuaceratops niei*: 100 cm (3.3 ft)

Lightest ceratopsians

1. *Liaoceratops yanzigouensis*: 2 kg (4.4 lb)
2. *Yamaceratops dorngobiensis*: 2 kg (4.4 lb)
3. *Psittacosaurus sinensis*: 4.1–6 kg (9.0–13.2 lb)
4. *Psittacosaurus lujiatunensis*: 5 kg (11 lb)
5. *Yinlong downsi*: 5.5–10 kg (12–22 lb)
6. *Micropachycephalosaurus hongtuyanensis*: 5.9 kg (13 lb)
7. *Chaoyangsaurus youngi*: 6 kg (13 lb)
8. *Xuanhuaceratops niei*: 6 kg (13 lb)
9. *Psittacosaurus gobiensis*: 6–9.4 kg (13–21 lb)
10. *Bagaceratops rozhdestvenskyi*: 7 kg (15 lb)

Pachycephalosaurs

Longest pachycephalosaurs

Size by overall length, including tail, of all pachycephalosaurs measuring 3 metres (9.8 ft) or more in length.

1. *Pachycephalosaurus wyomingensis*: 4.5–7 m (15–23 ft)
2. *Stygimoloch spinifer*: 3 m (9.8 ft)
3. *Gravitholus albertae*: 3 m (9.8 ft)?

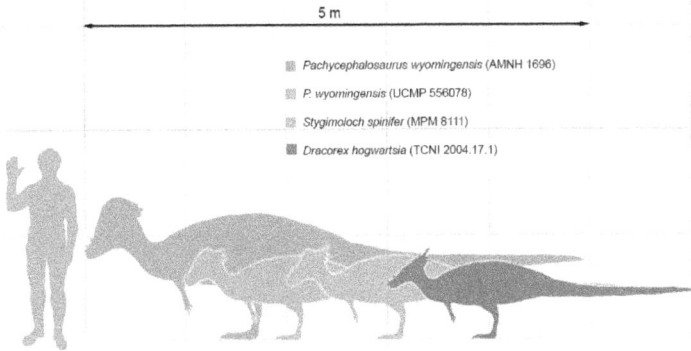

Figure 43: *Size comparison of an adult P. wyomingensis (green), potential growth stages, and a human*

Shortest pachycephalosaurs

Size by overall length, including tail, of all pachycephalosaurs measuring 2 metres (6 ft 7 in) or less in length as adults.

1. *Wannanosaurus yansiensis*: 60 cm (2.0 ft)
2. *Colepiocephale lambei*: 1.8 m (5.9 ft)
3. *Texacephale langstoni*: 2 m (6.6 ft)

Thyreophorans

Longest thyreophorans

1. *Stegosaurus ungulatus*: 7–9 m (23–30 ft)
2. *Stegosaurus stenops*: 6.5–9 m (21–30 ft)
3. *Ankylosaurus magniventris*: 6.25–8 m (20.5–26.2 ft)
4. *Cedarpelta bilbeyhallorum*: 5–9 m (16–30 ft)
5. *Dacentrurus armatus*: 7–8 m (23–26 ft)[87]
6. *Tarchia gigantea*: 4.5–8 m (15–26 ft)
7. *Sauropelta edwardsorum*: 5–7.6 m (16–25 ft)
8. *Dyoplosaurus acutosquameus*: 7 m (23 ft)?
9. *Tuojiangosaurus multispinus*: 6.5–7 m (21–23 ft)
10. *Wuerhosaurus homheni*: 6.1–7 m (20–23 ft)

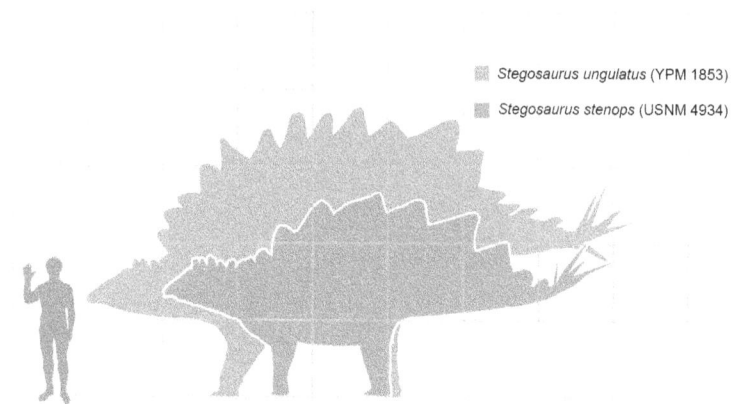

Stegosaurus ungulatus (YPM 1853)
Stegosaurus stenops (USNM 4934)

Figure 44: *Size of Stegosaurus ungulatus (orange) and S. stenops (green) compared to a human*

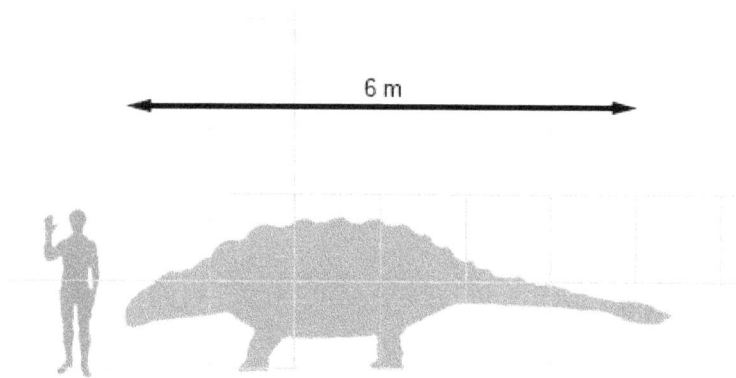

6 m

Figure 45: *Estimated size of Ankylosaurus compared to a human.*

Heaviest thyreophorans

1. *Ankylosaurus magniventris*: 4.8–8 t (5.3–8.8 short tons)
2. *Dacentrurus armatus*: 5–7.4 t (5.5–8.2 short tons)
3. *Stegosaurus ungulatus*: 3.8–7 t (4.2–7.7 short tons)
4. *Stegosaurus stenops*: 2.6–5.3 t (2.9–5.8 short tons)
5. *Cedarpelta bilbeyhallorum*: 5 t (5.5 short tons)
6. *Hesperosaurus mjosi*: 3.5–5 t (3.9–5.5 short tons)
7. *Tuojiangosaurus multispinus*: 1.1–4.8 t (1.2–5.3 short tons)
8. *Wuerhosaurus homheni*: 4 t (4.4 short tons)

9. *Niobrarasaurus coleii*: 4 t (4.4 short tons)
10. *Gobisaurus domoculus*: 3.5 t (3.9 short tons)

Shortest thyreophorans

1. *Tatisaurus oehleri*: 1.2 m (3.9 ft)
2. *Scutellosaurus lawleri*: 1.2–1.3 m (3.9–4.3 ft)
3. *Dracopelta zbyszewskii*: 2–3 m (6.6–9.8 ft)
4. *Minmi paravertebra*: 2–3 m (6.6–9.8 ft)

Lightest thyreophorans

1. *Scutellosaurus lawleri*: 3 kg (6.6 lb)
2. *Emausaurus ernsti*: 50 kg (110 lb)
3. *Scelidosaurus harrisonii*: 64.5–270 kg (142–595 lb)
4. *Animantarx ramaljonesi*: 300 kg (660 lb)
5. *Struthiosaurus transylvanicus*: 300 kg (660 lb)
6. *Struthiosaurus austriacus*: 300 kg (660 lb)
7. *Gargoyleosaurus parkpinorum*: 300 kg (660 lb)
8. *Mymoorapelta maysi*: 300 kg (660 lb)
9. *Minmi paravertebra*: 300 kg (660 lb)

External links

Wikimedia Commons has media related to *Dinosauria size comparisons*.

- " The Biggest Carnivore: Dinosaur History Rewritten[88]
- Holtz, Thomas R., Jr.; Rey, Luis V. (2007). *Dinosaurs: the most complete, up-to-date encyclopedia for dinosaur lovers of all ages*[89] (PDF). New York: Random House. ISBN 978-0-375-82419-7. (Dinosaur size#References)
- "Dinosaur records", Czech article by [[Vladimír Socha[90]]; *Dinosaurus-Blog.com*, August 1st, 2016]

Reproductive biology

Dinosaur egg

Dinosaur eggs are the organic vessels in which a dinosaur embryo develops. When the first scientifically documented remains of dinosaurs were being described in England during the 1820s, it was presumed that dinosaurs had laid eggs because they were reptiles. In 1859, the first scientifically documented dinosaur egg fossils were discovered in France by Jean-Jacques Poech, although they were mistaken for giant bird eggs. The first scientifically recognized dinosaur egg fossils were discovered in 1923 by an American Museum of Natural History crew in Mongolia. Since then many new nesting sites have been found all over the world and a system of classification based on the structure of eggshell was developed in China before gradually diffusing into the West. Dinosaur eggshell can be studied in thin section and viewed under a microscope. The interior of a dinosaur egg can be studied using CAT scans or by gradually dissolving away the shell with acid. Sometimes the egg preserves the remains of the developing embryo inside. The oldest known dinosaur eggs and embryos are from *Massospondylus*, which lived during the Early Jurassic, about 190 million years ago.[91,92]

History

In 1859, the first scientifically documented dinosaur egg fossils were discovered in southern France by a Catholic priest and amateur naturalist named Father Jean-Jacques Pouech; he thought, however, that they were laid by giant birds.[93] The first scientifically recognized dinosaur egg fossils were discovered serendipitously in 1923 by an American Museum of Natural History crew while looking for evidence of early humans in Mongolia.[94] These eggs were mistakenly attributed to the locally abundant herbivore *Protoceratops*, but are now known to be *Oviraptor* eggs. Egg discoveries continued to mount

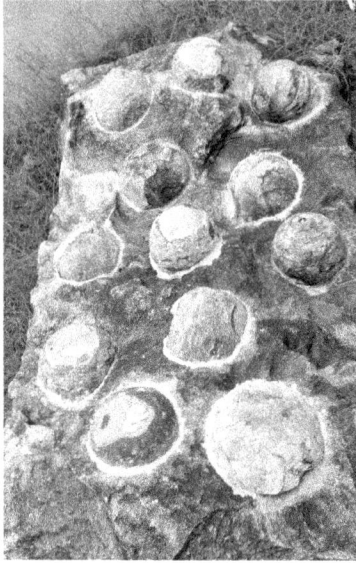

Figure 46: *Fossilized dinosaur eggs displayed at Indroda Dinosaur and Fossil Park*

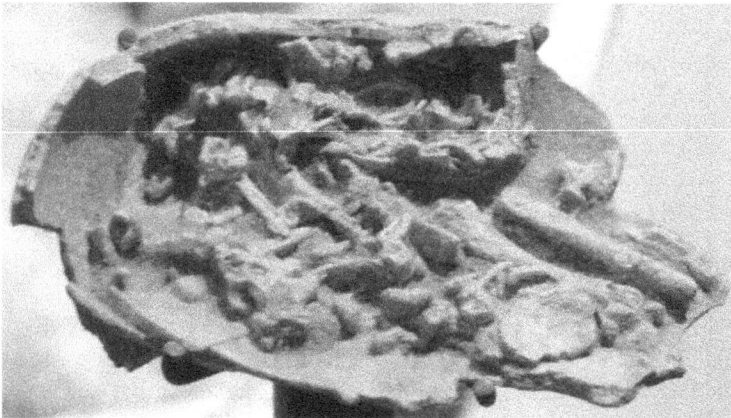

Figure 47: *A Citipati osmolskae egg with preserved embryo, at the AMNH.*

Figure 48: *Fossilized dinosaur egg from the
Gobi desert, National Museum in Prague*

all over the world, leading to the development of multiple competing classification schemes. In 1975 Chinese paleontologist Zhao Zi-Kui started a revolution in fossil egg classification by developing a system of "parataxonomy" based on the traditional Linnaean system which classified eggs based on their physical qualities rather than their hypothesized mothers. Zhao's new method of egg classification was hindered from adoption by Western scientists due to language barriers. However, in the early 1990s Russian paleontologist Konstantin Mikhailov brought attention to Zhao's work in the English language scientific literature.

Identification

Fossil dinosaur eggshell fragments can be recognized based on three important traits. Their thickness should be roughly uniform, they are usually slightly curved, and their surface is covered in tiny pores. Less frequently, the concave underside of the eggshell fragment will preserve bumps known as mammillae. Sometimes the embryo had absorbed so much of the calcium that the mammilae need a magnifying glass or microscope to be seen. However, there are many kinds of naturally occurring objects which can resemble fossil eggs. These can fool even professional paleontologists.

False eggs

Calculus: Calculi are egg-like objects formed in the stomachs of ruminants such as cattle, deer, elk, and goats. Calculus formation is a defense mechanism protecting the ruminant's stomach from damage if it swallows a foreign object while grazing. After ingestion, the object is covered by the same material composing bone, calcium phosphate, and eventually vomited out of the animal's system. These "stomach stones" tend to range in size from 1 to 6 centimeters. Larger sizes are known but very rare. Sometimes tiny dimples cover the surface of a stomach stone, which can fool observers into thinking they are the pores of an egg. Fossil egg expert Ken Carpenter has described stomach stones as the most egg-like natural objects, noting that they are "the trickiest [egg-like] objects to correctly identify". Calculi are so egg-like that on one occasion a detailed description of a stomach stone misidentified as a fossil egg was published in the scientific literature. Calculi can be distinguished from real egg fossils because when they are broken open, they show the layers of calcium phosphate and the foreign object at the core. Multiple layers of eggshell are known in pathological eggs, but these layers don't go all the way down to its core the way a stomach stone's do. Calculi are often suspiciously intact, unlike fossil eggs, which are usually damaged. Stomach stones also lack distinct shells with their attending structural components like continuous or prismatic layers, mammillae, and pores.

Concretions: Concretions are formed when decaying organisms change the chemistry of their immediate surroundings in a manner that is conducive to minerals precipitating out of solution. These minerals accumulate in a mass roughly shaped like the region of altered chemistry. Sometimes the mass produced is egg-shaped. Most egg-shaped concretions have uniform interiors, however some form through the accumulation of mineral in layers. These layered concretions can be even harder to recognize than those with uniform interiors because the layers can resemble egg white and yolk. The yellow of the false yolk comes from minerals like limonite, siderite, and sulfur.

Concretions also generally lack distinct shells, although sometimes they can appear to have them if their outside surfaces have been case-hardened. Since their interiors are softer, erosion can separate the two, creating eggshell pseudofossils. Real egg fossils should preserve eggshell structures like pores, mammillae, and prismatic or continuous layers, which are not present in concretions. Any given concretion is unlikely to be exactly the same size as any other, so associations of egg-like objects of different sizes are probably not real eggs at all. Concretions can also be far larger than any real egg so an apparently unnaturally large "egg" has probably been misidentified.

Insect trace fossils: Sometimes the living or breeding chambers of an insect burrow are so perfectly egg-shaped that even a paleontologist can mistake a

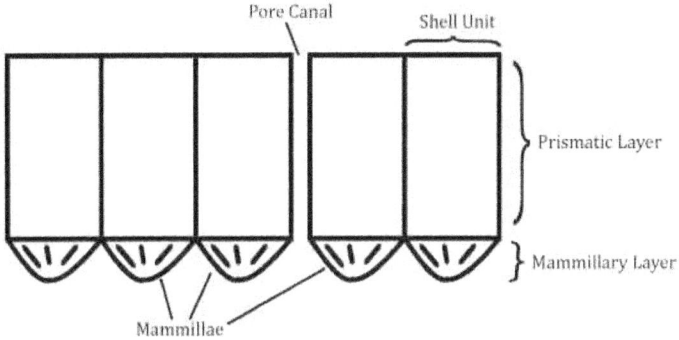

Figure 49: *Diagram of a two-layered eggshell.*

natural cast of these chambers for a fossil egg. Insect burrow fossils can sometimes be distinguished from real egg fossils by the presence of "scratch marks" on their surface left by the insect during the burrow's original excavation. Fossil insect pupae can also resemble eggs. After death and burial, the decomposition of a deceased pupa would leave a gap in the sediment that could be filled with minerals carried by groundwater, forming an egg-like cast. These pseudo-eggs can be recognized by their small size (usually not much longer than a centimeter or two) and lack of an eggshell with its typical anatomy.

Stones: The erosive effects of water can sometimes round rocks into egg-like shapes.

Structure

Paleontologists' knowledge of the structure of dinosaur eggs is limited to the hard shell. However, it can be inferred that dinosaur eggs had an amnion, chorion, and an allantois, the three major membranes in modern bird and reptile eggs. Dinosaur eggs vary greatly in size and shape, but even the largest dinosaur eggs (*Megaloolithus*) are smaller than the largest known bird eggs, which were laid by the extinct elephant bird. Dinosaur eggs range in shape from spherical to highly elongated (some specimens three times longer than they are wide). Some elongated eggs are symmetrical, whereas others have one rounded end and one pointed end (similar to bird eggs). Most elongated eggs were laid by theropods and have an avian-like eggshell, whereas the spherical eggs typically represent non-theropod dinosaurs.

Fossil dinosaur eggshells, like modern bird and reptile eggshells, are made up of calcium carbonate crystal units. The basic arrangement and structure of these eggshell units (called the ultrastructure) is used to divide fossil eggs into several basic types, including the spherulitic, prismatic, and ornithoid basic types, which contain dinosaurs. Dinosaur eggs further classified by the microstructural aspects of the crystalline structure of the eggshell units and by the type of their pores and their shell ornamentation.

Layers

Dinosaur eggshells are divided into one, two, or three layers of distinct ultrastructure.

The innermost layer, known as the mammillary layer or the cone layer, is only found in theropod eggs (the prismatic and ornithoid basic types). It is composed of cone-shaped structures called mammillae at the base of each shell unit. Mammillae are the first part of the eggshell to form. Each mammilla forms from crystals radiating outward from an organic core until they touch neighboring mammillae and grow upwards into the next layer.[95] In spherulitic eggs, the eggs of non-theropod dinosaurs, the eggshell units grow upward from their organic cores; the base of each eggshell unit is rounded, but is not a true mammilla because it does not have a distinct ultrastructure from the top of the unit.

The second layer is alternately called the prismatic layer, the columnar layer, the continuous layer, the crystalline layer, the cryptoprismatic layer,[96] the palisade layer, the spongy layer, or the single layer. In this layer, the shell units can be distinct, partially fused together, or entirely continuous. In some dinosaur eggs, the prismatic layer exhibits squamatic ultrastructure, where the prismatic structure is obscured by a rough texture resembling lizard skin.

Though rare in non-avian dinosaurs, some theropod eggs and most bird eggs have a third layer (known as the external layer) made up of vertical calcite crystals.

Pore canals

In all eggs, the embryo must breathe. In amniotes (including dinosaurs), pore canals cutting through the eggshell allow gas exchange between the embryo and the outside world. Dinosaur eggshells exhibit a lot of diversity in pore size, density, and shape. One early attempt at classification of dinosaurian eggs, proposed by the Soviet paleontologist A. Sochava, was based on grouping eggs by their pore systems. This system was abandoned when it was discovered that different eggs could have very similar pores, but pore systems do play an important role in modern eggshell parataxonomy. The density and width of the pores, combined with the eggshell's thickness can be used to predict the gas conductance of a dinosaur's egg. This can provide both information about nesting behavior and about the climate: eggs buried in sediment have higher rates of gas conductance than those laid in the open, and eggs laid in arid environments have lower gas conductance (to prevent water loss) than those laid in more humid conditions.[97]

Paleontologist and fossil egg expert Kenneth Carpenter catalogued six types of pore systems:

1. Angusticanaliculate - Long, narrow, straight pores with low pore density. These eggs would have a low gas exchange rate, and therefore they were typically laid in dry areas.
2. Tubocanaliculate - Large diameter pores with funnel-shaped openings on both inner and outer surfaces of the shell. These eggs would have a high gas exchange rate, and therefore were probably buried in humid mounds.
3. Multicanaliculate - Numerous large, branching, and closely spaced pore canals. They have a high gas exchange rate, so like tubocanaliculate eggs they were probably also buried humid mounds.
4. Prolatocanaliculate - Pores vary in width throughout their length. Gas exchange water loss rates are variable, so these eggs could have been laid in many different environments. This type is subdivided into foveocanaliculate with larger pore openings, and lagenocanaliculate with narrower pore openings.
5. Rimocanaliculate - Very narrow slitlike pore canals. This pore system is seen in modern ostriches, so these eggs were laid in open nests, similar to how ostriches do today.
6. Obliquicanaliculate - These canals cut diagonally through multiple eggshell units instead of going between them like in other pore systems. Obliquicanaliculate pores are only found in a single oogenus: *Preprismatoolithus*.

Ornamentation

Unlike most modern eggs, many dinosaur eggs had a rough texture formed by nodes and ridges ornamenting the surface of their shell. This is predominant in Cretaceous dinosaur eggs, but very rare in eggs from the Jurassic or Triassic. Because of the lack of modern analogues, the purpose of eggshell ornamentation is unknown, but many functions have been proposed. Possibly, they provided extra strength to the eggshell without having pore canals too long for adequate gas exchange. They could also have helped keep substrate away from the pore openings of eggs that were buried, but modern turtles and crocodylians which bury their eggs have smooth eggshells, so this adaptation is not necessary for animals which bury their eggs. Another hypothesis, proposed by R. M. Mellon in 1982 in his senior thesis at Princeton University, is that the ridges and nodes would have formed pathways for gas to flow across the surface of the eggshell, preventing accumulation of too much CO_2 and aiding the flow of oxygen and water vapor.

Since it varies from egg to egg, the texture of an eggshell's ornamentation is useful for classification. Six types of ornamentation were catalogued by Carpenter in 1999:

1. Compactituberculate - The dome-shaped tops of the shell units form a dense covering of nodes on the surface of the eggshell. This type of ornamentation is most commonly seen in megaloolithids.
2. Sagenotuberculate - The nodes and ridges form a netlike pattern interspersed with pits and grooves.
3. Dispersituberculate - Scattered nodes. This ornamentation is seen on the poles of elongated eggs, which may have allowed accumulations CO_2 at the poles to escape between the nodes.
4. Lineartuberculate - Ridges, and chains of ridges and nodes form lines parallel to the long axis of the egg.
5. Ramotuberculate - Irregular chains of nodes, typically found as a transition between the lineartuberculate midsection and dispersituberculate ends of elongated eggs.
6. Anastomotuberculate - Ridges similar to lineartuberculate, but instead form wavy, branching, or anastomosing patterns resembling the water ripple marks in sand.

Classification

The classification of dinosaur eggs is based on the structure of the egg shells viewed in thin section via microscope, although new techniques such as electron backscatter diffraction have been used. There are three main categories of dinosaur eggs: (sauropods and hadrosaurs,) Prismatic, and ornithoid (theropods, including modern birds).

Oogenera

Oogenera are taxonomic names for types of eggshell. Nearly three dozen oogenera have been named for dinosaur eggs:

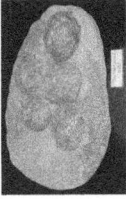

Figure 50: Therizinosaur nest and eggs in from Dinosaurland in Lyme Regis, England.

- Ageroolithus
- Apheloolithus
- Boletuoolithus[98]
- Cairanoolithus[99]
- Continuoolithus
- Dendroolithus
- Dictyoolithus[100]
- Dispersituberoolithus
- Ellipsoolithus[101]
- Elongatoolithus[102]

- Faveoolithus
- Heishanoolithus[103]
- Laevisoolithus
- Macroolithus[104]
- Macroelongatoolithus[105]
- Megaloolithus[106]
- Nanshiungoolithus[107]
- Oblongoolithus
- Ovaloolithus[108]
- Pachycorioolithus

- Paraspheroolithus[109]
- Phaceloolithus
- Placoolithus[110]
- Porituberoolithus
- Polyclonoolithus
- Preprismatoolithus
- Prismatoolithus[111]
- Protoceratopsidovum[112]
- Pseudogeckoolithus
- Shixingoolithus[113]

- Sphaerovum
- Spheroolithus[114]
- Spheruprismatoolithus[115]
- Spongioolithus[115]
- Stromatoolithus
- Subtiliolithus
- Tacuarembovum
- Trachoolithus[116]
- Tristraguloolithus
- Youngoolithus

Embryos

Dinosaur embryos, the animal inside the eggs, are very rare but useful to understand ontogeny, heterochrony, and dinosaur systematics. Embryo fossils are known from:

* *Beibeilong*
* *Citipati*
* *Heyuannia*
* *Lufengosaurus*
* *Lourinhanosaurus*
* *Massospondylus*
* *Maiasaura*
* *Troodon*

Taphonomy

The formation of fossil eggs begins with the original egg itself. Not all eggs that end up fossilizing experience the death of their embryo beforehand. Fossil eggs with open tops are common and could result from the preservation of eggs that hatched successfully. Dinosaur eggs whose embryos died were likely victims of similar causes to those that kill embryos in modern reptile and bird eggs. Typical causes of death include congenital problems, diseases, suffocation from being buried too deep, inimical temperatures, or too much or too little water.

Whether or not hatching was successful, burial would begin with sediments gradually entering any large openings in the shell. Even intact eggs are likely to fill with sediment once they crack under the strain of deep burial. Sometimes, though, fossilization can begin fast enough to prevent the eggs from being cracked. If the water table is high enough dissolved minerals like calcite can percolate through the pores of the eggshell. When the egg is completely filled it can become sturdy enough to withstand the weight of the overlying sediments. Not all fossil egg specimens are of complete specimens, however. Individual pieces of eggshell are much more robust than the entire egg and can be transported intact long distances from where they were originally laid.

When the egg is buried deeply enough, the bacteria decomposing it no longer have access to oxygen and need to power their metabolisms with different substances. These physiological changes in the decomposers also alter the local environment in a way that allows certain minerals to be deposited, while others remain in solution. Generally, however, a fossilizing egg's shell keeps the same calcite it had in life, which allows scientists to study its original structure millions of years after the developing dinosaur hatched or died. However, eggs can also sometimes be altered after burial. This process is called diagenesis. One form of diagenesis is a microscopic cross-hatched pattern imposed on the eggshell by the pressure of being buried deeply. If the pressure gets severe enough, sometimes the eggshell's internal microscopic structure can be completely destroyed. Diagenesis can also happen chemically in addition to physically. The chemical conditions of a decomposing egg can make it easy for silica to be incorporated into eggshell and damage its structure. When iron-bearing substances alter eggshell it can be obvious because compounds like hematite, pyrite, and iron sulfide can turn the shell blackish or rusty colors.

Depositional environments

Dinosaur eggs are known from a variety of depositional environments.

Beach sands: Beach sands were a good place for dinosaurs to lay their eggs because the sand would be effective at absorbing and holding enough heat to incubate the eggs. One ancient beach deposit in northeastern Spain actually preserves about 300,000 fossil dinosaur eggs.

Floodplains: Dinosaurs often laid their eggs on ancient floodplains. The mudstones deposited at these sites are therefore excellent sources of dinosaur egg fossils.

Sand dunes: Many dinosaur eggs have been recovered from sandstone deposits that formed in the ancient dune fields of what are now northern China and Mongolia. The presence of *Oviraptor* preserved in their life brooding position suggests that the eggs, nests, and parents may have been rapidly buried by sandstorms.

Excavation and preparation

Usually the first evidence of fossil dinosaur eggs to be discovered are shell fragments that have eroded away from the original eggs and been transported downhill by the elements. If the source eggs can be found the area must be examined for more unexposed eggs. If the paleontologists are fortunate enough to have found a nest, the number and arrangement of the eggs must be estimated. Excavation must proceed to significant depth since many dinosaur nests include multiple layers of eggs. As the underside of the nest is excavated, it would be covered by material like newspaper, tin foil, or tissue. Afterwards, the entire block is covered in multiple layers of plaster-soaked strips of burlap. When the plaster is dried, the block is undercut the rest of the way and turned over.

The fine work of cleaning the egg fossils is performed in a laboratory. Preparation usually begins from the underside of the block, which tends to be the best preserved. Because of their fragility, cleaning fossil eggs requires patience and skill. Scientists use delicate instruments like dental picks, needles, small pneumatic engraving tools, and X-Acto knives. Scientists must determine at what point to stop cleaning based on their own criteria. If eggs are fully extracted they can be more fully studied individually at the cost of information regarding the spatial relationships between eggs or if the eggs had hatched. Commercial fossil dealers tend to expose only the bottom of the eggs since the topsides might be damaged by hatching and therefore less visually appealing to potential customers.

Research techniques

Acid dissolution

Acids can be used to learn more about fossil eggs. Diluted acetic acid or EDTA can be used to expose the microstructure of shell that has been damaged by weathering. Acids are also used to extract embryo skeletons from the egg encasing them. Even fossilized soft tissue like muscle and cartilage as well as fat globules from the original egg yolk can be uncovered using this method. Amateur paleontologist Terry Manning has been credited with groundbreaking work developing this technique.Wikipedia:Citation needed First, the paleontologist must submerge the egg in a very dilute phosphoric acid bath. Since the acid solution can penetrate the egg, every few days the specimen must be soaked in distilled water to prevent the acid from damaging the embryo before it is even exposed. If embryonic fossil bone is revealed after drying from the water bath, the exposed fossils must be delicately cleaned with fine instruments like needles and paint brushes. The exposed bone is then coated with plastic preservatives like Acryloid B67, Paraloid B72, or Vinac B15 to protect it from the acid when submerged for another round. The complete process can take months before the whole embryo is revealed. Even then only about 20% of the eggs subjected to the process reveal any embryo fossils at all.

CAT scans

CAT scans can be used to infer the 3D structure of a fossil egg's interior by compiling images taken of slices through the egg in small regular increments. Scientists have tried to use CAT scans to look for embryo fossils contained inside the egg without having to damage the egg itself by physically extracting them. However, as of Ken Carpenter's 1999 book on dinosaur eggs, *Eggs, Nests, and Baby Dinosaurs*, all alleged embryos discovered using this method were actually false alarms. Variations in the type of infilling mineral or cement binding the infilling sediment into rock sometimes resemble bones in CAT scan images. Sometimes eggshell fragments that fell back into the egg when it hatched have been mistaken for embryonic bones. The use of CAT scans to search for embryonic remains is actually conceptually flawed since embryonic bones have not yet mineralized. Since the infilling sediment is their only source of minerals they will be preserved at basically the same density and therefore have poor visibility in the scan. The validity of this issue has been confirmed by performing Cat scans on fossil eggs known to have embryos inside and noting their poor visibility in the scan images. The only truly reliable way to discover a dinosaur embryo is to cut the egg open or dissolve some of its eggshell away.

Cathodoluminescence

Cathodoluminescence is the most important tool paleontologists have for revealing whether or not the calcium in fossil eggshell has been altered. Calcite in eggshell is either pure or rich in calcium carbonate. However, the calcite composing the egg can be altered after burial to include significant calcium content. Cathodoluminescence causes calcite altered in this fashion to glow orange.

Gel electrophoresis

Gel electrophoresis has been used in attempts to identify the amino acids present in the organic components of dinosaur eggshell. Contact with human skin can contaminate eggs with foreign amino acids, so only untouched eggs can be investigated using this technique. EDTA can be used to dissolve the calcite of the eggshell while leaving the shell's organic content intact. The resultant organic residue would be blended and then implanted into gel. Electricity would then be run through the sample, causing the amino acids to migrate through the gel until they stop at levels determined by their physical properties. Protein silver stain is then used to dye the amino acids and make them visible. The bands of amino acids from the dinosaur eggs can then be compared with the banding of samples with known composition for identification.

Gel electrophoresis is not necessarily a perfect means of discovering the amino acid composition of dinosaur eggshell because sometimes the amount or type of amino acids present could be altered during or after preservation. One potential confounding factor would be the heating of deeply buried egg fossils, which can break down amino acids. Another potential source of error is groundwater, which can leach away amino acids. These issues cast doubt as to whether the results these sorts of studies give are reliable as the actual composition of the eggshell's organic material in life. However, studies applying these techniques have made suggestive findings, including amino acid profiles in dinosaur eggs similar to those in modern birds.

Geneva lens measure

The Geneva Lens Measure is a device used to measure curved surfaces. It is most commonly used by opticians to measure lenses but can also be used by paleontologists to estimate the life size of dinosaur eggs from shell fragments. The instrument can be used to help estimate the size of fossil eggshells by measuring their curved surfaces. Since most eggs aren't perfectly round measurements from multiple parts of the egg with varying shell curvatures may be needed to get a full idea of the egg's size. Ideally an eggshell fragment being used to estimate the full size of an egg should be more than 3 cm long. Smaller eggshell fragments are better suited to other methods of study, like the Obrig radius dial gauge. The Geneva Lens measure gives units in diopters which must be converted to the radius in millimeters. Use of the Geneva Lens Measure to estimate the size of a fossil egg was first done by Sauer· on fossil ostrich eggs.

Light microscopy

Light microscopy can be used to magnify the structure of dinosaur eggshell for scientific research. To do so an eggshell fragment must be embedded in epoxy resin and sliced into a thin section with a thin-bladed rock saw. This basic method was invented by French paleontologist Paul Gervais and has remained almost unchanged ever since. Horizontally cut thin sections are called tangential thin sections while vertically cut thin sections are called radial sections. Regardless of direction, the sample must be abraded by fine-grit sand or emery paper until it is translucent. Then the structure of the shell's calcite crystals or pores can be examined under a petrographic microscope. The calcite crystal structure of dinosaur eggshell can be classified by their effect on polarized light. Calcite is capable of acting as a polarizing light filter. When a microscopic thin section sample is rotated relative to polarized light it can eventually block all the light and seem opaque. This phenomenon is called extinction. Different varieties of dinosaur eggs with their different calcite crystal structures have different light extinction properties that can be used to identify and distinguish even eggs that seem very similar on the surface. To reconstruct the three-dimensional structures of the shell's pore channels scientists require a series of multiple radial sections.

Scanning electron microscopy

Scanning electron microscopy is used to view dinosaur eggshell under even greater magnification than is possible with light microscopy. However, this does not mean that scanning electron microscopy is necessarily the superior research method. Since both techniques provide differing amounts and types of information they can be used together synergistically to provide a more complete understanding of the specimen under scrutiny. Eggshell specimens best suited for scanning electron microscopy are those recently broken because such a break will usually occur along the plane of the eggshell's calcite crystal lattice. First, a small specimen would be covered with a very thin layer of gold or platinum. The specimen would then be bombarded with electrons. The electrons bounce back off the metal and due to their small size, can be used to form a detailed image of the specimen.

Mass spectrometry

Mass spectrometry is a method for determining eggshell composition that uses a device called a mass spectrometer. First, the eggshell sample must be powdered and placed in the mass spectrometer's vacuum chamber. The powder is vaporized by the heat of an intense laser beam. A stream of electrons then bombard the gaseous eggshell molecules, which breaks down the molecules in the eggshell and imbues them with a positive charge. A magnetic field then sorts them by mass before they are detected by the spectrometer. One application of mass spectrometry has been to study the isotope ratios of dinosaur eggshell in order to ascertain their diets and living conditions. However this research is complicated by the fact that isotope ratios can be altered post mortem before or during fossilization. Bacterial decomposition can alter carbon isotope ratios in eggs and groundwater can alter the oxygen isotope ratios of eggshell.

X rays

X-ray equipment, like CAT scans, are used to study the interior of fossil eggs. Unlike CAT scans, x-ray imaging condenses the entire interior of the egg into a single two-dimensional image rather than a series of images documenting the interior in three dimensions. X-ray imaging in the context of dinosaur research has generally been used to look for evidence of embryonic fossils contained inside the egg. However, as of Kenneth Carpenter's 1999 book *Eggs, Nests, and Baby Dinosaurs*, all putative embryos discovered using x-rays have been misidentifications. This is because the use of x-rays to find embryos is conceptually flawed. Embryo bones are incompletely developed and will generally lack their own mineral content, as such the only source of minerals for these bones is the sediment that fills the egg after burial. The fossilized bones will therefore have the same density as the sediment filling the interior of the egg which served as the source for their mineral content and will be poorly visible in an x-ray image. So far the only reliable method for examining embryonic fossils preserved in dinosaur eggs is to physically extract them through means such as acid dissolution.

X-rays can be used to chemically analyze dinosaur eggshell. This technique requires pure shell samples, so the fossil must be completely free of its surrounding rock matrix. The shell must then be further cleaned by an ultrasonic bath. The sample can then be bombarded by electrons emitted by the same sort of probe used by scanning electron microscopes. Upon impact with the samples x-rays are emitted that can be used to identify the composition of the shell.

X-ray diffraction is a method for determining eggshell composition that uses X-rays to directly bombard powdered eggshell. Upon impact some of the x-rays will be diffracted at different angles and intensities depending on the specific elements present in the eggshell.

Allosterics

In order to test out how allosterics played a part in dinosaur egg size, scientists used modern day animal species such as birds, crocodiles, and tortoises in their experiment. They set the bird group as the representing the theropods with the reptiles representing the sauropod group. The laid eggs of each species where compared with one another over the course of the study as well as against the fossilized eggs. The results that was retrieved from the experiment was that while sauropods laid smaller eggs in greater amounts each year, dinosaur of the theropod group was revealed to lay larger eggs less frequently over the years, similar to modern birds today.

Footnotes

References

- Carpenter, Kenneth (1999). *Eggs, Nests, and Baby Dinosaurs: A Look at Dinosaur Reproduction (Life of the Past)*, Indiana University Press; ISBN 0-253-33497-7.
- Deeming, D. C. and M. W. J. Ferguson (eds.) 1991. Egg incubation: its effect on embryonic development in birds and reptiles. Cambridge University Press, UK. 448pp.
- Glut, Donald F. (2003), "Appendix: Dinosaur Tracks and Eggs", *Dinosaurs: The Encyclopedia. 3rd Supplement*, Jefferson, North Carolina: McFarland & Company, Inc., pp. 613–652, ISBN 0-7864-1166-X
- Horner, John R.; Weishampel, David B. (1996). "A comparative embryological study of two ornithischian dinosaurs - a correction". *Nature*. **383**: 256–257.

• Mateus, I; Mateus, H; Antunes, MT; Mateus, O; Taquet, P; Ribeiro, V; Manuppella, G (1998). "Upper Jurassic theropod dinosaur embryos from Lourinhã (Portugal)". *Memórias da Academia das Ciências de Lisboa.* **37**: 101–110.

• Moskvitch, Katia. "Eggs with the Oldest Known Embryos of a Dinosaur Found"[117]. BBC News. November 12, 2010.

• de Ricqlès, A.; Mateus, O.; Antunes, M. T.; Taquet, P. (2001). "Histomorphogenesis of embryos of Upper Jurassic theropods from Lourinhã (Portugal)". *Comptes Rendus de l'Académie des Sciences, Série IIA.* **332** (10): 647–656. Bibcode: 2001CRASE.332..647D[118]. doi: 10.1016/s1251-8050(01)01580-4[119].

• Reisz, Robert R.; Scott, Diane; Sues, Hans-Dieter; Evans, David C.; Raath, Michael A. (2005). "Embryos of an Early Jurassic prosauropod dinosaur and their evolutionary significance". *Science.* **309** (5735): 761–764. Bibcode: 2005Sci...309..761R[120]. doi: 10.1126/science. 1114942[121].

• Skinner, Justin. "ROM Puts Oldest Dinosaur Eggs Ever Discovered on Display"[122]. insidetoronto.com. May 6, 2010.

• "What are dinosaur eggs?"[123], *University of Bristol Earth Sciences*, retrieved June 20, 2013

External links

• ⚘ Media related to Dinosauria eggs at Wikimedia Commons

Physiology

Physiology of dinosaurs

Preliminary note: In this article "dinosaur" means "non-avian dinosaur," since birds are a monophyletic taxon within the clade Dinosauria and most experts regard birds as dinosaurs.

The **physiology of dinosaurs** has historically been a controversial subject, particularly their thermoregulation. Recently, many new lines of evidence have been brought to bear on dinosaur physiology generally, including not only metabolic systems and thermoregulation, but on respiratory and cardiovascular systems as well.

During the early years of dinosaur paleontology, it was widely considered that they were sluggish, cumbersome, and sprawling cold-blooded lizards. However, with the discovery of much more complete skeletons in western United States, starting in the 1870s, scientists could make more informed interpretations of dinosaur biology and physiology. Edward Drinker Cope, opponent of Othniel Charles Marsh in the Bone Wars, propounded at least some dinosaurs as active and agile, as seen in the painting of two fighting "Laelaps" produced under his direction by Charles R. Knight.

In parallel, the development of Darwinian evolution, and the discoveries of *Archaeopteryx* and *Compsognathus*, led Thomas Henry Huxley to propose that dinosaurs were closely related to birds. Despite these considerations, the image of dinosaurs as large reptiles had already taken root, and most aspects of their paleobiology were interpreted as being typically reptilian for the first half of the twentieth century. Beginning in the 1960s and with the advent of the Dinosaur Renaissance, views of dinosaurs and their physiology have changed dramatically, including the discovery of feathered dinosaurs in Early Cretaceous age deposits in China, indicating that birds evolved from highly agile maniraptoran dinosaurs.

Figure 51: *Reconstruction of Megalosaurus from 1854, in Crystal Palace, London*

History of study

Early interpretations of dinosaurs: 1820s to early 1900s

The study of dinosaurs began in the 1820s in England. Pioneers in the field, such as William Buckland, Gideon Mantell, and Richard Owen, interpreted the first, very fragmentary remains as belonging to large quadrupedal beasts. Their early work can be seen today in the Crystal Palace Dinosaurs, constructed in the 1850s, which present known dinosaurs as elephantine lizard-like reptiles. Despite these reptilian appearances, Owen speculated that dinosaur heart and respiratory systems were more similar to that of a mammal than a reptile.

Changing views and the dinosaur renaissance

In the late 1960s, similar ideas reappeared, beginning with John Ostrom's work on *Deinonychus* and bird evolution. His student, Bob Bakker, popularized the changing thought in a series of papers beginning with *The superiority of dinosaurs* in 1968.[124] In these publications, he argued strenuously that dinosaurs were warm-blooded and active animals, capable of sustained periods of high activity. In most of his writings Bakker framed his arguments as new evidence leading to a revival of ideas popular in the late 19th century, frequently referring to an ongoing *dinosaur renaissance*. He used a variety of anatomical and statistical arguments to defend his case, the methodology of which was fiercely debated among scientists.

Figure 52: *The 1897 painting of "Laelaps"*
(now Dryptosaurus) by Charles R. Knight

These debates sparked interest in new methods for ascertaining the palaeobiology of extinct animals, such as bone histology, which have been successfully applied to determining the growth-rates of many dinosaurs.

Today, it is generally thought that many or perhaps all dinosaurs had higher metabolic rates than living reptiles, but also that the situation is more complex and varied than Bakker originally proposed. For example, while smaller dinosaurs may have been true endotherms, the larger forms could have been inertial homeotherms, or that many dinosaurs could have had intermediate metabolic rates.

Feeding and digestion

The earliest dinosaurs were almost certainly predators, and shared several predatory features with their nearest non-dinosaur relatives like *Lagosuchus*, including: relatively large, curved, blade-like teeth in large, wide-opening jaws that closed like scissors; relatively small abdomens, as carnivores do not require large digestive systems. Later dinosaurs regarded as predators sometimes grew much larger, but retained the same set of features. Instead of chewing their food, these predators swallowed it whole.

The feeding habits of ornithomimosaurs and oviraptorosaurs are a mystery: although they evolved from a predatory theropod lineage, they have small jaws and lack the blade-like teeth of typical predators, but there is no evidence of their diet or how they ate and digested it.

Features of other groups of dinosaurs indicate they were herbivores. These features include:

• Jaws that only slightly opened and closed so that all the teeth met at the same time
• Large abdomens that could accommodate large amounts of vegetation and store it for the long time it takes to digest vegetation
• Guts that likely contained Endosymbiotic micro-organisms that digest cellulose, as no known animal can digest this tough material directly

Sauropods, which were herbivores, did not chew their food, as their teeth and jaws appear suitable only for stripping leaves off plants. Ornithischians, also herbivores, show a variety of approaches. The armored ankylosaurs and stegosaurs had small heads and weak jaws and teeth, and are thought to have fed in much the same way as sauropods. The pachycephalosaurs had small heads and weak jaws and teeth, but their lack of large digestive systems suggests a different diet, possibly fruits, seeds, or young shoots, which would have been more nutritious to them than leaves.

On the other hand, ornithopods such as *Hypsilophodon*, *Iguanodon* and various hadrosaurs had horny beaks for snipping off vegetation and jaws and teeth that were well-adapted for chewing. The horned ceratopsians had similar mechanisms.

It has often been suggested that at least some dinosaurs used swallowed stones, known as gastroliths, to aid digestion by grinding their food in muscular gizzards, and that this was a feature they shared with birds. In 2007 Oliver Wings reviewed references to gastroliths in scientific literature and found considerable confusion, starting with the lack of an agreed and objective definition of "gastrolith". He found that swallowed hard stones or grit can assist digestion in birds that mainly feed on grain but may not be essential—and that birds that eat insects in summer and grain in winter usually get rid of the stones and grit in summer. Gastroliths have often been described as important for sauropod dinosaurs, whose diet of vegetation required very thorough digestion, but Wings concluded that this idea was incorrect: gastroliths are found with only a small percentage of sauropod fossils; where they have been found, the amounts are too small and in many cases the stones are too soft to have been effective in grinding food; most of these gastroliths are highly polished, but gastroliths used by modern animals to grind food are roughened by wear and corroded by stomach acids; hence the sauropod gastroliths were probably swallowed accidentally. On the other hand, he concluded that gastroliths found with fossils of advanced theropod dinosaurs such as *Sinornithomimus* and *Caudipteryx* resemble those of birds, and that the use of gastroliths for grinding food may have appeared early in the group of dinosaurs from which these dinosaurs and birds both evolved.

Reproductive biology

When laying eggs, female birds grow a special type of bone in their limbs between the hard outer bone and the marrow.[125] This medullary bone, which is rich in calcium, is used to make eggshells, and the birds that produced it absorb it when they have finished laying eggs. Medullary bone has been found in fossils of the theropods *Tyrannosaurus* and *Allosaurus* and of the ornithopod *Tenontosaurus*.

Because the line of dinosaurs that includes *Allosaurus* and *Tyrannosaurus* diverged from the line that led to *Tenontosaurus* very early in the evolution of dinosaurs, the presence of medullary bone in both groups suggests that dinosaurs in general produced medullary tissue. On the other hand, crocodilians, which are dinosaurs' second closest extant relatives after birds, do not produce medullary bone. This tissue may have first appeared in ornithodires, the Triassic archosaur group from which dinosaurs are thought to have evolved.

Medullary bone has been found in specimens of sub-adult size, which suggests that dinosaurs reached sexual maturity before they were full-grown. Sexual maturity at sub-adult size is also found in reptiles and in medium- to large-sized mammals, but birds and small mammals reach sexual maturity only after they are full-grown—which happens within their first year. Early sexual maturity is also associated with specific features of animals' life cycles: the young are born relatively well-developed rather than helpless; and the death-rate among adults is high.

Respiratory system

Air sacs

From about 1870 onwards scientists have generally agreed that the post-cranial skeletons of many dinosaurs contained many air-filled cavities (postcranial skeletal pneumaticity, especially in the vertebrae. Pneumatization of the skull (such as paranasal sinuses) is found in both synapsids and archosaurs, but postcranial pneumatization is found only in birds, non-avian saurischian dinosaurs, and pterosaurs.

For a long time these cavities were regarded simply as weight-saving devices, but Bakker proposed that they were connected to air sacs like those that make birds' respiratory systems the most efficient of all animals'.

Inhalation

Exhalation

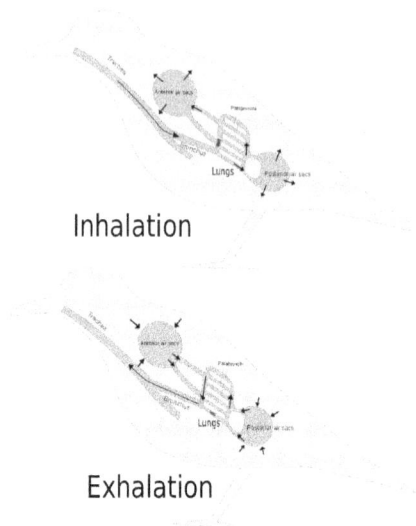

Figure 53: *Birds' lungs obtain fresh air during both exhalation and inhalation, because the air sacs do all the "pumping" and the lungs simply absorb oxygen.*

John Ruben *et al.* (1997, 1999, 2003, 2004) disputed this and suggested that dinosaurs had a "tidal" respiratory system (in and out) powered by a crocodile-like hepatic piston mechanism – muscles attached mainly to the pubis pull the liver backwards, which makes the lungs expand to inhale; when these muscles relax, the lungs return to their previous size and shape, and the animal exhales. They also presented this as a reason for doubting that birds descended from dinosaurs.

Critics have claimed that, without avian air sacs, modest improvements in a few aspects of a modern reptile's circulatory and respiratory systems would enable the reptile to achieve 50% to 70% of the oxygen flow of a mammal of similar size, and that lack of avian air sacs would not prevent the development of endothermy. Very few formal rebuttals have been published in scientific journals of Ruben *et al.*'s claim that dinosaurs could not have had avian-style air sacs; but one points out that the *Sinosauropteryx* fossil on which they based much of their argument was severely flattened and therefore it was impossible to tell whether the liver was the right shape to act as part of a hepatic piston mechanism. Some recent papers simply note without further comment that Ruben *et al.* argued against the presence of air sacs in dinosaurs.

Researchers have presented evidence and arguments for air sacs in sauropods, "prosauropods", coelurosaurs, ceratosaurs, and the theropods *Aerosteon* and

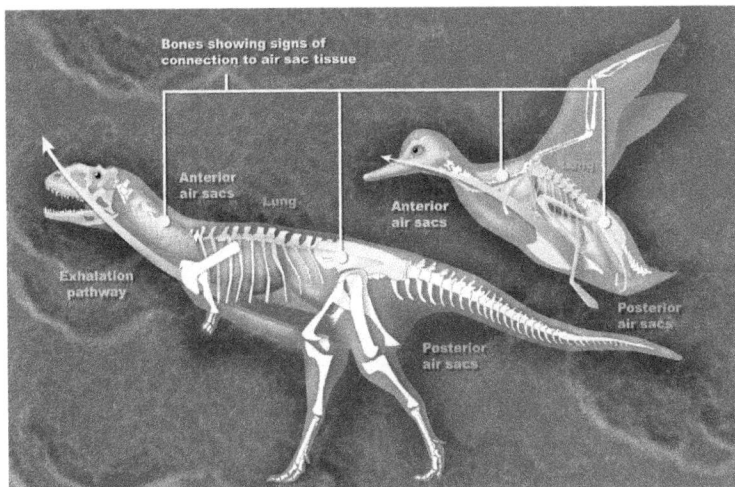

Figure 54: *Comparison between the air sacs of Majungasaurus and a bird*

Coelophysis.

In advanced sauropods ("neosauropods") the vertebrae of the lower back and hip regions show signs of air sacs. In early sauropods only the cervical (neck) vertebrae show these features. If the developmental sequence found in bird embryos is a guide, air sacs actually evolved before the channels in the skeleton that accommodate them in later forms.[126]

Evidence of air sacs has also been found in theropods. Studies indicate that fossils of coelurosaurs,[127] ceratosaurs, and the theropods *Coelophysis* and *Aerosteon* exhibit evidence of air sacs. *Coelophysis*, from the late Triassic, is one of the earliest dinosaurs whose fossils show evidence of channels for air sacs. *Aerosteon*, a Late Cretaceous allosaur, had the most bird-like air sacs found so far.

Early sauropodomorphs, including the group traditionally called "prosauropods", may also have had air sacs. Although possible pneumatic indentations have been found in *Plateosaurus* and *Thecodontosaurus*, the indentations are very small. One study in 2007 concluded that prosauropods likely had abdominal and cervical air sacs, based on the evidence for them in sister taxa (theropods and sauropods). The study concluded that it was impossible to determine whether prosauropods had a bird-like flow-through lung, but that the air sacs were almost certainly present. A further indication for the presence of air sacs and their use in lung ventilation comes from a reconstruction of the air exchange volume (the volume of air exchanged with each breath) of *Plateosaurus*, which when expressed as a ratio of air volume per body weight at 29 ml/kg is similar to values of geese and other birds, and much higher than typical mammalian values.

So far no evidence of air sacs has been found in ornithischian dinosaurs. But this does not imply that ornithischians could not have had metabolic rates comparable to those of mammals, since mammals also do not have air sacs.

Three explanations have been suggested for the development of air sacs in dinosaurs:

• Increase in respiratory capacity. This is probably the most common hypothesis, and fits well with the idea that many dinosaurs had fairly high metabolic rates.
• Improving balance and maneuvrability by lowering the center of gravity and reducing rotational inertia. However this does not explain the expansion of air sacs in the quadrupedal sauropods.
• As a cooling mechanism. It seems that air sacs and feathers evolved at about the same time in coelurosaurs. If feathers retained heat, their owners would have required a means of dissipating excess heat. This idea is plausible but needs further empirical support.

Calculations of the volumes of various parts of the sauropod *Apatosaurus'* respiratory system support the evidence of bird-like air sacs in sauropods:

• Assuming that *Apatosaurus*, like dinosaurs' nearest surviving relatives crocodilians and birds, did not have a diaphragm, the dead-space volume of a 30-ton specimen would be about 184 liters. This is the total volume of the mouth, trachea and air tubes. If the animal exhales less than this, stale air is not expelled and is sucked back into the lungs on the following inhalation.
• Estimates of its tidal volume – the amount of air moved into or out of the lungs in a single breath – depend on the type of respiratory system the animal had: 904 liters if avian; 225 liters if mammalian; 19 liters if reptilian.

On this basis, *Apatosaurus* could not have had a reptilian respiratory system, as its tidal volume would have been less than its dead-space volume, so that stale air was not expelled but was sucked back into the lungs. Likewise, a mammalian system would only provide to the lungs about $225 - 184 = 41$ liters of fresh, oxygenated air on each breath. *Apatosaurus* must therefore have had either a system unknown in the modern world or one like birds', with multiple air sacs and a flow-through lung. Furthermore, an avian system would only need a lung volume of about 600 liters while a mammalian one would have required about 2,950 liters, which would exceed the estimated 1,700 liters of space available in a 30-ton *Apatosaurus'* chest.

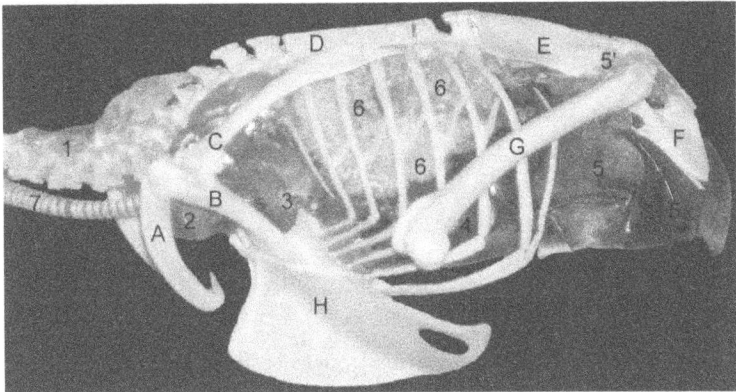

Figure 55: *The uncinate processes are the small white spurs about halfway along the ribs. The rest of this diagram shows the air sacs and other parts of a bird's respiratory system: 1 cervical air sac, 2 clavicular air sac, 3 cranial thoracal air sac, 4 caudal thoracal air sac, 5 abdominal air sac (5' diverticulus into pelvic girdle), 6 lung, 7 trachea*

Dinosaur respiratory systems with bird-like air sacs may have been capable of sustaining higher activity levels than mammals of similar size and build can sustain. In addition to providing a very efficient supply of oxygen, the rapid airflow would have been an effective cooling mechanism, which is essential for animals that are active but too large to get rid of all the excess heat through their skins.

The palaeontologist Peter Ward has argued that the evolution of the air sac system, which first appears in the very earliest dinosaurs, may have been in response to the very low (11%) atmospheric oxygen of the Carnian and Norian ages of the Triassic Period.[128]

Uncinate processes on the ribs

Birds have spurs called "uncinate processes" on the rear edges of their ribs, and these give the chest muscles more leverage when pumping the chest to improve oxygen supply. The size of the uncinate processes is related to the bird's lifestyle and oxygen requirements: they are shortest in walking birds and longest in diving birds, which need to replenish their oxygen reserves quickly when they surface. Non-avian maniraptoran dinosaurs also had these uncinate processes, and they were proportionately as long as in modern diving birds, which indicates that maniraptorans needed a high-capacity oxygen supply.[129]

Plates that may have functioned the same way as uncinate processes have been observed in fossils of the ornithischian dinosaur *Thescelosaurus*, and have been interpreted as evidence of high oxygen consumption and therefore high metabolic rate.[130]

Nasal turbinates

Nasal turbinates are convoluted structures of thin bone in the nasal cavity. In most mammals and birds these are present and lined with mucous membranes that perform two functions. They improve the sense of smell by increasing the area available to absorb airborne chemicals, and they warm and moisten inhaled air, and extract heat and moisture from exhaled air to prevent desiccation of the lungs.

John Ruben and others have argued that no evidence of nasal turbinates has been found in dinosaurs. All the dinosaurs they examined had nasal passages that were too narrow and short to accommodate nasal turbinates, so dinosaurs could not have sustained the breathing rate required for a mammal-like or bird-like metabolic rate while at rest, because their lungs would have dried out. However, objections have been raised against this argument. Nasal turbinates are absent or very small in some birds (e.g. ratites, Procellariiformes and Falconiformes) and mammals (e.g. whales, anteaters, bats, elephants, and most primates), although these animals are fully endothermic and in some cases very active. Other studies conclude that nasal turbinates are fragile and seldom found in fossils. In particular none have been found in fossil birds.

In 2014 Jason Bourke and others in *Anatomical Record* reported finding nasal turbinates in pachycephalosaurs.

Cardiovascular system

In principle one would expect dinosaurs to have had two-part circulations driven by four-chambered hearts, since many would have needed high blood pressure to deliver blood to their heads, which were high off the ground, but vertebrate lungs can only tolerate fairly low blood pressure. In 2000, a skeleton of *Thescelosaurus*, now on display at the North Carolina Museum of Natural Sciences, was described as including the remnants of a four-chambered heart and an aorta. The authors interpreted the structure of the heart as indicating an elevated metabolic rate for *Thescelosaurus*, not reptilian cold-bloodedness. Their conclusions have been disputed; other researchers published a paper where they assert that the heart is really a concretion of entirely mineral "cement". As they note: the anatomy given for the object is incorrect, for example the alleged "aorta" is narrowest where it meets the "heart" and lacks arteries branching from it; the "heart" partially engulfs one of the ribs and has an internal structure of concentric layers in some places; and another concretion is preserved behind the right leg. The original authors defended their position;

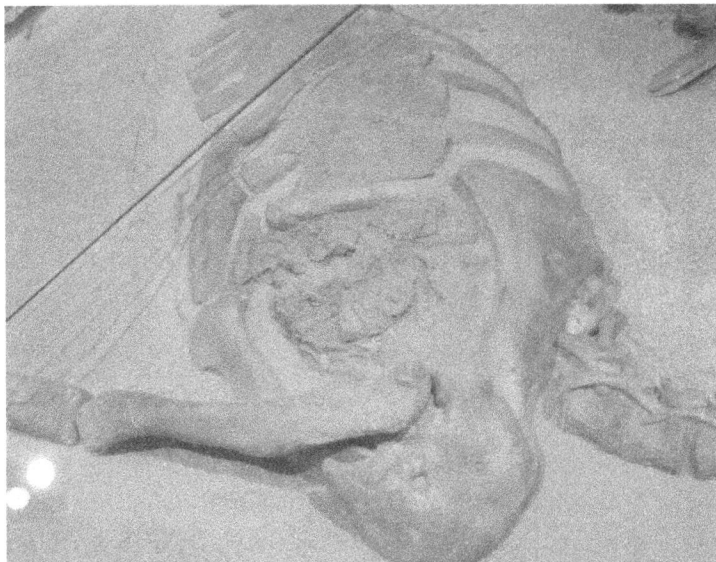

Figure 56: *The possible heart of "Willo" the thescelosaur (center).*

they agreed that the chest did contain a type of concretion, but one that had formed around and partially preserved the more muscular portions of the heart and aorta.

Regardless of the object's identity, it may have little relevance to dinosaurs' internal anatomy and metabolic rate. Both modern crocodilians and birds, the closest living relatives of dinosaurs, have four-chambered hearts, although modified in crocodilians, and so dinosaurs probably had them as well. However such hearts are not necessarily tied to metabolic rate.[131]

Growth and lifecycle

No dinosaur egg has been found that is larger than a basketball and embryos of large dinosaurs have been found in relatively small eggs, e.g. Maiasaura. Like mammals, dinosaurs stopped growing when they reached the typical adult size of their species, while mature reptiles continued to grow slowly if they had enough food. Dinosaurs of all sizes grew faster than similarly sized modern reptiles; but the results of comparisons with similarly sized "warm-blooded" modern animals depend on their sizes:[132]

Weight (kg)	Comparative growth rate of dinosaurs	Modern animals in this size range
0.22	Slower than marsupials	Rat
1 – 20	Similar to marsupials, slower than precocial birds (those that are born capable of running)	From guinea pig to Andean condor
100 – 1000	Faster than marsupials, similar to precocial birds, slower than placental mammals	From red kangaroo to polar bear
1500 – 3500	Similar to most placental mammals	From American bison to rhinoceros
25000 and over	Very fast, similar to modern whales; but about half that of a scaled-up altricial bird (one that is born helpless) – if one could scale up a bird to 25,000 kilograms (25 long tons; 28 short tons)	Whales

Tyrannosaurus rex showed a "teenage growth spurt":

- ½ ton at age 10
- very rapid growth to around 2 tons in the mid-teens (about ½ ton per year).
- negligible growth after the second decade.

A 2008 study of one skeleton of the hadrosaur *Hypacrosaurus* concluded that this dinosaur grew even faster, reaching its full size at the age of about 15; the main evidence was the number and spacing of growth rings in its bones. The authors found this consistent with a life-cycle theory that prey species should grow faster than their predators if they lose a lot of juveniles to predators and the local environment provides enough resources for rapid growth.

It appears that individual dinosaurs were rather short-lived, e.g. the oldest (at death) *Tyrannosaurus* found so far was 28 and the oldest sauropod was 38. Predation was probably responsible for the high death rate of very young dinosaurs and sexual competition for the high death rate of sexually mature dinosaurs.

Metabolism

Scientific opinion about the life-style, metabolism and temperature regulation of dinosaurs has varied over time since the discovery of dinosaurs in the mid-19th century. The activity of metabolic enzymes varies with temperature, so temperature control is vital for any organism, whether endothermic or ectothermic. Organisms can be categorized as poikilotherms (poikilo – changing), which are tolerant of internal temperature fluctuations, and homeotherms (homeo – same), which must maintain a constant core temperature. Animals can be further categorized as endotherms, which regulate their temperature

Body mass (kilograms)

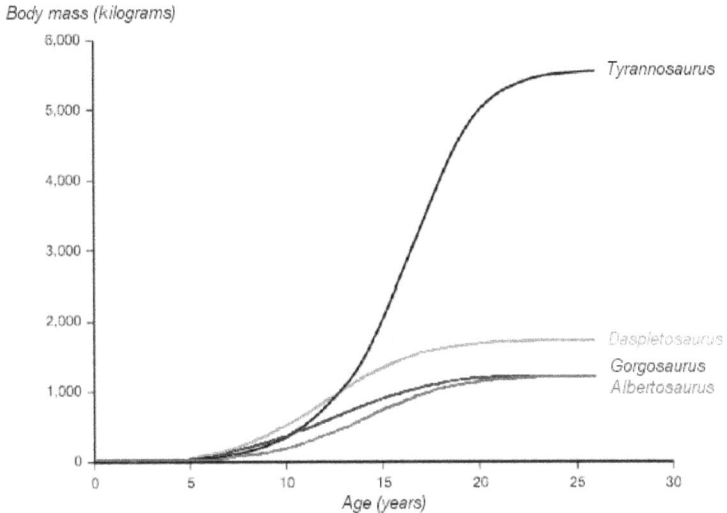

Figure 57: *A graph showing the hypothesized growth curves (body mass versus age) of four tyrannosaurids. Tyrannosaurus rex is drawn in black. Based on Erickson et al. 2004.*

internally, and ectotherms, which regulate temperature by the use of external heat sources.

What the debate is about

"Warm-bloodedness" is a complex and rather ambiguous term, because it includes some or all of:

- **Homeothermy**, i.e. maintaining a fairly constant body temperature. Modern endotherms maintain a variety of temperatures: 28 °C (82 °F) to 30 °C (86 °F) in monotremes and sloths; 33 °C (91 °F) to 36 °C (97 °F) in marsupials; 36 °C (97 °F) to 38 °C (100 °F) in most placentals; and around 41 °C (106 °F) in birds.
- **Tachymetabolism**, i.e. maintaining a high metabolic rate, particularly when at rest. This requires a fairly high and stable body temperature, since biochemical processes run about half as fast if an animal's temperature drops by 10C°; most enzymes have an optimum operating temperature and their efficiency drops rapidly outside the preferred range.
- **Endothermy**, i.e. the ability to generate heat internally, for example by "burning" fat, rather than via behaviors such as basking or muscular activity. Although endothermy is in principle the most reliable way

to maintain a fairly constant temperature, it is expensive; for example modern mammals need 10 to 13 times as much food as modern reptiles.

Large dinosaurs may also have maintained their temperatures by inertial homeothermy, also known as "bulk homeothermy" or "mass homeothermy". In other words, the thermal capacity of such large animals was so high that it would take two days or more for their temperatures to change significantly, and this would have smoothed out variations caused by daily temperature cycles. This smoothing effect has been observed in large turtles and crocodilians, but *Plateosaurus*, which weighed about 700 kilograms (1,500 lb), may have been the smallest dinosaur in which it would have been effective. Inertial homeothermy would not have been possible for small species nor for the young of larger species. Vegetation fermenting in the guts of large herbivores can also produce considerable heat, but this method of maintaining a high and stable temperature would not have been possible for carnivores or for small herbivores or the young of larger herbivores.

Since the internal mechanisms of extinct creatures are unknowable, most discussion focuses on homeothermy and tachymetabolism.

Assessment of metabolic rates is complicated by the distinction between the rates while resting and while active. In all modern reptiles and most mammals and birds the maximum rates during all-out activity are 10 to 20 times higher than minimum rates while at rest. However, in a few mammals these rates differ by a factor of 70. Theoretically it would be possible for a land vertebrate to have a reptilian metabolic rate at rest and a bird-like rate while working flat out. However, an animal with such a low resting rate would be unable to grow quickly. The huge herbivorous sauropods may have been on the move so constantly in search of food that their energy expenditure would have been much the same irrespective of whether their resting metabolic rates were high or low.

Metabolic options

The main possibilities are that:

• Dinosaurs were cold-blooded, like modern reptiles, except that the large size of many would have stabilized their body temperatures.
• They were warm-blooded, more like modern mammals or birds than modern reptiles.
• They were neither cold-blooded nor warm-blooded in modern terms, but had metabolisms that were different from and in some ways intermediate between those of modern cold-blooded and warm-blooded animals.
• They included animals with two or three of these types of metabolism.

Dinosaurs were around for about 150 million years, so it is very likely that different groups evolved different metabolisms and thermoregulatory regimes, and that some developed different physiologies from the first dinosaurs.

If all or some dinosaurs had intermediate metabolisms, they may have had the following features:

- Low resting metabolic rates—which would reduce the amount of food they needed and allow them to use more of that food for growth than do animals with high resting metabolic rates.
- Inertial homeothermy
- The ability to control heat loss by expanding and contracting blood vessels just under the skin, as many modern reptiles do.
- Two-part circulations driven by four-chambered hearts.
- High aerobic capacity, allowing sustained activity.

Robert Reid has suggested that such animals could be regarded as "failed endotherms". He envisaged both dinosaurs and the Triassic ancestors of mammals passing through a stage with these features. Mammals were forced to become smaller as archosaurs came to dominate ecological niches for medium to large animals. Their decreasing size made them more vulnerable to heat loss because it increased their ratios of surface area to mass, and thus forced them to increase internal heat generation and thus become full endotherms. On the other hand, dinosaurs became medium to very large animals and thus were able to retain the "intermediate" type of metabolism.

Bone structure

Armand de Ricqlès discovered Haversian canals in dinosaur bones, and argued that they were evidence of endothermy in dinosaurs. These canals are common in "warm-blooded" animals and are associated with fast growth and an active life style because they help to recycle bone to facilitate rapid growth and repair damage caused by stress or injuries.[133] Dense secondary Haversian bone, which is formed during remodeling, is found in many living endotherms as well as dinosaurs, pterosaurs and therapsids. Secondary Haversian canals are correlated with size and age, mechanical stress and nutrient turnover. The presence of secondary Haversian canals suggests comparable bone growth and lifespans in mammals and dinosaurs.[134] Bakker argued that the presence of fibrolamellar bone (produced quickly and having a fibrous, woven appearance) in dinosaur fossils was evidence of endothermy.

However, as a result of other, mainly later research, bone structure is not considered a reliable indicator of metabolism in dinosaurs, mammals or reptiles:

- Dinosaur bones often contain lines of arrested growth (LAGs), formed by alternating periods of slow and fast growth; in fact many studies count growth rings to estimate the ages of dinosaurs. The formation of growth rings is usually driven by seasonal changes in temperature, and this seasonal influence has sometimes been regarded as a sign of slow metabolism and ectothermy. But growth rings are found in polar bears and in mammals that hibernate. The relationship between LAGs and seasonal growth dependency remains unresolved.[135]
- Fibrolamellar bone is fairly common in young crocodilians and sometimes found in adults.
- Haversian bone has been found in turtles, crocodilians and tortoises, but is often absent in small birds, bats, shrews and rodents.

Nevertheless, de Ricqlès persevered with studies of the bone structure of dinosaurs and archosaurs. In mid-2008 he co-authored a paper that examined bone samples from a wide range of archosaurs, including early dinosaurs, and concluded that:[136]

- Even the earliest archosauriformes may have been capable of very fast growth, which suggests they had fairly high metabolic rates. Although drawing conclusions about the earliest archosauriformes from later forms is tricky, because species-specific variations in bone structure and growth rate are very likely, there are research strategies than can minimize the risk that such factors will cause errors in the analysis.
- Archosaurs split into three main groups in the Triassic: ornithodirans, from which dinosaurs evolved, remained committed to rapid growth; crocodilians' ancestors adopted more typical "reptilian" slow growth rates; and most other Triassic archosaurs had intermediate growth rates.

Metabolic rate, blood pressure and flow

Endotherms rely highly on aerobic metabolism and have high rates of oxygen consumption during activity and rest. The oxygen required by the tissues is carried by the blood, and consequently blood flow rates and blood pressures at the heart of warm-blooded endotherms are considerably higher than those of cold-blooded ectotherms. It is possible to measure the minimum blood pressures of dinosaurs by estimating the vertical distance between the heart and the top of the head, because this column of blood must have a pressure at the bottom equal to the hydrostatic pressure derived from the density of blood and gravity. Added to this pressure is that required to move the blood through the circulatory system. It was pointed out in 1976 that, because of their height, many dinosaurs had minimum blood pressures within the endothermic range, and that they must have had four-chambered hearts to separate the high pressure circuit to the body from the low pressure circuit to the lungs. It was not

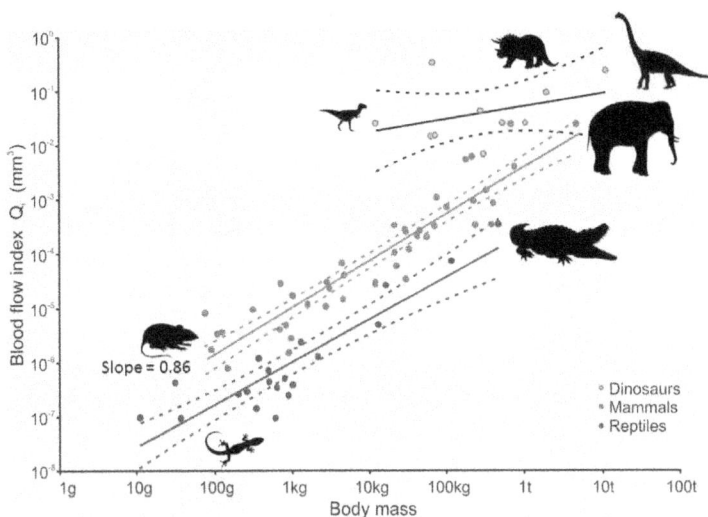

Figure 58: *Foramen blood flow index, derived from the size of the nutrient foramen of the femurs of mammals, reptiles and dinosaurs*

clear whether these dinosaurs had high blood pressure simply to support the blood column or to support the high blood flow rates required by endothermy or both.

However, recent analysis of the tiny holes in fossil leg bones of dinosaurs provides a gauge for blood flow rate and hence metabolic rate. The holes are called nutrient foramina, and the nutrient artery is the major blood vessel passing through to the interior of the bone, where it branches into tiny vessels of the Haversian canal system. This system is responsible for replacing old bone with new bone, thereby repairing microbreaks that occur naturally during locomotion. Without this repair, microbreaks would build up, leading to stress fractures and ultimately catastrophic bone failure. The size of the nutrient foramen provides an index of blood flow through it, according to the Hagen-Poiseuille equation. The size is also related to the body size of animal, of course, so this effect is removed by analysis of allometry. Blood flow index of the nutrient foramen of the femurs in living mammals increases in direct proportion to the animals' maximum metabolic rates, as measured during maximum sustained locomotion. Mammalian blood flow index is about 10 times greater than in ectothermic reptiles. Ten species of fossil dinosaurs from five taxonomic groups reveal indices even higher than in mammals, when body size is accounted for, indicating that they were highly active, aerobic animals.

Thus high blood flow rate, high blood pressure, a four-chambered heart and sustained aerobic metabolism are all consistent with endothermy.

Growth rates

Dinosaurs grew from small eggs to several tons in weight relatively quickly. A natural interpretation of this is that dinosaurs converted food into body weight very quickly, which requires a fairly fast metabolism both to forage actively and to assimilate the food quickly. Developing bone found in juveniles is distinctly porous, which has been linked to vascularization and bone deposition rate, all suggesting growth rates close to those observed in modern birds.

But a preliminary study of the relationship between adult size, growth rate, and body temperature concluded that larger dinosaurs had higher body temperatures than smaller ones had; *Apatosaurus*, the largest dinosaur in the sample, was estimated to have a body temperature exceeding 41 °C (106 °F), whereas smaller dinosaurs were estimated to have body temperatures around 25 °C (77 °F) – for comparison, normal human body temperature is about 37 °C (99 °F). Based on these estimations, the study concluded that large dinosaurs were inertial homeotherms (their temperatures were stabilized by their sheer bulk) and that dinosaurs were ectothermic (in colloquial terms, "cold-blooded", because they did not generate as much heat as mammals when not moving or digesting food).[137] These results are consistent with the relationship between dinosaurs' sizes and growth rates (described above). Studies of the sauropodomorph *Massospondylus* and early theropod *Syntarsus* (*Megapnosaurus*) reveal growth rates of 3 kg/year and 17 kg/year, respectively, much slower than those estimated of Maiasaura and observed in modern birds.

Oxygen isotope ratios in bone

The ratio of the isotopes [16]O and [18]O in bone depends on the temperature the bone formed at: the higher the temperature, the more [16]O. Barrick and Showers (1999) analyzed the isotope ratios in two theropods that lived in temperate regions with seasonal variation in temperature, *Tyrannosaurus* (USA) and *Giganotosaurus* (Argentina):

• dorsal vertebrae from both dinosaurs showed no sign of seasonal variation, indicating that both maintained a constant core temperature despite seasonal variations in air temperature.

• ribs and leg bones from both dinosaurs showed greater variability in temperature and a lower average temperature as the distance from the vertebrae increased.

Barrick and Showers concluded that both dinosaurs were endothermic but at lower metabolic levels than modern mammals, and that inertial homeothermy was an important part of their temperature regulation as adults. Their similar analysis of some Late Cretaceous ornithischians in 1996 concluded that these animals showed a similar pattern.

However this view has been challenged. The evidence indicates homeothermy, but by itself cannot prove endothermy. Secondly, the production of bone may not have been continuous in areas near the extremities of limbs – in allosaur skeletons lines of arrested growth ("LAGs"; rather like growth rings) are sparse or absent in large limb bones but common in the fingers and toes. While there is no absolute proof that LAGs are temperature-related, they could mark times when the extremities were so cool that the bones ceased to grow. If so, the data about oxygen isotope ratios would be incomplete, especially for times when the extremities were coolest. Oxygen isotope ratios may be an unreliable method of estimating temperatures if it cannot be shown that bone growth was equally continuous in all parts of the animal.

Predator–prey ratios

Bakker argued that:

- cold-blooded predators need much less food than warm-blooded ones, so a given mass of prey can support far more cold-blooded predators than warm-blooded ones.
- the ratio of the total mass of predators to prey in dinosaur communities was much more like that of modern and recent warm-blooded communities than that of recent or fossil cold-blooded communities.
- hence predatory dinosaurs were warm-blooded. And since the earliest dinosaurs (e.g. *Staurikosaurus*, *Herrerasaurus*) were predators, all dinosaurs must have been warm-blooded.

This argument was criticized on several grounds and is no longer taken seriously (the following list of criticisms is far from exhaustive):

- Estimates of dinosaur weights vary widely, and even a small variation can make a large difference to the calculated predator–prey ratio.
- His sample may not have been representative. Bakker obtained his numbers by counting museum specimens, but these have a bias towards rare or especially well-preserved specimens, and do not represent what exists in fossil beds. Even fossil beds may not accurately represent the actual populations, for example smaller and younger animals have less robust bones and are therefore less likely to be preserved.

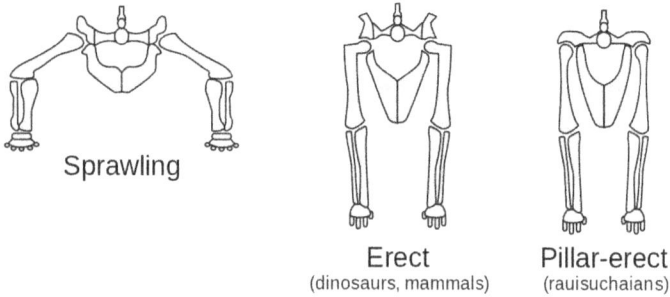

Figure 59: *Hip joints and limb postures.*

- There are no published predator–prey ratios for large ectothermic predators, because such predators are very rare and mostly occur only on fairly small islands. Large ectothermic herbivores are equally rare. So Bakker was forced to compare mammalian predator–prey ratios with those of fish and invertebrate communities, where life expectancies are much shorter and other differences also distort the comparison.
- The concept assumes that predator populations are limited only by the availability of prey. However other factors such as shortage of nesting sites, cannibalism or predation of one predator on another can hold predator populations below the limit imposed by prey biomass, and this would misleadingly reduce the predator–prey ratio.
- Ecological factors can misleadingly reduce the predator–prey ratio, for example: a predator might prey on only some of the "prey" species present; disease, parasites and starvation might kill some of the prey animals before the predators get a chance to hunt them.
- It is very difficult to state precisely what preys on what. For example, the young of herbivores may be preyed upon by lizards and snakes while the adults are preyed on by mammals. Conversely the young of many predators live largely on invertebrates and switch to vertebrates as they grow.

Posture and gait

Dinosaurs' limbs were erect and held under their bodies, rather than sprawling out to the sides like those of lizards and newts. The evidence for this is the angles of the joint surfaces and the locations of muscle and tendon attachments on the bones. Attempts to represent dinosaurs with sprawling limbs result in creatures with dislocated hips, knees, shoulders and elbows.[138]

Carrier's constraint states that air-breathing vertebrates with two lungs that flex their bodies sideways during locomotion find it difficult to move and breathe at the same time. This severely limits stamina, and forces them to spend more time resting than moving.

Sprawling limbs require sideways flexing during locomotion (except for tortoises and turtles, which are very slow and whose armor keeps their bodies fairly rigid). However, despite Carrier's constraint, sprawling limbs are efficient for creatures that spend most of their time resting on their bellies and only move for a few seconds at a time—because this arrangement minimizes the energy costs of getting up and lying down.

Erect limbs increase the costs of getting up and lying down, but avoid Carrier's constraint. This indicates that dinosaurs were active animals because natural selection would have favored the retention of sprawling limbs if dinosaurs had been sluggish and spent most of their waking time resting. An active lifestyle requires a metabolism that quickly regenerates energy supplies and breaks down waste products which cause fatigue, i.e., it requires a fairly fast metabolism and a considerable degree of homeothermy.

Additionally, an erect posture demands precise balance, the result of a rapidly functioning neuromuscular system. This suggests endothermic metabolism, because an ectothermic animal would be unable to walk or run, and thus to evade predators, when its core temperature was lowered. Other evidence for endothermy includes limb length (many dinosaurs possessed comparatively long limbs) and bipedalism, both found today only in endotherms.[139] Many bipedal dinosaurs possessed gracile leg bones with a short thigh relative to calf length. This is generally an adaptation to frequent sustained running, characteristic of endotherms which, unlike ectotherms, are capable of producing sufficient energy to stave off the onset of anaerobic metabolism in the muscle.[140]

Bakker and Ostrom both pointed out that all dinosaurs had erect hindlimbs and that all quadrupedal dinosaurs had erect forelimbs; and that among living animals only the endothermic ("warm-blooded") mammals and birds have erect limbs (Ostrom acknowledged that crocodilians' occasional "high walk" was a partial exception). Bakker claimed this was clear evidence of endothermy in dinosaurs, while Ostrom regarded it as persuasive but not conclusive.

A 2009 study supported the hypothesis that endothermy was widespread in at least larger non-avian dinosaurs, and that It was plausibly ancestral for all dinosauriforms, based on the biomechanics of running.

Figure 60: *Skin impression of the hadrosaur Edmontosaurus*

Feathers

There is now no doubt that many theropod dinosaur species had feathers, including *Shuvuuia*, *Sinosauropteryx* and *Dilong* (an early tyrannosaur). These have been interpreted as insulation and therefore evidence of warm-bloodedness.

But impressions of feathers have only been found in coelurosaurs (which includes the ancestors of both birds and tyrannosaurs), so at present feathers give us no information about the metabolisms of the other major dinosaur groups, e.g. coelophysids, ceratosaurs, carnosaurs, sauropods or ornithischians.

In fact the fossilised skin of *Carnotaurus* (an abelisaurid and therefore not a coelurosaur) shows an unfeathered, reptile-like skin with rows of bumps. But an adult *Carnotaurus* weighed about 1 ton, and mammals of this size and larger have either very short hair or naked skins, so perhaps the skin of *Carnotaurus* tells us nothing about whether smaller non-coelurosaurid theropods had feathers.

Skin-impressions of *Pelorosaurus* and other sauropods (dinosaurs with elephantine bodies and long necks) reveal large hexagonal scales, and some sauropods, such as *Saltasaurus*, had bony plates in their skin. The skin of ceratopsians consisted of large polygonal scales, sometimes with scattered circular plates.[141] "Mummified" remains and skin impressions of hadrosaurids reveal pebbly scales. It is unlikely that the ankylosaurids, such as *Euoplocephalus*, had insulation, as most of their surface area was covered in bony knobs and plates. Likewise there is no evidence of insulation in the stegosaurs. Thus insulation, and the elevated metabolic rate behind evolving them, may have been limited to the theropods, or even just a subset of theropods. Worth mentioning is that filaments similar to feathers has been found on three species of small ornithischians, those being *Psittacosaurus*, *Tianyulong* and *Kulindadromeus*, but whether these are true feathers, or the result of convergent evolution is unclear.

Polar dinosaurs

Dinosaur fossils have been found in regions that were close to the poles at the relevant times, notably in southeastern Australia, Antarctica and the North Slope of Alaska. There is no evidence of major changes in the angle of the Earth's axis, so polar dinosaurs and the rest of these ecosystems would have had to cope with the same extreme variation of day length through the year that occurs at similar latitudes today (up to a full day with no darkness in summer, and a full day with no sunlight in winter).[142]

Studies of fossilized vegetation suggest that the Alaska North Slope had a maximum temperature of 13 °C (55 °F) and a minimum temperature of 2 °C (36 °F) to 8 °C (46 °F) in the last 35 million years of the Cretaceous (slightly cooler than Portland, Oregon but slightly warmer than Calgary, Alberta). Even so, the Alaska North Slope has no fossils of large cold-blooded animals such as lizards and crocodilians, which were common at the same time in Alberta, Montana, and Wyoming. This suggests that at least some non-avian dinosaurs were warm-blooded. It has been proposed that North American polar dinosaurs may have migrated to warmer regions as winter approached, which would allow them to inhabit Alaska during the summers even if they were cold-blooded. But a round trip between there and Montana would probably have used more energy than a cold-blooded land vertebrate produces in a year; in other words the Alaskan dinosaurs would have to be warm-blooded, irrespective of whether they migrated or stayed for the winter. A 2008 paper on dinosaur migration by Phil R. Bell and Eric Snively proposed that most polar dinosaurs, including theropods, sauropods, ankylosaurians, and hypsilophodonts, probably overwintered, although hadrosaurids like *Edmontosaurus* were probably capable of annual 2,600 km (1,600 mi) round trips.

It is more difficult to determine the climate of southeastern Australia when the dinosaur fossil beds were laid down 115 to 105[143] million years ago, towards the end of the Early Cretaceous: these deposits contain evidence of permafrost, ice wedges, and hummocky ground formed by the movement of

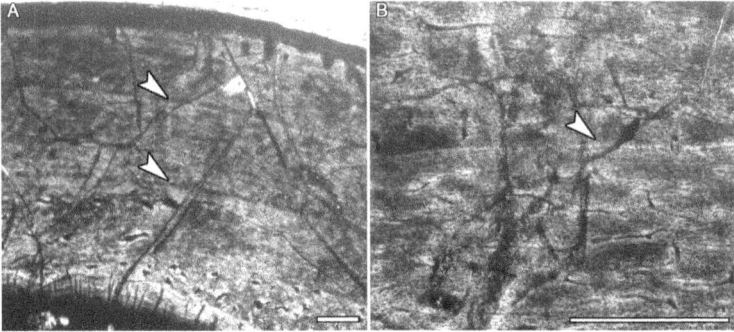

Figure 61: *Bone microstructure of polar hyp-
silophodontid approaching skeletal maturity*

subterranean ice, which suggests mean annual temperatures ranged between
–6 °C (21 °F) and 5 °C (41 °F); oxygen isotope studies of these deposits give
a mean annual temperature of 1.5 °C (34.7 °F) to 2.5 °C (36.5 °F). However
the diversity of fossil vegetation and the large size of some of fossil trees exceed what is found in such cold environments today, and no-one has explained
how such vegetation could have survived in the cold temperatures suggested
by the physical indicators – for comparison Fairbanks, Alaska presently has
a mean annual temperature of 2.9 °C (37.2 °F). An annual migration from
and to southeastern Australia would have been very difficult for fairly small
dinosaurs in such as *Leaellynasaura*, a herbivore about 60 centimetres (2.0 ft)
to 90 centimetres (3.0 ft) long, because seaways to the north blocked the pas-
sage to warmer latitudes. Bone samples from *Leaellynasaura* and *Timimus*,
an ornithomimid about 3.5 metres (11 ft) long and 1.5 metres (4.9 ft) high
at the hip, suggested these two dinosaurs had different ways of surviving the
cold, dark winters: the *Timimus* sample had lines of arrested growth (LAGs
for short; similar to growth rings), and it may have hibernated; but the *Leaellynasaura* sample showed no signs of LAGs, so it may have remained active
throughout the winter.[144] A 2011 study focusing on hypsilophodont and theropod bones also concluded that these dinosaurs did not hibernate through the
winter, but stayed active.[145]

Evidence for behavioral thermoregulation

Some dinosaurs, e.g. *Spinosaurus* and *Ouranosaurus*, had on their backs
"sails" supported by spines growing up from the vertebrae. (This was also
true, incidentally, for the synapsid *Dimetrodon*.) Such dinosaurs could have
used these sails to:

• take in heat by basking with the "sails" at right angles to the sun's rays.

- to lose heat by using the "sails" as radiators while standing in the shade or while facing directly towards or away from the sun.

But these were a very small minority of known dinosaur species. One common interpretation of the plates on stegosaurs' backs is as heat exchangers for thermoregulation, as the plates are filled with blood vessels, which, theoretically, could absorb and dissipate heat.

This might have worked for a stegosaur with large plates, such as *Stegosaurus*, but other stegosaurs, such as *Wuerhosaurus*, *Tuojiangosaurus* and *Kentrosaurus* possessed much smaller plates with a surface area of doubtful value for thermo-regulation. However, the idea of stegosaurian plates as heat exchangers has recently been questioned.

Other evidence

Endothermy demands frequent respiration, which can result in water loss. In living birds and mammals, water loss is limited by pulling moisture out of exhaled air with mucous-covered respiratory turbinates, tissue-covered bony sheets in the nasal cavity. Several dinosaurs have olfactory turbinates, used for smell, but none have yet been identified with respiratory turbinates.[146]

Because endothermy allows refined neuromuscular control, and because brain matter requires large amounts of energy to sustain, some speculate that increased brain size indicates increased activity and, thus, endothermy. The encephalization quotient (EQ) of dinosaurs, a measure of brain size calculated using brain endocasts, varies on a spectrum from bird-like to reptile-like. Using EQ alone, coelosaurs appear to have been as active as living mammals, while theropods and ornithopods fall somewhere between mammals and reptiles, and other dinosaurs resemble reptiles.

A study published by Roger Seymour in 2013 added more support to the idea that dinosaurs were endothermic. After studying saltwater crocodiles, Seymour found that even if their large sizes could provide stable and high body temperatures, during activity the crocodile's ectothermic metabolism provided less aerobic abilities and generate only 14% of the total muscle power of a similar sized endothermic mammal before full fatigue. Seymour reasoned that dinosaurs would have needed to be endothermic since they would have needed better aerobic abilities and higher power generation to compete with and dominate over mammals as active land animals throughout the Mesozoic era.

The crocodilian puzzle and early archosaur metabolism

It appears that the earliest dinosaurs had the features that form the basis for arguments for warm-blooded dinosaurs—especially erect limbs. This raises the question "How did dinosaurs become warm-blooded?" The most obvious possible answers are:

- "Their immediate ancestors (archosaurs) were cold-blooded, and dinosaurs began developing warm-bloodedness very early in their evolution." This implies that dinosaurs developed a significant degree of warm-bloodedness in a very short time, possibly less than 20M years. But in mammals' ancestors the evolution of warm-bloodedness seems to have taken much longer, starting with the beginnings of a secondary palate around the beginning of the mid-Permian and going on possibly until the appearance of hair about 164M years ago in the mid Jurassic[147]).
- "Dinosaurs' immediate ancestors (archosaurs) were at least fairly warm-blooded, and dinosaurs evolved further in that direction." This answer raises 2 problems: (**A**) The early evolution of archosaurs is still very poorly understood – large numbers of individuals and species are found from the start of the Triassic but only 2 species are known from the very late Permian (*Archosaurus rossicus* and *Protorosaurus speneri*); (**B**) Crocodilians evolved shortly before dinosaurs and are closely related to them, but are cold-blooded (see below).

Crocodilians present some puzzles if one regards dinosaurs as active animals with fairly constant body temperatures. Crocodilians evolved shortly before dinosaurs and, second to birds, are dinosaurs' closest living relatives – but modern crocodilians are cold-blooded. This raises some questions:

- If dinosaurs were to a large extent "warm-blooded", when and how fast did warm-bloodedness evolve in their lineage?
- Modern crocodilians are cold-blooded but have several features associated with warm-bloodedness. How did they acquire these features?

Modern crocodilians are cold-blooded but can move with their limbs erect, and have several features normally associated with warm-bloodedness because they improve the animal's oxygen supply:

- 4-chambered hearts. Mammals and birds have four-chambered hearts. Non-crocodilian reptiles have three-chambered hearts, which are less efficient because they allow oxygenated and de-oxygenated blood to mix and therefore send some de-oxygenated blood out to the body instead of to the lungs. Modern crocodilians' hearts are four-chambered, but are smaller relative to body size and run at lower pressure than those of modern mammals and birds. They also have a bypass that makes then functionally three-chambered when under water, conserving oxygen.

Figure 62: *Reconstruction of Terrestrisuchus,*
a very slim, leggy Triassic crocodylomorph.

- a diaphragm, which aids breathing.
- a secondary palate, which allows the animal to eat and breathe at the same time.
- a hepatic piston mechanism for pumping the lungs. This is different from the lung-pumping mechanisms of mammals and birds but similar to what some researchers claim to have found in some dinosaurs.

So why did natural selection favor these features, which are important for active warm-blooded creatures but of little apparent use to cold-blooded aquatic ambush predators that spend most of their time floating in water or lying on river banks?

It was suggested in the late 1980s that crocodilians were originally active, warm-blooded predators and that their archosaur ancestors were warm-blooded. More recently, developmental studies indicate that crocodilian embryos develop fully four-chambered hearts first—then develop the modifications that make their hearts function as three-chambered under water. Using the principle that ontogeny recapitulates phylogeny, the researchers concluded that the original crocodilians had fully 4-chambered hearts and were therefore warm-blooded and that later crocodilians developed the bypass as they reverted to being cold-blooded aquatic ambush predators.[148]

More recent research on archosaur bone structures and their implications for growth rates also suggests that early archosaurs had fairly high metabolic rates and that the Triassic ancestors of crocodilians dropped back to more typically "reptilian" metabolic rates.

If this view is correct, the development of warm-bloodedness in archosaurs (reaching its peak in dinosaurs) and in mammals would have taken more similar amounts of time. It would also be consistent with the fossil evidence:

- The earliest crocodilians, e.g. *Terrestrisuchus*, were slim, leggy terrestrial predators.
- Erect limbs appeared quite early in archosaurs' evolution, and those of rauisuchians are very poorly adapted for any other posture.

External links

- Thermophysiology and Biology of Giganotosaurus: Comparison with Tyrannosaurus[149] by RE Barrick and WJ Showers (1999)
- Heart of a Dinosaur Is Reported Found[150]
- Crocodile evolution no heart-warmer[151]

Origin of birds

Origin of birds

The scientific question of within which larger group of animals birds evolved, has traditionally been called the **origin of birds**. The present scientific consensus is that birds are a group of theropod dinosaurs that originated during the Mesozoic Era.

A close relationship between birds and dinosaurs was first proposed in the nineteenth century after the discovery of the primitive bird *Archaeopteryx* in Germany. Birds and extinct non-avian dinosaurs share many unique skeletal traits. Moreover, fossils of more than thirty species of non-avian dinosaur have been collected with preserved feathers. There are even very small dinosaurs, such as *Microraptor* and *Anchiornis*, which have long, vaned, arm and leg feathers forming wings. The Jurassic basal avialan *Pedopenna* also shows these long foot feathers. Witmer in 2009 concluded that this evidence is sufficient to demonstrate that avian evolution went through a four-winged stage. Fossil evidence also demonstrates that birds and dinosaurs shared features such as hollow, pneumatized bones, gastroliths in the digestive system, nest-building and brooding behaviors.

Although the origin of birds has historically been a contentious topic within evolutionary biology, only a few scientists still debate the dinosaurian origin of birds, suggesting descent from other types of archosaurian reptiles. Within the consensus that supports dinosaurian ancestry, the exact sequence of evolutionary events that gave rise to the early birds within maniraptoran theropods is disputed. The origin of bird flight is a separate but related question for which there are also several proposed answers.

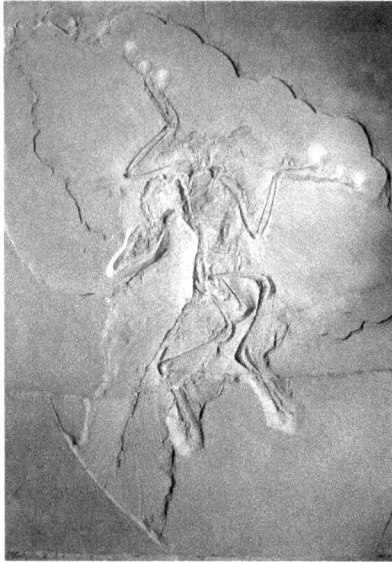

Figure 63: *The Berlin specimen of Archaeopteryx lithographica*

Research history

Huxley, *Archaeopteryx* and early research

Scientific investigation into the origin of birds began shortly after the 1859 publication of Charles Darwin's *On the Origin of Species*. In 1860, a fossilized feather was discovered in Germany's Late Jurassic Solnhofen limestone. Christian Erich Hermann von Meyer described this feather as *Archaeopteryx lithographica* the next year. Richard Owen described a nearly complete skeleton in 1863, recognizing it as a bird despite many features reminiscent of reptiles, including clawed forelimbs and a long, bony tail.

Biologist Thomas Henry Huxley, known as "Darwin's Bulldog" for his tenacious support of the new theory of evolution by means of natural selection, almost immediately seized upon *Archaeopteryx* as a transitional fossil between birds and reptiles. Starting in 1868, and following earlier suggestions by Karl Gegenbaur, and Edward Drinker Cope,[152] Huxley made detailed comparisons of *Archaeopteryx* with various prehistoric reptiles and found that it was most similar to dinosaurs like *Hypsilophodon* and *Compsognathus*. The discovery in the late 1870s of the iconic "Berlin specimen" of *Archaeopteryx*, complete with a set of reptilian teeth, provided further evidence. Huxley was the first to propose an evolutionary relationship between birds and dinosaurs. Although

Figure 64: *Thomas Henry Huxley (1825–1895).*

Huxley was opposed by the very influential Owen, his conclusions were accepted by many biologists, including Baron Franz Nopcsa, while others, notably Harry Seeley, argued that the similarities were due to convergent evolution.

Heilmann and the thecodont hypothesis

A turning point came in the early twentieth century with the writings of Gerhard Heilmann of Denmark. An artist by trade, Heilmann had a scholarly interest in birds and from 1913 to 1916, expanding on earlier work by Othenio Abel, published the results of his research in several parts, dealing with the anatomy, embryology, behavior, paleontology, and evolution of birds. His work, originally written in Danish as *Vor Nuvaerende Viden om Fuglenes Afstamning*, was compiled, translated into English, and published in 1926 as *The Origin of Birds*.

Like Huxley, Heilmann compared *Archaeopteryx* and other birds to an exhaustive list of prehistoric reptiles, and also came to the conclusion that theropod dinosaurs like *Compsognathus* were the most similar. However, Heilmann noted that birds had clavicles (collar bones) fused to form a bone called the furcula ("wishbone"), and while clavicles were known in more primitive reptiles, they had not yet been recognized in dinosaurs. Since he was a firm believer in Dollo's law, which states that evolution is not reversible, Heilmann

Figure 65: *Heilmann's hypothetical illustration of a pair of fighting 'Proaves' from 1916*

could not accept that clavicles were lost in dinosaurs and re-evolved in birds. He was therefore forced to rule out dinosaurs as bird ancestors and ascribe all of their similarities to convergent evolution. Heilmann stated that bird ancestors would instead be found among the more primitive "thecodont" grade of reptiles. Heilmann's extremely thorough approach ensured that his book became a classic in the field, and its conclusions on bird origins, as with most other topics, were accepted by nearly all evolutionary biologists for the next four decades.

Clavicles are relatively delicate bones and therefore in danger of being destroyed or at least damaged beyond recognition. Nevertheless, some fossil theropod clavicles had actually been excavated before Heilmann wrote his book but these had been misidentified.[153] The absence of clavicles in dinosaurs became the orthodox view despite the discovery of clavicles in the primitive theropod *Segisaurus* in 1936. The next report of clavicles in a dinosaur was in a Russian article in 1983.[154]

Contrary to what Heilmann believed, paleontologists now accept that clavicles and in most cases furculae are a standard feature not just of theropods but of saurischian dinosaurs. Up to late 2007 ossified furculae (i.e. made of bone rather than cartilage) have been found in all types of theropods except the most

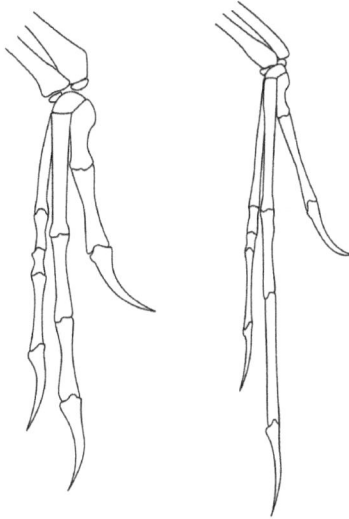

Figure 66: *The similarity of the forelimbs of Deinonychus (left) and Archaeopteryx (right) led John Ostrom to revive the link between dinosaurs and birds.*

basal ones, *Eoraptor* and *Herrerasaurus*.[155] The original report of a furcula in the primitive theropod *Segisaurus* (1936) was confirmed by a re-examination in 2005. Joined, furcula-like clavicles have also been found in *Massospondylus*, an Early Jurassic sauropodomorph.

Ostrom, *Deinonychus* and the dinosaur renaissance

The tide began to turn against the 'thecodont' hypothesis after the 1964 discovery of a new theropod dinosaur in Montana. In 1969, this dinosaur was described and named *Deinonychus* by John Ostrom of Yale University. The next year, Ostrom redescribed a specimen of *Pterodactylus* in the Dutch Teyler Museum as another skeleton of *Archaeopteryx*. The specimen consisted mainly of a single wing and its description made Ostrom aware of the similarities between the wrists of *Archaeopteryx* and *Deinonychus*.

In 1972, British paleontologist Alick Walker hypothesized that birds arose not from 'thecodonts' but from crocodile ancestors like *Sphenosuchus*. Ostrom's work with both theropods and early birds led him to respond with a series of publications in the mid-1970s in which he laid out the many similarities between birds and theropod dinosaurs, resurrecting the ideas first put forth by Huxley over a century before. Ostrom's recognition of the dinosaurian ancestry

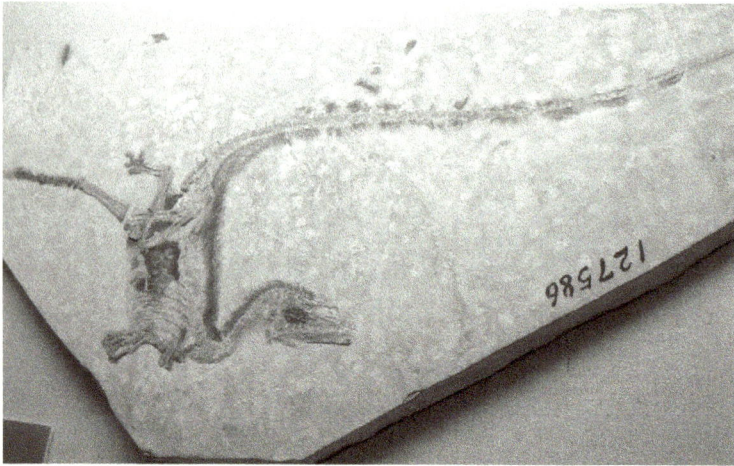

Figure 67: *Fossil of Sinosauropteryx prima*

of birds, along with other new ideas about dinosaur metabolism, activity levels, and parental care, began what is known as the dinosaur renaissance, which began in the 1970s and continues to this day.

Ostrom's revelations also coincided with the increasing adoption of phylogenetic systematics (cladistics), which began in the 1960s with the work of Willi Hennig. Cladistics is a method of arranging species based strictly on their evolutionary relationships, using a statistical analysis of their anatomical characteristics. In the 1980s, cladistic methodology was applied to dinosaur phylogeny for the first time by Jacques Gauthier and others, showing unequivocally that birds were a derived group of theropod dinosaurs. Early analyses suggested that dromaeosaurid theropods like *Deinonychus* were particularly closely related to birds, a result that has been corroborated many times since.

Feathered dinosaurs in China

The early 1990s saw the discovery of spectacularly preserved bird fossils in several Early Cretaceous geological formations in the northeastern Chinese province of Liaoning. In 1996, Chinese paleontologists described *Sinosauropteryx* as a new genus of bird from the Yixian Formation, but this animal was quickly recognized as a theropod dinosaur closely related to *Compsognathus*. Surprisingly, its body was covered by long filamentous structures. These were dubbed 'protofeathers' and considered homologous with the more advanced feathers of birds, although some scientists disagree with this assessment. Chinese and North American scientists described *Caudipteryx* and

Protarchaeopteryx soon after. Based on skeletal features, these animals were non-avian dinosaurs, but their remains bore fully formed feathers closely resembling those of birds. "Archaeoraptor", described without peer review in a 1999 issue of *National Geographic*, turned out to be a smuggled forgery, but legitimate remains continue to pour out of the Yixian, both legally and illegally. Feathers or "protofeathers" have been found on a wide variety of theropods in the Yixian, and the discoveries of extremely bird-like dinosaurs, as well as dinosaur-like primitive birds, have almost entirely closed the morphological gap between theropods and birds.

Digit homology

There is a debate between embryologists and paleontologists whether the hands of theropod dinosaurs and birds are essentially different, based on phalangeal counts, a count of the number of phalanges (fingers) in the hand. This is an important and fiercely debated area of research because its results may challenge the consensus that birds are descendants of dinosaurs.

Embryologists and some paleontologists who oppose the bird-dinosaur link have long numbered the digits of birds II-III-IV on the basis of multiple studies of the development in the egg. This is based on the fact that in most amniotes, the first digit to form in a 5-fingered hand is digit IV, which develops a primary axis. Therefore, embryologists have identified the primary axis in birds as digit IV, and the surviving digits as II-III-IV. The fossils of advanced theropod (Tetanurae) hands appear to have the digits I-II-III (some genera within Avetheropoda also have a reduced digit IV[156]). If this is true, then the II-III-IV development of digits in birds is an indication against theropod (dinosaur) ancestry. However, with no ontogenical (developmental) basis to definitively state which digits are which on a theropod hand (because no non-avian theropods can be observed growing and developing today), the labelling of the theropod hand is not absolutely conclusive.

Paleontologists have traditionally identified avian digits as I-II-III. They argue that the digits of birds number I-II-III, just as those of theropod dinosaurs do, by the conserved phalangeal formula. The phalangeal count for archosaurs is 2-3-4-5-3; many archosaur lineages have a reduced number of digits, but have the same phalangeal formula in the digits that remain. In other words, paleontologists assert that archosaurs of different lineages tend to lose the same digits when digit loss occurs, from the outside to the inside. The three digits of dromaeosaurs, and *Archaeopteryx* have the same phalangeal formula of I-II-III as digits I-II-III of basal archosaurs. Therefore, the lost digits would be V and IV. If this is true, then modern birds would also possess digits I-II-III. Also, one 1999 publication proposed a frame-shift in the digits of the theropod line leading to birds (thus making digit I into digit II, II to III, and so forth).[157] However, such frame shifts are rare in amniotes and—to be consistent with the theropod origin of birds—would have had to occur solely in the bird-theropod lineage forelimbs and not the hindlimbs (a condition unknown in any animal).[158] This is called *Lateral Digit Reduction* (LDR) versus *Bilateral Digit Reduction* (BDR) (see also *Limusaurus*[159])

A small minority, including ornithologists Alan Feduccia and Larry Martin, continues to assert that birds are instead the descendants of earlier archosaurs, such as *Longisquama* or *Euparkeria*. Embryological studies of bird developmental biology have raised questions about digit homology in bird and dinosaur forelimbs. However, due to the cogent evidence provided by comparative anatomy and phylogenetics, as well as the dramatic feathered dinosaur fossils from China, the idea that birds are derived dinosaurs, first championed by Huxley and later by Nopcsa and Ostrom, enjoys near-unanimous support among today's paleontologists.

Thermogenic muscle hypothesis

A 2011 publication suggested that selection for the expansion of skeletal muscle, rather than the evolution of flight, was the driving force for the emergence of this clade. Muscles became larger in prospectively endothermic saurians, according to this hypothesis, as a response to the loss of the vertebrate mitochondrial uncoupling protein, UCP1, which is thermogenic. In mammals, UCP1 functions within brown adipose tissue to protect newborns against hypothermia. In modern birds, skeletal muscle serves a similar function and is presumed to have done so in their ancestors. In this view, bipedality and other avian skeletal alterations were side effects of muscle hyperplasia, with further evolutionary modifications of the forelimbs, including adaptations for flight or swimming, and vestigiality, being secondary consequences of two-leggedness.

Phylogeny

Archaeopteryx has historically been considered the first bird, or *Urvogel*. Although newer fossil discoveries filled the gap between theropods and *Archaeopteryx*, as well as the gap between *Archaeopteryx* and modern birds, phylogenetic taxonomists, in keeping with tradition, almost always use *Archaeopteryx* as a specifier to help define Aves. Aves has more rarely been defined as a crown group consisting only of modern birds. Nearly all palaeontologists regard birds as coelurosaurian theropod dinosaurs. Within Coelurosauria, multiple cladistic analyses have found support for a clade named Maniraptora, consisting of therizinosauroids, oviraptorosaurs, troodontids, dromaeosaurids, and birds. Of these, dromaeosaurids and troodontids are usually united in the clade Deinonychosauria, which is a sister group to birds (together forming the node-clade Eumaniraptora) within the stem-clade Paraves.

Other studies have proposed alternative phylogenies, in which certain groups of dinosaurs usually considered non-avian may have evolved from avian ancestors. For example, a 2002 analysis found that oviraptorosaurs were basal avians. Alvarezsaurids, known from Asia and the Americas, have been variously classified as basal maniraptorans, paravians, the sister taxon of ornithomimosaurs, as well as specialized early birds. The genus *Rahonavis*, originally described as an early bird, has been identified as a non-avian dromaeosaurid in several studies. Dromaeosaurids and troodontids themselves have also been suggested to lie within Aves rather than just outside it.

Features linking birds and dinosaurs

Many anatomical features are shared by birds and theropod dinosaurs.

Feathers

Archaeopteryx, the first good example of a "feathered dinosaur", was discovered in 1861. The first specimen was found in the Solnhofen limestone in southern Germany, which is a *lagerstätte*, a rare and remarkable geological formation known for its superbly detailed fossils. *Archaeopteryx* is a transitional fossil, with features clearly intermediate between those of non-avian theropod dinosaurs and birds. Discovered just two years after Darwin's seminal *Origin of Species*, its discovery spurred the nascent debate between proponents of evolutionary biology and creationism. This early bird is so dinosaur-like that, without a clear impression of feathers in the surrounding rock, at least one specimen was mistaken for *Compsognathus*.

File:Parts of feather modified.jpg

Parts of a feather

Since the 1990s, a number of additional feathered dinosaurs have been found, providing even stronger evidence of the close relationship between dinosaurs and modern birds. The first of these were initially described as simple filamentous *protofeathers*, which were reported in dinosaur lineages as primitive as compsognathids and tyrannosauroids. However, feathers indistinguishable from those of modern birds were soon after found in non-avialan dinosaurs as well.

A small minority of researchers have claimed that the simple filamentous "protofeather" structures are simply the result of the decomposition of collagen fiber under the dinosaurs' skin or in fins along their backs, and that species with unquestionable feathers, such as oviraptorosaurs and dromaeosaurs are

Figure 68: *Fossil cast of NGMC 91, a probable specimen of Sinornithosaurus*

not dinosaurs, but true birds unrelated to dinosaurs.[160] However, a majority of studies have concluded that feathered dinosaurs are in fact dinosaurs, and that the simpler filaments of unquestionable theropods represent simple feathers. Some researchers have demonstrated the presence of color-bearing melanin in the structures—which would be expected in feathers but not collagen fibers. Others have demonstrated, using studies of modern bird decomposition, that even advanced feathers appear filamentous when subjected to the crushing forces experienced during fossilization, and that the supposed "protofeathers" may have been more complex than previously thought.[161] Detailed examination of the "protofeathers" of *Sinosauropteryx prima* showed that individual feathers consisted of a central quill (*rachis*) with thinner *barbs* branching off from it, similar to but more primitive in structure than modern bird feathers.

Skeleton

Because feathers are often associated with birds, feathered dinosaurs are often touted as the missing link between birds and dinosaurs. However, the multiple skeletal features also shared by the two groups represent the more important link for paleontologists. Furthermore, it is increasingly clear that the relationship between birds and dinosaurs, and the evolution of flight, are more complex topics than previously realized. For example, while it was once believed that birds evolved from dinosaurs in one linear progression, some scientists, most notably Gregory S. Paul, conclude that dinosaurs such as the dromaeosaurs may have evolved from birds, losing the power of flight while keeping their feathers in a manner similar to the modern ostrich and other ratites.

Comparisons of bird and dinosaur skeletons, as well as cladistic analysis, strengthens the case for the link, particularly for a branch of theropods called maniraptors. Skeletal similarities include the neck, pubis, wrist (semi-lunate carpal), arm and pectoral girdle, shoulder blade, clavicle, and breast bone.

A study comparing embryonic, juvenile and adult archosaur skulls concluded that bird skulls are derived from those of theropod dinosaurs by progenesis, a type of paedomorphic heterochrony, which resulted in retention of juvenile characteristics of their ancestors.

Lungs

Large meat-eating dinosaurs had a complex system of air sacs similar to those found in modern birds, according to an investigation led by Patrick M. O'Connor of Ohio University. In theropod dinosaurs (carnivores that walked on two legs and had birdlike feet) flexible soft tissue air sacs likely pumped air through the stiff lungs, as is the case in birds. "What was once formally considered unique to birds was present in some form in the ancestors of birds", O'Connor said.

Heart

Computed tomography (CT) scans conducted in 2000 of the chest cavity of a specimen of the ornithopod *Thescelosaurus* found the apparent remnants of complex four-chambered hearts, much like those found in today's mammals and birds. The idea is controversial within the scientific community, coming under fire for bad anatomical science or simply wishful thinking.

A study published in 2011 applied multiple lines of inquiry to the question of the object's identity, including more advanced CT scanning, histology, X-ray diffraction, X-ray photoelectron spectroscopy, and scanning electron microscopy. From these methods, the authors found that: the object's internal structure does not include chambers but is made up of three unconnected areas of lower density material, and is not comparable to the structure of an ostrich's heart; the "walls" are composed of sedimentary minerals not known to be produced in biological systems, such as goethite, feldspar minerals, quartz, and gypsum, as well as some plant fragments; carbon, nitrogen, and phosphorus, chemical elements important to life, were lacking in their samples; and cardiac cellular structures were absent. There was one possible patch with animal cellular structures. The authors found their data supported identification

Figure 69: *Comparison between the air sacs of Majungasaurus and a bird (duck)*

as a concretion of sand from the burial environment, not the heart, with the possibility that isolated areas of tissues were preserved.

The question of how this find reflects metabolic rate and dinosaur internal anatomy is moot, though, regardless of the object's identity. Both modern crocodilians and birds, the closest living relatives of dinosaurs, have four-chambered hearts (albeit modified in crocodilians), so dinosaurs probably had them as well; the structure is not necessarily tied to metabolic rate.[162]

Sleeping posture

Fossils of the troodonts *Mei* and *Sinornithoides* demonstrate that the dinosaurs slept like certain modern birds, with their heads tucked under their arms.[163] This behavior, which may have helped to keep the head warm, is also characteristic of modern birds.

Reproductive biology

When laying eggs, female birds grow a special type of bone in their limbs. This medullary bone forms as a calcium-rich layer inside the hard outer bone, and is used as a calcium source to make eggshells. The presence of endosteally derived bone tissues lining the interior marrow cavities of portions of a *Tyrannosaurus rex* specimen's hind limb suggested that *T. rex* used similar reproductive strategies, and revealed that the specimen is female. Further research

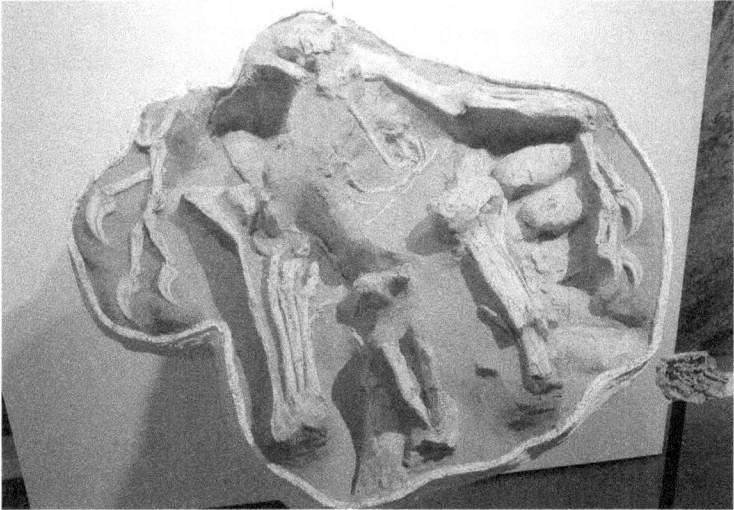

Figure 70: *A nesting Citipati osmolskae specimen, at the American Museum of Natural History in New York City*

has found medullary bone in the theropod *Allosaurus* and ornithopod *Tenontosaurus*. Because the line of dinosaurs that includes *Allosaurus* and *Tyrannosaurus* diverged from the line that led to *Tenontosaurus* very early in the evolution of dinosaurs, this suggests that dinosaurs in general produced medullary tissue.

Brooding and care of young

Several *Citipati* specimens have been found resting over the eggs in its nest in a position most reminiscent of brooding.

Numerous dinosaur species, for example *Maiasaura*, have been found in herds mixing both very young and adult individuals, suggesting rich interactions between them.

A dinosaur embryo was found without teeth, which suggests some parental care was required to feed the young dinosaur, possibly the adult dinosaur regurgitated food into the young dinosaur's mouth (*see* altricial). This behaviour is seen in numerous bird species; parent birds regurgitate food into the hatchling's mouth.

Gizzard stones

Both birds and dinosaurs use gizzard stones. These stones are swallowed by animals to aid digestion and break down food and hard fibres once they enter the stomach. When found in association with fossils, gizzard stones are called gastroliths. Gizzard stones are also found in some fish (mullets, mud shad, and the gillaroo, a type of trout) and in crocodiles.

Molecular evidence

On several occasions, the extraction of DNA and proteins from Mesozoic dinosaurs fossils has been claimed, allowing for a comparison with birds. Several proteins have putatively been detected in dinosaur fossils, including hemoglobin.

In the March 2005 issue of *Science*, Dr. Mary Higby Schweitzer and her team announced the discovery of flexible material resembling actual soft tissue inside a 68-million-year-old *Tyrannosaurus rex* leg bone of specimen MOR 1125 from the Hell Creek Formation in Montana. The seven collagen types obtained from the bone fragments, compared to collagen data from living birds (specifically, a chicken), suggest that older theropods and birds are closely related.[164] The soft tissue allowed a molecular comparison of cellular anatomy and protein sequencing of collagen tissue published in 2007, both of which indicated that *T. rex* and birds are more closely related to each other than either is to *Alligator*.[165] A second molecular study robustly supported the relationship of birds to dinosaurs, though it did not place birds within Theropoda, as expected. This study utilized eight additional collagen sequences extracted from a femur of the "mummified" *Brachylophosaurus canadensis* specimen MOR 2598, a hadrosaur. However, these results have been very controversial. No other peptides of a Mesozoic age have been reported. In 2008, it was suggested that the presumed soft tissue was in fact a bacterial microfilm.[166] In response, it was argued that these very microfilms protected the soft tissue.[167] Another objection was that the results could have been caused by contamination.[168] In 2015, under more controlled conditions safeguarding against contamination, the peptides were still identified.[169] In 2017, a study found that a peptide was present in the bone of the modern ostrich that was identical to that found in the *Tyrannosaurus* and *Brachylophosaurus* specimens, highlighting the danger of a cross-contamination.[170]

The successful extraction of ancient DNA from dinosaur fossils has been reported on two separate occasions, but upon further inspection and peer review, neither of these reports could be confirmed.

Figure 71: *Reconstruction of Rahonavis, a ground-dwelling feathered dinosaur that some researchers think was well equipped for flight*

Origin of bird flight

Debates about the origin of bird flight are almost as old as the idea that birds evolved from dinosaurs, which arose soon after the discovery of *Archaeopteryx* in 1862. Two theories have dominated most of the discussion since then: the cursorial ("from the ground up") theory proposes that birds evolved from small, fast predators that ran on the ground; the arboreal ("from the trees down") theory proposes that powered flight evolved from unpowered gliding by arboreal (tree-climbing) animals. A more recent theory, "wing-assisted incline running" (WAIR), is a variant of the cursorial theory and proposes that wings developed their aerodynamic functions as a result of the need to run quickly up very steep slopes such as trees, which would help small feathered dinosaurs escape from predators.

In March 2018, scientists reported that *Archaeopteryx* was likely capable of flight, but in a manner substantially different from that of modern birds.

Cursorial ("from the ground up") theory

The cursorial theory of the origin of flight was first proposed by Samuel Wendell Williston, and elaborated upon by Baron Nopcsa. This hypothesis proposes that some fast-running animals with long tails used their arms to keep their balance while running. Modern versions of this theory differ in many details from the Williston-Nopcsa version, mainly as a result of discoveries since Nopcsa's time.

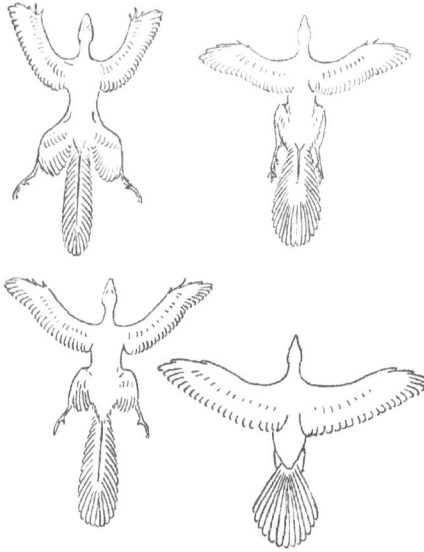

Figure 72: *Proposed development of flight in a book from 1922:*
Tetrapteryx, Archaeopteryx, Hypothetical Stage, Modern Bird

Nopcsa theorized that increasing the surface area of the outstretched arms could have helped small cursorial predators keep their balance, and that the scales of the forearms elongated, evolving into feathers. The feathers could also have been used to trap insects or other prey. Progressively, the animals leapt for longer distances, helped by their evolving wings. Nopcsa also proposed three stages in the evolution of flight. First, animals developed passive flight, in which developing wing structures served as a sort of parachute. Second, they achieved active flight by flapping the wings. He used *Archaeopteryx* as an example of this second stage. Finally, birds gained the ability to soar.

Current thought is that feathers did not evolve from scales, as feathers are made of different proteins. More seriously, Nopcsa's theory assumes that feathers evolved as part of the evolution of flight, and recent discoveries prove that assumption is false.

Feathers are very common in coelurosaurian dinosaurs (including the early tyrannosauroid *Dilong*). Modern birds are classified as coelurosaurs by nearly all palaeontologists, though not by a few ornithologists.[171,172] The modern version of the "from the ground up" hypothesis argues that birds' ancestors were small, *feathered*, ground-running predatory dinosaurs (rather like roadrunners in their hunting style[173]) that used their forelimbs for balance while pursuing prey, and that the forelimbs and feathers later evolved in ways that provided gliding and then powered flight. The most widely suggested original functions of feathers include thermal insulation and competitive displays, as in modern birds.

All of the *Archaeopteryx* fossils come from marine sediments, and it has been suggested that wings may have helped the birds run over water in the manner of the *Jesus Christ Lizard* (common basilisk).[174]

Most recent refutations of the "from the ground up" hypothesis attempt to refute the modern version's assumption that birds are modified coelurosaurian dinosaurs. The strongest attacks are based on embryological analyses that conclude that birds' wings are formed from digits 2, 3, and 4, (corresponding to the index, middle, and ring fingers in humans. The first of a bird's three digits forms the alula, which they use to avoid stalling in low-speed flight—for example, when landing). The hands of coelurosaurs, however, are formed by digits 1, 2, and 3 (thumb and first two fingers in humans).[175] However, these embryological analyses were immediately challenged on the embryological grounds that the "hand" often develops differently in clades that have lost some digits in the course of their evolution, and that birds' "hands" do develop from digits 1, 2, and 3. This debate is complex and not yet resolved - see "Digit homology".

Wing-assisted incline running

The wing-assisted incline running (WAIR) hypothesis was prompted by observation of young chukar chicks, and proposes that wings developed their aerodynamic functions as a result of the need to run quickly up very steep slopes such as tree trunks, for example to escape from predators.[176] This makes it a specialized type of cursorial ("from the ground up") theory. Note that in this scenario birds need *downforce* to give their feet increased grip.[177] But early birds, including *Archaeopteryx*, lacked the shoulder mechanism by which modern birds' wings produce swift, powerful upstrokes. Since the downforce WAIR depends on is generated by upstrokes, it seems that early birds were incapable of WAIR. Because WAIR is a behavioural trait without osteological specializations, the phylogenetic placement of the flight stroke before the divergence of Neornithes makes it impossible to determine if WAIR is ancestral to the avian flight stroke or derived from it.

Arboreal ("from the trees down") theory

Most versions of the arboreal hypothesis state that the ancestors of birds were very small dinosaurs that lived in trees, springing from branch to branch. This small dinosaur already had feathers, which were co-opted by evolution to produce longer, stiffer forms that were useful in aerodynamics, eventually producing wings. Wings would have then evolved and become increasingly refined

Figure 73: *The four-winged Microraptor, a member of the Dromaeosauridae, a group of dinosaurs closely related to birds*

as devices to give the leaper more control, to parachute, to glide, and to fly in stepwise fashion. The arboreal hypothesis also notes that, for arboreal animals, aerodynamics are far more energy efficient, since such animals simply fall to achieve minimum gliding speeds.[178,179]

Several small dinosaurs from the Jurassic or Early Cretaceous, all with feathers, have been interpreted as possibly having arboreal and/or aerodynamic adaptations. These include *Scansoriopteryx*, *Epidexipteryx*, *Microraptor*, *Pedopenna*, and *Anchiornis*. *Anchiornis* is particularly important to this subject, as it lived at the beginning of the Late Jurassic, long before *Archaeopteryx*.

Analysis of the proportions of the toe bones of the most primitive birds *Archaeopteryx* and *Confuciusornis*, compared to those of living species, suggest that the early species may have lived both on the ground and in trees.[180]

One study suggested that the earliest birds and their immediate ancestors did not climb trees. This study determined that the amount of toe claw curvature of early birds was more like that seen in modern ground-foraging birds than in perching birds.

Diminished significance of *Archaeopteryx*

Archaeopteryx was the first and for a long time the only known feathered Mesozoic animal. As a result, discussion of the evolution of birds and of bird flight centered on *Archaeopteryx* at least until the mid-1990s.

There has been debate about whether *Archaeopteryx* could really fly. It appears that *Archaeopteryx* had the brain structures and inner-ear balance sensors that

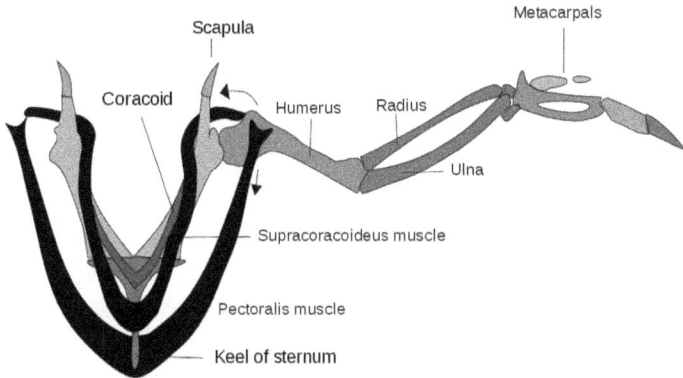

Figure 74: *The supracoracoideus works using a pulley-like system to lift the wing while the pectorals provide the powerful downstroke.*

birds use to control their flight. *Archaeopteryx* also had a wing feather arrangement like that of modern birds and similarly asymmetrical flight feathers on its wings and tail. But *Archaeopteryx* lacked the shoulder mechanism by which modern birds' wings produce swift, powerful upstrokes (see diagram above of supracoracoideus pulley); this may mean that it and other early birds were incapable of flapping flight and could only glide.

But the discovery since the early 1990s of many feathered dinosaurs means that *Archaeopteryx* is no longer the key figure in the evolution of bird flight. Other small feathered coelurosaurs from the Cretaceous and Late Jurassic show possible precursors of avian flight. These include *Rahonavis*, a ground-runner with a *Velociraptor*-like raised sickle claw on the second toe, that some paleontologists assume to have been better adapted for flight than *Archaeopteryx*, *Scansoriopteryx*, an arboreal dinosaur that may support the "from the trees down" theory, and *Microraptor*, an arboreal dinosaur possibly capable of powered flight but, if so, more like a biplane, as it had well-developed feathers on its legs. As early as 1915, some scientists argued that the evolution of bird flight may have gone through a four-winged (or *tetrapteryx*) stage.

Secondary flightlessness in dinosaurs

<templatestyles src="Template:Clade/styles.css" />

Coelurosaurs <templatestyles src="Template:Clade/styles.css" />
   Tyrannosauroids

    <templatestyles src="Template:Clade/styles.css" />
    Ornithomimosaurs

      <templatestyles src="Template:Clade/styles.css" />
      Alvarezsaurids

        <templatestyles src="Template:Clade/styles.css" />
        <templatestyles src="Template:Clade/styles.css" />

          Therizinosauroids

        Oviraptosaurs

        <templatestyles src="Template:Clade/styles.css" />
          Archaeopteryx and *Rahonavis*
          (birds)

      Deinony-   <templatestyles src="Template:Clade/styles.css" />
      chosaurs   Troodontids

          <templatestyles src="Template:Clade/styles.css" />
          <templatestyles src="Template:Clade/styles.css" />

          Confuciusornis
          (bird)

          Microraptor
          (dromaeosaur)

        Dromaeosaurs

Simplified cladogram from Mayr *et al.* (2005)
Groups usually regarded as birds are in bold type.

A hypothesis, credited to Gregory Paul and propounded in his books *Predatory Dinosaurs of the World* (1988) and *Dinosaurs of the Air* (2002), suggests that some groups of non-flying carnivorous dinosaurs - especially deinonychosaurs, but perhaps others such as oviraptorosaurs, therizinosaurs, alvarezsaurids and ornithomimosaurs - actually descend from birds. Paul also proposed that the bird ancestor of these groups was more advanced in its flight adaptations than *Archaeopteryx*. The hypothesis would mean that *Archaeopteryx* is less closely related to extant birds than these dinosaurs are.[181]

Paul's hypothesis received additional support when Mayr *et al.* (2005) analyzed a new, tenth specimen of *Archaeopteryx*, and concluded that *Archaeopteryx* was the sister clade to the Deinonychosauria, but that the more advanced bird *Confuciusornis* was within the Dromaeosauridae. This result supports Paul's hypothesis, suggesting that the Deinonychosauria and the Troodontidae are part of Aves, the bird lineage proper, and secondarily flightless. This paper, however, excluded all other birds and thus did not sample their character distributions. The paper was criticized by Corfe and Butler (2006) who found the authors could not support their conclusions statistically. Mayr *et al.* agreed that the statistical support was weak, but added that it is also weak for the alternative scenarios.

Current cladistic analyses do not support Paul's hypothesis about the position of *Archaeopteryx*. Instead, they indicate that *Archaeopteryx* is closer to birds, within the clade *Avialae*, than it is to deinonychosaurs or oviraptorosaurs. However, some fossils support the version of this theory that holds that some non-flying carnivorous dinosaurs may have had flying ancestors. In particular, *Microraptor*, *Pedopenna*, and *Anchiornis* all have winged feet, share many features, and lie close to the base of the clade Paraves. This suggests that the ancestral paravian was a four-winged glider, and that larger Deinonychosaurs secondarily lost the ability to glide, while the bird lineage increased in aerodynamic ability as it progressed. *Deinonychus* may also display partial volancy, with the young being capable of flight or gliding and the adults being flightless.[182] In 2018, a study concluded that the last common ancestor of the Pennaraptora had joint surfaces on the fingers, and between the metatarsus and the wrist, that were optimised to stabilise the hand in flight. This was seen as an indication for secondary flightlessness in heavy basal members of that group[183]

References

<templatestyles src="Template:Refbegin/styles.css" />

- Barsbold, Rinchen (1983): O ptich'ikh chertakh v stroyenii khishchnykh dinozavrov. ["Avian" features in the morphology of predatory dinosaurs]. *Transactions of the Joint Soviet Mongolian Paleontological Expedition* **24**: 96-103. [Original article in Russian.] Translated by W. Robert Welsh, copy provided by Kenneth Carpenter and converted by Matthew Carrano. PDF fulltext[184]
- Borenstein, Seth (July 31, 2014). "Study traces dinosaur evolution into early birds"[185]. *AP News*. Retrieved August 3, 2014.
- Bostwick, Kimberly S. (2003): Bird origins and evolution: data accumulates, scientists integrate, and yet the "debate" still rages. *Cladistics* **19**: 369–371. doi: 10.1016/S0748-3007(03)00069-0[186] PDF fulltext[187]
- Dingus, Lowell & Rowe, Timothy (1997): *The Mistaken Extinction: Dinosaur Evolution and the Origin of Birds*. W. H. Freeman and Company, New York. ISBN 0-7167-2944-X
- Dinosauria On-Line[188] (1995): Archaeopteryx's Relationship With Modern Birds[189]. Retrieved 2006-09-30.

- Dinosauria On-Line[188] (1996): Dinosaurian Synapomorphies Found In *Archaeopteryx*[190]. Retrieved 2006-09-30.
- Heilmann, G. (1926): *The Origin of Birds*. Witherby, London. ISBN 0-486-22784-7 (1972 Dover reprint)
- Mayr, Gerald; Pohl, B. & Peters, D. S. (2005): A Well-Preserved *Archaeopteryx* Specimen with Theropod Features. *Science* **310**(5753): 1483-1486. doi: 10.1126/science.1120331[191]
- Olson, Storrs L. (1985): The fossil record of birds. *In:* Farner, D.S.; King, J.R. & Parkes, Kenneth C. (eds.): *Avian Biology* **8**: 79-238. Academic Press, New York.

External links

- DinoBuzz[192] A popular-level discussion of the dinosaur-bird hypothesis
- *Archaeopteryx* - FAQs[193] from the Usenet newsgroup talk.origins.
- Dinosaurs among us[194] Article and Video[195] American Museum of Natural History exhibit of dinosaur evolution leading to birds

Wikimedia Commons has media related to *Aves fossils*.

Feathered dinosaurs

Feathered dinosaur

Since scientific research began on dinosaurs in the early 1800s, dinosaurs were generally believed to be most closely related to squamata ("scaled reptiles"). The word "dinosaur" itself, coined in 1842 by paleontologist Richard Owen, comes from the Greek for "fearsome lizard". This view began to shift during the so-called dinosaur renaissance in scientific research in the late 1960s, and by the mid-1990s significant evidence had emerged that birds are dinosaurs which are now believed to have descended directly from the theropod group.

Among extinct dinosaurs, feathers or feather-like integument have been discovered on dozens of genera via both direct and indirect fossil evidence. The vast majority of feather discoveries have been for coelurosaurian theropods. However, integument has also been discovered on at least three ornithischians, raising the likelihood that proto-feathers were also present in earlier dinosaurs.

In 2017, Baron, Norman, and Barrett proposed that feathers or featherlike structures may have originated with the common ancestor of the Ornithoscelida, a group of dinosaurs which includes both theropods and ornithischians, the only two known dinosaurian clades in which feathers have been observed so far. It is possible that feathers first developed in an even earlier group, in light of the discovery of pycnofibers of pterosaurs. Crocodilians also possess beta keratin similar to those of birds, which suggests that they evolved from common ancestral genes.

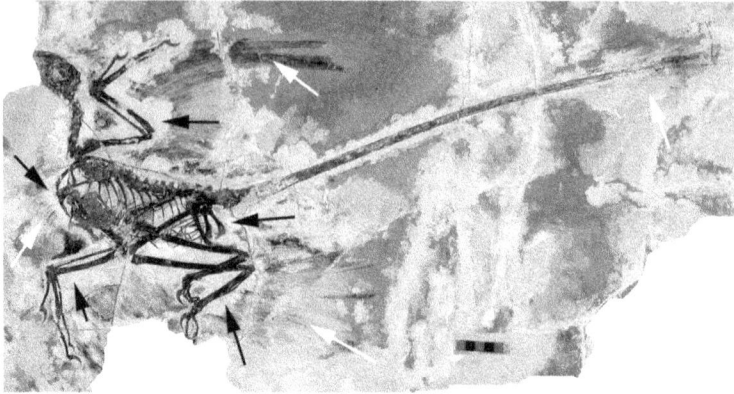

Figure 75: *Fossil of Microraptor gui includes impressions of feathered wings (see arrows)*

History of research

Early

Shortly after the 1859 publication of Charles Darwin's *On the Origin of Species*, British biologist Thomas Henry Huxley proposed that birds were descendants of dinosaurs. He compared the skeletal structure of *Compsognathus*, a small theropod dinosaur, and the 'first bird' *Archaeopteryx lithographica* (both of which were found in the Upper Jurassic Bavarian limestone of Solnhofen). He showed that, apart from its hands and feathers, *Archaeopteryx* was quite similar to *Compsognathus*. Thus *Archaeopteryx* represents a transitional fossil. In 1868 he published *On the Animals which are most nearly intermediate between Birds and Reptiles*, making the case.[196] The first restoration of a feathered dinosaur was Thomas Henry Huxley's depiction in 1876 of a feathered *Compsognathus* to accompany a lecture on the evolution of birds he delivered in New York in which he speculated that the aforementioned dinosaur might have been in possession of feathers. The leading dinosaur expert of the time, Richard Owen, disagreed, claiming *Archaeopteryx* as the first bird outside dinosaur lineage. For the next century, claims that birds were dinosaur descendants faded, with more popular bird-ancestry hypotheses including 'crocodylomorph' and 'thecodont' ancestors, rather than dinosaurs or other archosaurs.

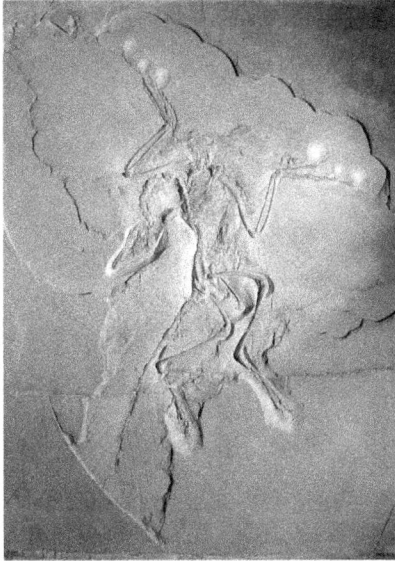

Figure 76: *The Berlin Archaeopteryx*

'Dinosaur renaissance'

In 1969, John Ostrom described *Deinonychus antirrhopus*, a theropod that he had discovered in Montana in 1964 and whose skeletal resemblance to birds seemed unmistakable. Ostrom became a leading proponent of the theory that birds are direct descendants of dinosaurs. Further comparisons of bird and dinosaur skeletons, as well as cladistic analysis strengthened the case for the link, particularly for a branch of theropods called maniraptors. Skeletal similarities include the neck, the pubis, the wrists (semi-lunate carpal), the 'arms' and pectoral girdle, the shoulder blade, the clavicle and the breast bone. In all, over a hundred distinct anatomical features are shared by birds and theropod dinosaurs.Wikipedia:Citation needed Other researchers drew on these shared features and other aspects of dinosaur biology and began to suggest that at least some theropod dinosaurs were feathered.

At the same time, paleoartists began to create modern restorations of highly active dinosaurs. In 1969, Robert T. Bakker drew a running *Deinonychus*. His student Gregory S. Paul depicted non-avian maniraptoran dinosaurs with feathers and protofeathers, starting in the late 1970s. In 1975, Eleanor M. Kish began to paint accurate images of dinosaurs, her *Hypacrosaurus* being the first one shown with its camouflage.

Figure 77: *Sinosauropteryx fossil, the first fossil of a definitively non-avialan dinosaur with feathers*

Before the discovery of feathered dinosaur fossils, the evidence was limited to Huxley and Ostrom's comparative anatomy. Some mainstream ornithologists, including Smithsonian Institution curator Storrs L. Olson, disputed the links, specifically citing the lack of fossil evidence for feathered dinosaurs.Wikipedia:Citation needed By the 1990s, however, most paleontologists considered birds to be surviving dinosaurs and referred to 'non-avian dinosaurs' (all extinct), to distinguish them from birds (Avialae).

Fossil discoveries

One of the earliest discoveries of possible feather impressions by non-avian dinosaurs is an ichnofossil (*Fulicopus lyellii*) of the 195-199 million year old Portland Formation in the northeastern United States. Gierlinski (1996, 1997, 1998) and Kondrat (2004) have interpreted traces between two footprints in this fossil as feather impressions from the belly of a squatting dilophosaurid. Although some reviewers have raised questions about the naming and interpretation of this fossil, if correct, this early Jurassic fossil is the oldest known evidence of feathers, almost 30 million years older than the next-oldest-known evidence.[197]

After a century of hypotheses without conclusive evidence, well-preserved fossils of feathered dinosaurs were discovered during the 1990s, and more continue to be found. The fossils were preserved in a Lagerstätte—a sedimentary deposit exhibiting remarkable richness and completeness in its fossils—in Liaoning, China. The area had repeatedly been smothered in volcanic

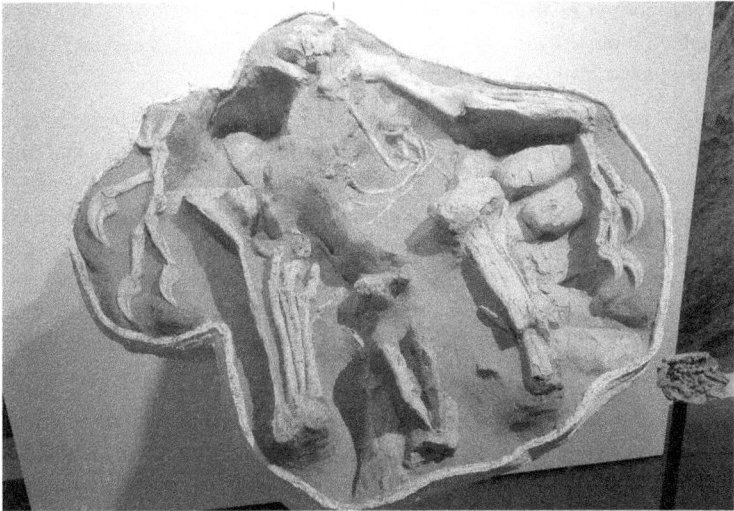

Figure 78: *A nesting Citipati osmolskae specimen, at the AMNH*

ash produced by eruptions in Inner Mongolia 124 million years ago, during the Early Cretaceous epoch. The fine-grained ash preserved the living organisms that it buried in fine detail. The area was teeming with life, with millions of leaves, angiosperms (the oldest known), insects, fish, frogs, salamanders, mammals, turtles, and lizards discovered to date.

The most important discoveries at Liaoning have been a host of feathered dinosaur fossils, with a steady stream of new finds filling in the picture of the dinosaur–bird connection and adding more to theories of the evolutionary development of feathers and flight. Turner *et al.* (2007) reported quill knobs from an ulna of *Velociraptor mongoliensis*, and these are strongly correlated with large and well-developed secondary feathers.

Behavioural evidence, in the form of an oviraptorosaur on its nest, showed another link with birds. Its forearms were folded, like those of a bird. Although no feathers were preserved, it is likely that these would have been present to insulate eggs and juveniles.[198]

Not all of the Chinese fossil discoveries proved valid however. In 1999, a supposed fossil of an apparently feathered dinosaur named *Archaeoraptor liaoningensis*, found in Liaoning Province, northeastern China, turned out to be a forgery. Comparing the photograph of the specimen with another find, Chinese paleontologist Xu Xing came to the conclusion that it was composed of two portions of different fossil animals. His claim made *National Geographic* review their research and they too came to the same conclusion. The bottom portion of the "*Archaeoraptor*" composite came from a legitimate feathered dromaeosaurid now known as *Microraptor*, and the upper portion from a previously known primitive bird called *Yanornis*.

In 2011, samples of amber were discovered to contain preserved feathers from 75 to 80 million years ago during the Cretaceous era, with evidence that they were from both dinosaurs and birds. Initial analysis suggests that some of the feathers were used for insulation, and not flight. More complex feathers were revealed to have variations in coloration similar to modern birds, while simpler protofeathers were predominantly dark. Only 11 specimens are currently known. The specimens are too rare to be broken open to study their melanosomes, but there are plans for using non-destructive high-resolution X-ray imaging.

In 2016, the discovery was announced of a feathered dinosaur tail preserved in amber that is estimated to be 99 million years old. Lida Xing, a researcher from the China University of Geosciences in Beijing, found the specimen at an amber market in Myanmar. It is the first definitive discovery of dinosaur material in amber.

In March 2018, scientists reported that *Archaeopteryx* was likely capable of flight, but in a manner substantially different from that of modern birds.

Current knowledge

Non-avian dinosaur species preserved with evidence of feathers

Several non-avian dinosaurs are now known to have been feathered. Direct evidence of feathers exists for several species. In all examples, the evidence described consists of feather impressions, except those genera inferred to have had feathers based on skeletal or chemical evidence, such as the presence of quill knobs (the anchor points for wing feathers on the forelimb) or a pygostyle (the fused vertebrae at the tail tip which often supports large feathers).

Primitive feather types

Integumentary structures that gave rise to the feathers of birds are seen in the dorsal spines of reptiles and fish. A similar stage in their evolution to the complex coats of birds and mammals can be observed in living reptiles such as iguanas and *Gonocephalus* agamids. Feather structures are thought to have proceeded from simple hollow filaments through several stages of increasing complexity, ending with the large, deeply rooted feathers with strong pens (rachis), barbs and barbules that birds display today.

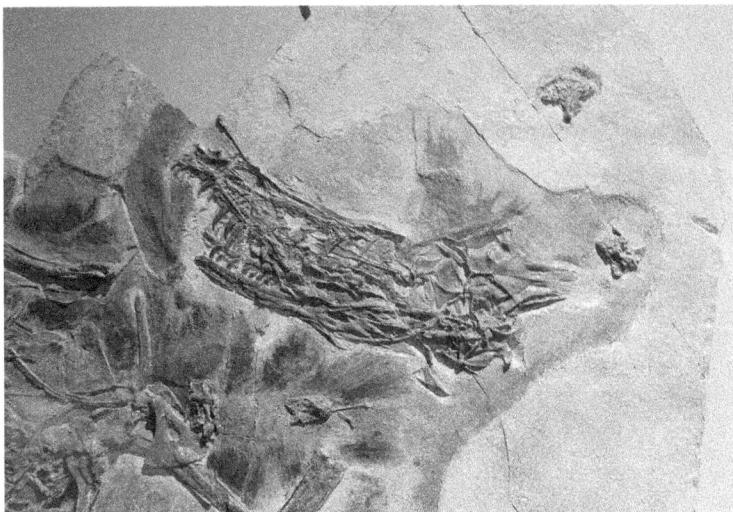

Figure 79: *Fossil of Sinornithosaurus millenii,*
the first evidence of feathers in dromaeosaurids

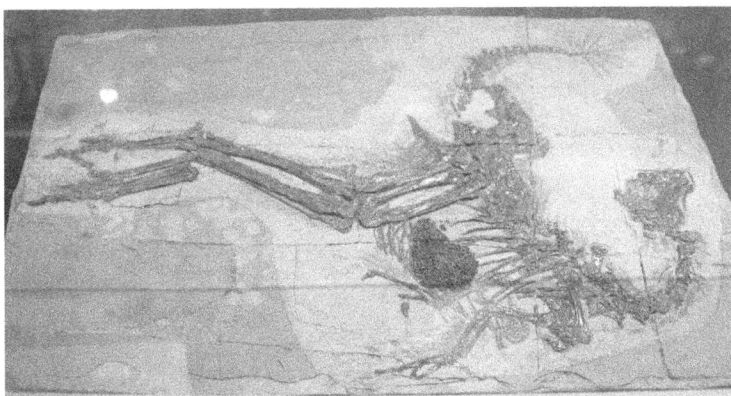

Figure 80: *Cast of a Caudipteryx fossil with*
feather impressions and stomach content

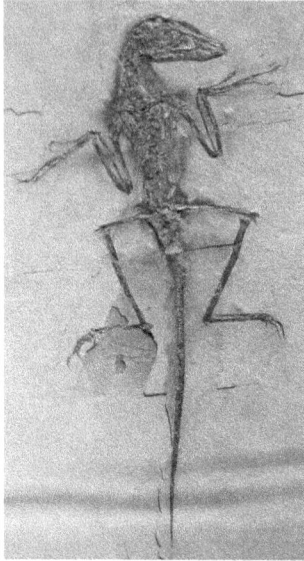

Figure 81: *Fossil cast of a Sinornithosaurus millenii*

Figure 82: *Jinfengopteryx elegans fossil*

According to Prum's (1999) proposed model, at stage I, the follicle originates with a cylindrical epidermal depression around the base of the feather papilla. The first feather resulted when undifferentiated tubular follicle collar developed out of the old keratinocytes being pushed out. At stage II, the inner, basilar layer of the follicle collar differentiated into longitudinal barb ridges with unbranched keratin filaments, while the thin peripheral layer of the collar became the deciduous sheath, forming a tuft of unbranched barbs with a basal calamus. Stage III consists of two developmental novelties, IIIa and IIIb, as either could have occurred first. Stage IIIa involves helical displacement of barb ridges arising within the collar. The barb ridges on the anterior midline of the follicle fuse together, forming the rachis. The creation of a posterior barb locus follows, giving an indeterminate number of barbs. This resulted in a feather with a symmetrical, primarily branched structure with a rachis and unbranched barbs. In stage IIIb, barbules paired within the peripheral barbule plates of the barb ridges, create branched barbs with rami and barbules. This resulting feather is one with a tuft of branched barbs without a rachis. At stage IV, differentiated distal and proximal barbules produce a closed, pennaceous vane. A closed vane develops when pennulae on the distal barbules form a hooked shape to attach to the simpler proximal barbules of the adjacent barb. Stage V developmental novelties gave rise to additional structural diversity in the closed pennaceous feather. Here, asymmetrical flight feathers, bipinnate plumulaceous feathers, filoplumes, powder down, and bristles evolved.

Some evidence suggests that the original function of simple feathers was insulation. In particular, preserved patches of skin in large, derived, tyrannosauroids show scutes, while those in smaller, more primitive, forms show feathers. This may indicate that the larger forms had complex skins, with both scutes and filaments, or that tyrannosauroids may be like rhinos and elephants, having filaments at birth and then losing them as they developed to maturity. An adult *Tyrannosaurus rex* weighed about as much as an African elephant. If large tyrannosauroids were endotherms, they would have needed to radiate heat efficiently.[199] However, due to the different structural properties of feathers compared to fur, as well as a larger surface area per cubic square meter, it is extremely unlikely even the largest theropods would suffer overheating issues from an extensive feather coat.Wikipedia:Citation needed

There is an increasing body of evidence that supports the display hypothesis, which states that early feathers were colored and increased reproductive success. Coloration could have provided the original adaptation of feathers, implying that all later functions of feathers, such as thermoregulation and flight, were co-opted. This hypothesis has been supported by the discovery of pigmented feathers in multiple species. Supporting the display hypothesis is the fact that fossil feathers have been observed in a ground-dwelling herbivorous dinosaur clade, making it unlikely that feathers functioned as predatory

tools or as a means of flight.[200] Additionally, some specimens have iridescent feathers. Pigmented and iridescent feathers may have provided greater
attractiveness to mates, providing enhanced reproductive success when compared to non-colored feathers. Current research shows that it is plausible that
theropods would have had the visual acuity necessary to see the displays. In a
study by Stevens (2006), the binocular field of view for *Velociraptor* has been
estimated to be 55 to 60 degrees, which is about that of modern owls. Visual acuity for *Tyrannosaurus* has been predicted to be anywhere from about
that of humans to 13 times that of humans. However, as both *Velociraptor*
and *Tyrannosaurus* have a rather extended evolutionary relationship with the
more basal theropods, it is unclear how much of this visual acuity data can be
extrapolated.Wikipedia:Citation needed

The idea that precursors of feathers appeared before they were co-opted for
insulation is already stated in Gould and Vrba, 1982. The original benefit
might have been metabolic. Feathers are largely made of the keratin protein
complex, which has disulfide bonds between amino acids that give it stability
and elasticity. The metabolism of amino acids containing sulfur can be toxic;
however, if the sulfur amino acids are not catabolized at the final products
of urea or uric acid but used for the synthesis of keratin instead, the release
of hydrogen sulfide is extremely reduced or avoided. For an organism whose
metabolism works at high internal temperatures of 40 °C or greater, it can
be extremely important to prevent the excess production of hydrogen sulfide.
This hypothesis could be consistent with the need for high metabolic rate of
theropod dinosaurs.

It is not known with certainty at what point in archosaur phylogeny the earliest simple "protofeathers" arose, or whether they arose once or independently
multiple times. Filamentous structures are clearly present in pterosaurs, and
long, hollow quills have been reported in specimens of the ornithischian dinosaurs *Psittacosaurus* and *Tianyulong*. In 2009, Xu et al. noted that the
hollow, unbranched, stiff integumentary structures found on a specimen of
Beipiaosaurus were strikingly similar to the integumentary structures of *Psittacosaurus* and pterosaurs. They suggested that all of these structures may have
been inherited from a common ancestor much earlier in the evolution of archosaurs, possibly in an ornithodire from the Middle Triassic or earlier. More
recently, findings in Russia of the basal neornithischian *Kulindadromeus* report
that although the lower leg and tail seemed to be scaled, "varied integumentary
structures were found directly associated with skeletal elements, supporting
the hypothesis that simple filamentous feathers, as well as compound feather-
like structures comparable to those in theropods, were widespread amongst the
whole dinosaur clade."

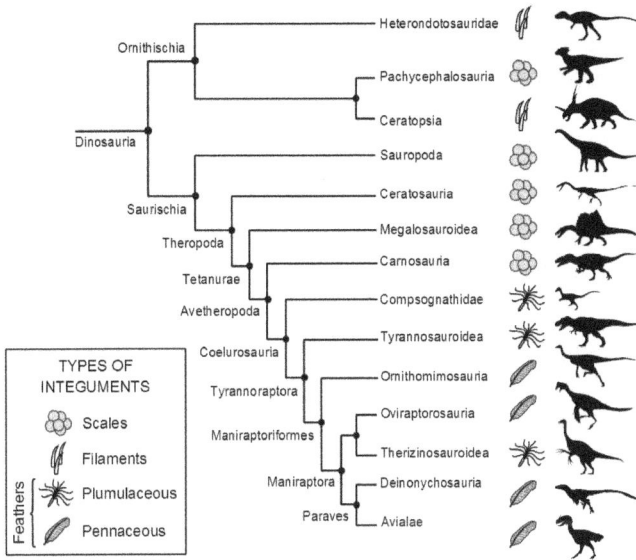

Figure 83: *Cladogram showing distribution of feathers in Dinosauria, as of 2015*

Display feathers are also known from dinosaurs that are very primitive members of the bird lineage, or Avialae. The most primitive example is *Epidexipteryx*, which had a short tail with extremely long, ribbon-like feathers. Oddly enough, the fossil does not preserve wing feathers, suggesting that *Epidexipteryx* was either secondarily flightless, or that display feathers evolved before flight feathers in the bird lineage. Plumaceous feathers are found in nearly all lineages of Theropoda common in the northern hemisphere, and pennaceous feathers are attested as far down the tree as the Ornithomimosauria. The fact that only adult *Ornithomimus* had wing-like structures suggests that pennaceous feathers evolved for mating displays.

Phylogeny and the inference of feathers in other dinosaurs

Fossil feather impressions are extremely rare and they require exceptional preservation conditions to form. Therefore, only a few non-avian feathered dinosaur genera have been identified. All fossil feather specimens have been found to show certain similarities. Due to these similarities and through developmental research, many scientists believe that feathers have only evolved once in dinosaurs.Wikipedia:Citation needed Feathers would then have been passed down to all later, more derived species, unless some lineages lost feathers secondarily. If a dinosaur falls at a point on an evolutionary tree within the known feather-bearing lineages, then its ancestors had feathers, and it is quite possible that it did as well.Wikipedia:Citation needed This technique, called phylogenetic bracketing, can also be used to infer the type of feathers a species may have had, since the developmental history of feathers is now reasonably well-known. All feathered species had filamentaceous or plumaceous (downy) feathers, with pennaceous feathers found among the more bird-like groups. The following cladogram is adapted from Godefroit *et al.*, 2013.

Grey denotes a clade that is not known to contain any feathered specimen at the time of writing (although this does not imply that members of the clade lacked feathers).

<templatestyles src="Template:Clade/styles.css" />

Neotheropoda <templatestyles src="Template:Clade/styles.css" />

Dilophosauridae

Ori-   <templatestyles src="Template:Clade/styles.css" />
on-   Megalosauroidea
ides

Avetheropoda <templatestyles src="Template:Clade/styles.css" />
              Carnosauria

Coelurosauria <templatestyles src="Template:Clade/styles.css" />
               Sciurumimus - filamentous feathers

Tyran- <templatestyles src="Template:Clade/styles.css" />
no-   Tyrannosauroidea (*Dilong, Yutyrannus*) – plumulaceous feathers
rap-
tora

        <templatestyles src="Template:Clade/styles.css" />
        Sinocalliopteryx – plumulaceous feathers

        <templatestyles src="Template:Clade/styles.css" />
        Compsognathidae (*Sinosauropteryx*, GMV 2124) – plumulaceous
        feathers

        <templatestyles src="Template:Clade/styles.css" />
        <templatestyles src="Template:Clade/styles.css" />

        Juravenator – filamentous feathers

        Ornitholestes

Mani-   <templatestyles src="Template:Clade/styles.css" />
rap-   Ornithomimosauria (*Ornithomimus, Deinocheirus*)
tori-   – plumulaceous feathers
formes

Mani-   <templatestyles src="Template:Clade/styles.css" />
rap-   Alvarezsauridae (*Shuvuuia*) – plumulaceous
tora   feathers

        <templatestyles src="Template:Clade/styles.css"
        />
        Therizinosauroidea (*Beipiaosaurus,
        Jianchangosaurus*) – plumulaceous
        feathers

Pen-   <templatestyles src="Template:Clade/-
nara-   styles.css" />
p-   Oviraptorosauria (*Avimimus,
tora   Nomingia, Caudipteryx, Simili-
        caudipteryx, Protarchaeopteryx,
        Ningyuansaurus, Citipati,
        Conchoraptor*) – pennaceous
        feathers

Par-   <templatestyles
aves   src="Template:Clade/styles.css"
        />
        Scansoriopterygidae (*Scan-
        soriopteryx, Epidexipteryx*) –
        pennaceous feathers

        <templatestyles
        src="Template:Clade/styles.css"
        />
        Eosinopteryx –
        pennaceous feathers

Eu-   <templatestyles
mani-   src="Template:Clade/-
rap-   styles.css" />
tora   Dromaeosauridae
        (*Sinornithosaurus,
        Microraptor,
        Velociraptor,
        Changyuraptor*) –
        pennaceous feathers

        <templatestyles
        src="Template:Clade/-
        styles.css" />

        Troodontidae
        (*Jinfengopteryx*)
        – pennaceous
        feathers
        Avialae (birds)

External links

- DinoBuzz[201], dinosaur-bird controversy explained, by UC Berkeley.
- Feathered Dinosaurs[202] on *In Our Time* at the BBC

Extinction of major groups

Cretaceous–Paleogene extinction event

The **Cretaceous–Paleogene (K–Pg) extinction event**,[203] also known as the **Cretaceous–Tertiary (K–T) extinction**,[204]</ref> was a sudden mass extinction of some three-quarters of the plant and animal species on Earth, approximately 66 million years ago. With the exception of some ectothermic species such as the leatherback sea turtle and crocodiles, no tetrapods weighing more than 25 kilograms (55 lb) survived. It marked the end of the Cretaceous period and with it, the entire Mesozoic Era, opening the Cenozoic Era that continues today.

In the geologic record, the K–Pg event is marked by a thin layer of sediment called the K–Pg boundary, which can be found throughout the world in marine and terrestrial rocks. The boundary clay shows high levels of the metal iridium, which is rare in the Earth's crust, but abundant in asteroids.

As originally proposed in 1980 by a team of scientists led by Luis Alvarez and Walter Alvarez, it is now generally thought that the K–Pg extinction was caused by the impact of a massive comet or asteroid 10 to 15 km (6.2 to 9.3 mi) wide, 66 million years ago, which devastated the global environment, mainly through a lingering impact winter which halted photosynthesis in plants and plankton. The impact hypothesis, also known as the Alvarez hypothesis, was bolstered by the discovery of the 180-kilometre-wide (112 mi) Chicxulub crater in the Gulf of Mexico in the early 1990s, which provided conclusive evidence that the K–Pg boundary clay represented debris from an asteroid impact. The fact that the extinctions occurred simultaneously provides strong evidence that they were caused by the asteroid. A 2016 drilling project into the Chicxulub peak ring confirmed that the peak ring comprised granite ejected within minutes from deep in the earth, but contained hardly any gypsum, the usual sulfate-containing sea floor rock in the region: the gypsum would have vaporized and

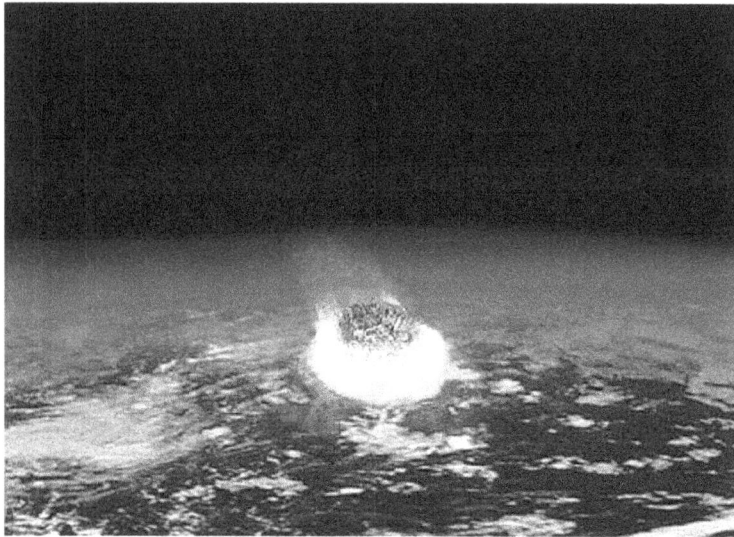

Figure 84: *An artist's rendering of an asteroid a few kilometers across colliding with the Earth. Such an impact can release the equivalent energy of several million nuclear weapons detonating simultaneously.*

Figure 85: *Badlands near Drumheller, Alberta, where erosion has exposed the K–Pg boundary*

Figure 86: *A Wyoming rock with an intermediate claystone layer that contains 1000 times more iridium than the upper and lower layers. Picture taken at the San Diego Natural History Museum*

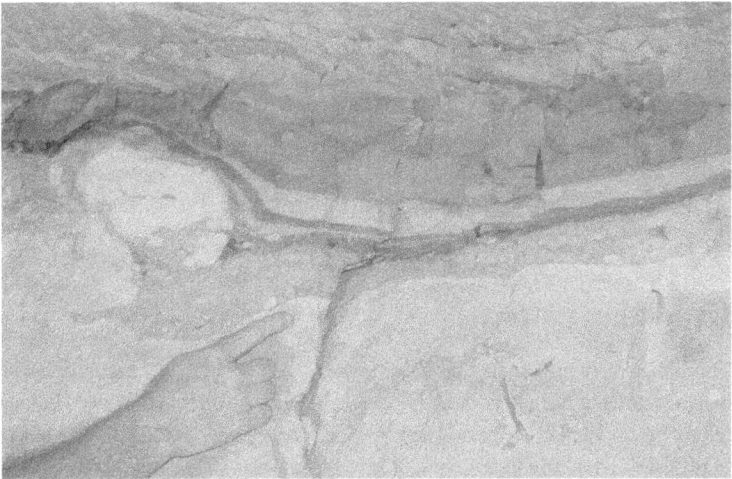

Figure 87: *Complex Cretaceous–Paleogene clay layer (gray) in the Geulhemmergroeve tunnels near Geulhem, The Netherlands. (Finger is below the actual Cretaceous-Paleogene boundary)*

dispersed as an aerosol into the atmosphere, causing longer term effects on the climate and food chain.

Other causal or contributing factors to the extinction may have been the Deccan Traps and other volcanic eruptions, climate change, and sea level change.

A wide range of species perished in the K–Pg extinction, the best-known being the non-avian dinosaurs. It also destroyed a plethora of other terrestrial organisms, including certain mammals, pterosaurs, birds, lizards, insects, and plants. In the oceans, the K–Pg extinction killed off plesiosaurs and the giant marine lizards (Mosasauridae), and devastated fish, sharks, mollusks (especially ammonites, which became extinct), and many species of plankton. It is estimated that 75% or more of all species on Earth vanished. Yet the extinction also provided evolutionary opportunities: in its wake, many groups underwent remarkable adaptive radiation—sudden and prolific divergence into new forms and species within the disrupted and emptied ecological niches. Mammals in particular diversified in the Paleogene, evolving new forms such as horses, whales, bats, and primates. Birds, fish, and perhaps lizards also radiated.

Microbiota

The K–Pg boundary represents one of the most dramatic turnovers in the fossil record for various calcareous nanoplankton that formed the calcium deposits for which the Cretaceous is named. The turnover in this group is clearly marked at the species level. Statistical analysis of marine losses at this time suggests that the decrease in diversity was caused more by a sharp increase in extinctions than by a decrease in speciation. The K–Pg boundary record of dinoflagellates is not so well understood, mainly because only microbial cysts provide a fossil record, and not all dinoflagellate species have cyst-forming stages, which likely causes diversity to be underestimated. Recent studies indicate that there were no major shifts in dinoflagellates through the boundary layer.

Extinction patterns

The blue graph shows the apparent *percentage* (not the absolute number) of marine animal genera becoming extinct during any given time interval. It does not represent all marine species, just those that are readily fossilized. The labels of the traditional "Big Five" extinction events and the more recently recognised End-Capitanian extinction event are clickable hyperlinks; see Extinction event for more details. *(source and image info)*

The K–Pg extinction event was severe, global, rapid, and selective, eliminating a vast number of species. Based on marine fossils, it is estimated that 75% or more of all species were made extinct. The event appears to have affected all continents at the same time. Non-avian dinosaurs, for example, are known from the Maastrichtian of North America, Europe, Asia, Africa, South America, and Antarctica, but are unknown from the Cenozoic anywhere in the world. Similarly, fossil pollen shows devastation of the plant communities in areas as far apart as New Mexico, Alaska, China, and New Zealand.

Despite the event's severity, there was significant variability in the rate of extinction between and within different clades. Species that depended on photosynthesis declined or became extinct as atmospheric particles blocked sunlight and reduced the solar energy reaching the ground. This plant extinction caused a major reshuffling of the dominant plant groups. Omnivores, insectivores, and carrion-eaters survived the extinction event, perhaps because of the increased availability of their food sources. No purely herbivorous or carnivorous mammals seem to have survived. Rather, the surviving mammals and birds fed on insects, worms, and snails, which in turn fed on detritus (dead plant and animal matter).

In stream communities, few animal groups became extinct because such communities rely less directly on food from living plants and more on detritus washed in from the land, protecting them from extinction. Similar, but more complex patterns have been found in the oceans. Extinction was more severe among animals living in the water column than among animals living on or in the sea floor. Animals in the water column are almost entirely dependent on primary production from living phytoplankton, while animals on the ocean floor always or sometimes feed on detritus. Coccolithophorids and mollusks (including ammonites, rudists, freshwater snails, and mussels), and those organisms whose food chain included these shell builders, became extinct or suffered heavy losses. For example, it is thought that ammonites were the principal food of mosasaurs, a group of giant marine reptiles that became extinct at the boundary. The largest air-breathing survivors of the event, crocodyliforms and champsosaurs, were semi-aquatic and had access to detritus. Modern crocodilians can live as scavengers and survive for months without food, and their young are small, grow slowly, and feed largely on invertebrates and dead organisms for their first few years. These characteristics have been linked to crocodilian survival at the end of the Cretaceous.

After the K–Pg extinction event, biodiversity required substantial time to recover, despite the existence of abundant vacant ecological niches.

Radiolaria have left a geological record since at least the Ordovician times, and their mineral fossil skeletons can be tracked across the K–Pg boundary.

There is no evidence of mass extinction of these organisms, and there is support for high productivity of these species in southern high latitudes as a result of cooling temperatures in the early Paleocene. Approximately 46% of diatom species survived the transition from the Cretaceous to the Upper Paleocene, a significant turnover in species but not a catastrophic extinction.

The occurrence of planktonic foraminifera across the K–Pg boundary has been studied since the 1930s. Research spurred by the possibility of an impact event at the K–Pg boundary resulted in numerous publications detailing planktonic foraminiferal extinction at the boundary, however, there is ongoing debate between groups that think the evidence indicates substantial extinction of these species at the K–Pg boundary, and those who think the evidence supports multiple extinctions and expansions through the boundary.

Numerous species of benthic foraminifera became extinct during the event, presumably because they depend on organic debris for nutrients, while biomass in the ocean is thought to have decreased. As the marine microbiota recovered, however, it is thought that increased speciation of benthic foraminifera resulted from the increase in food sources. Phytoplankton recovery in the early Paleocene provided the food source to support large benthic foraminiferal assemblages, which are mainly detritus-feeding. Ultimate recovery of the benthic populations occurred over several stages lasting several hundred thousand years into the early Paleocene.

Marine invertebrates

There is significant variation in the fossil record as to the extinction rate of marine invertebrates across the K–Pg boundary. The apparent rate is influenced by a lack of fossil records, rather than extinctions.

Ostracods, a class of small crustaceans that were prevalent in the upper Maastrichtian, left fossil deposits in a variety of locations. A review of these fossils shows that ostracod diversity was lower in the Paleocene than any other time in the Cenozoic. Current research cannot ascertain, however, whether the extinctions occurred prior to, or during, the boundary interval.

Approximately 60% of late-Cretaceous Scleractinia coral genera failed to cross the K–Pg boundary into the Paleocene. Further analysis of the coral extinctions shows that approximately 98% of colonial species, ones that inhabit warm, shallow tropical waters, became extinct. The solitary corals, which generally do not form reefs and inhabit colder and deeper (below the photic zone) areas of the ocean were less impacted by the K–Pg boundary. Colonial coral species rely upon symbiosis with photosynthetic algae, which collapsed due to the events surrounding the K–Pg boundary, however, the use of data from coral fossils to support K–Pg extinction and subsequent Paleocene recovery,

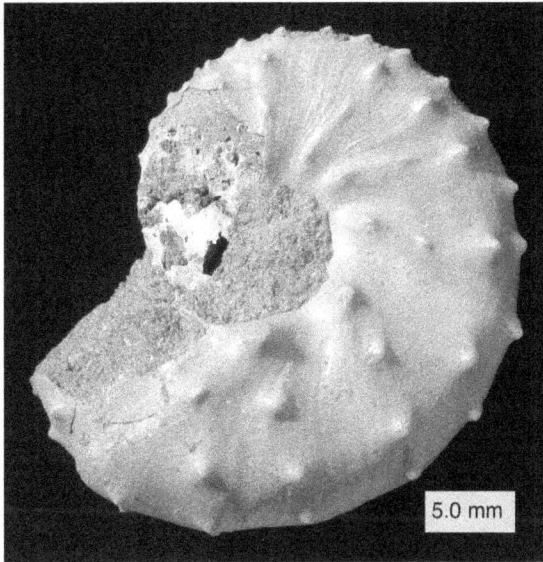

Figure 88: *Discoscaphites iris ammonite from the Owl Creek Formation (Upper Cretaceous), Owl Creek, Ripley, Mississippi*

must be weighed against the changes that occurred in coral ecosystems through the K–Pg boundary.

The numbers of cephalopod, echinoderm, and bivalve genera exhibited significant diminution after the K–Pg boundary. Most species of brachiopods, a small phylum of marine invertebrates, survived the K–Pg extinction event and diversified during the early Paleocene.

Except for nautiloids (represented by the modern order Nautilida) and coleoids (which had already diverged into modern octopodes, squids, and cuttlefish) all other species of the molluscan class Cephalopoda became extinct at the K–Pg boundary. These included the ecologically significant belemnoids, as well as the ammonoids, a group of highly diverse, numerous, and widely distributed shelled cephalopods. Researchers have pointed out that the reproductive strategy of the surviving nautiloids, which rely upon few and larger eggs, played a role in outsurviving their ammonoid counterparts through the extinction event. The ammonoids utilized a planktonic strategy of reproduction (numerous eggs and planktonic larvae), which would have been devastated by the K–Pg extinction event. Additional research has shown that subsequent to this elimination of ammonoids from the global biota, nautiloids began an evolutionary radiation into shell shapes and complexities theretofore known only from ammonoids.

Figure 89: *Rudist bivalves from the Late Cretaceous of the Omani Mountains, United Arab Emirates. Scale bar is 10 mm*

Approximately 35% of echinoderm genera became extinct at the K–Pg boundary, although taxa that thrived in low-latitude, shallow-water environments during the late Cretaceous had the highest extinction rate. Mid-latitude, deepwater echinoderms were much less affected at the K–Pg boundary. The pattern of extinction points to habitat loss, specifically the drowning of carbonate platforms, the shallow-water reefs in existence at that time, by the extinction event.

Other invertebrate groups, including rudists (reef-building clams) and inoceramids (giant relatives of modern scallops), also became extinct at the K–Pg boundary.

Fish

There are substantial fossil records of jawed fishes across the K–Pg boundary, which provide good evidence of extinction patterns of these classes of marine vertebrates. While the deep sea realm was able to remain seemingly unaffected, there was an equal loss between the open marine apex predators and the durophagous demersal feeders on the continental shelf.

Within cartilaginous fish, approximately 7 out of the 41 families of neoselachians (modern sharks, skates, and rays) disappeared after this event and batoids (skates and rays) lost nearly all the identifiable species, while more than 90% of teleost fish (bony fish) families survived.

In the Maastrichtian age, 28 shark families and 13 batoid families thrived, of which 25 and 9, respectively, survived the K-T boundary event. 47 of all neoselachian genera cross the K/T boundary, with 85% being sharks. Batoids display with 15% a comparably low survival rate.

There is evidence of a mass extinction of bony fishes at a fossil site immediately above the K–Pg boundary layer on Seymour Island near Antarctica, apparently precipitated by the K–Pg extinction event, however, the marine and freshwater environments of fishes mitigated environmental effects of the extinction event.

Terrestrial invertebrates

Insect damage to the fossilized leaves of flowering plants from fourteen sites in North America was used as a proxy for insect diversity across the K–Pg boundary and analyzed to determine the rate of extinction. Researchers found that Cretaceous sites, prior to the extinction event, had rich plant and insect-feeding diversity. During the early Paleocene, however, flora were relatively diverse with little predation from insects, even 1.7 million years after the extinction event.

Terrestrial plants

There is overwhelming evidence of global disruption of plant communities at the K–Pg boundary. Extinctions are seen both in studies of fossil pollen, and fossil leaves. In North America, the data suggests massive devastation and mass extinction of plants at the K–Pg boundary sections, although there were substantial megafloral changes before the boundary. In North America, approximately 57% of plant species became extinct. In high southern hemisphere latitudes, such as New Zealand and Antarctica, the mass die-off of flora caused no significant turnover in species, but dramatic and short-term changes in the relative abundance of plant groups. In some regions, the Paleocene recovery of plants began with recolonizations by fern species, represented as a fern spike in the geologic record; this same pattern of fern recolonization was observed after the 1980 Mount St. Helens eruption.

Due to the wholesale destruction of plants at the K–Pg boundary, there was a proliferation of saprotrophic organisms, such as fungi, that do not require photosynthesis and use nutrients from decaying vegetation. The dominance of fungal species lasted only a few years while the atmosphere cleared and plenty of organic matter to feed on was present. Once the atmosphere cleared, photosynthetic organisms, such as ferns and other plants, returned.

Figure 90: *Kronosaurus Hunt by Dmitry Bogdanov, 2008 – Large marine reptiles, including plesiosaurians such as these, became extinct at the end of the Cretaceous.*

Polyploidy appears to have enhanced the ability of flowering plants to survive the extinction, probably because the additional copies of the genome such plants possessed, allowed them to more readily adapt to the rapidly changing environmental conditions that followed the impact.

Amphibians

There is limited evidence for extinction of amphibians at the K–Pg boundary. A study of fossil vertebrates across the K–Pg boundary in Montana concluded that no species of amphibian became extinct. Yet there are several species of Maastrichtian amphibian, not included as part of this study, which are unknown from the Paleocene. These include the frog *Theatonius lancensis* and the albanerpetontid *Albanerpeton galaktion*; therefore, some amphibians do seem to have become extinct at the boundary. The relatively low levels of extinction seen among amphibians probably reflect the low extinction rates seen in freshwater animals.

Non-archosaurs

Choristodere

The choristoderes (semi-aquatic archosauromorphs) survived across the K–Pg boundary but would die out in the early Miocene. Studies on *Champsosaurus'* palatal teeth suggest that there were dietary changes among the various species across the KT event.

Turtles

More than 80% of Cretaceous turtle species passed through the K–Pg boundary. Additionally, all six turtle families in existence at the end of the Cretaceous survived into the Paleogene and are represented by living species.

Lepidosauria

The living non-archosaurian reptile taxa, lepidosaurians (lizards and tuataras), survived across the K–Pg boundary. Living lepidosaurs include the tuataras (the only living rhynchocephalians) and the squamates.

The rhynchocephalians were a widespread and relatively successful group of lepidosaurians during the early Mesozoic, but began to decline by the mid-Cretaceous, although they were very successful in the Late Cretaceous of South America. They are represented today by a single genus, located exclusively in New Zealand.

The order Squamata, which is represented today by lizards, including snakes and amphisbaenians (worm lizards), radiated into various ecological niches during the Jurassic and was successful throughout the Cretaceous. They survived through the K–Pg boundary and are currently the most successful and diverse group of living reptiles, with more than 6,000 extant species. Many families of terrestrial squamates became extinct at the boundary, such as monstersaurians and polyglyphanodonts, and fossil evidence indicates they suffered very heavy losses in the KT event, only recovering 10 million years after it. Giant non-archosaurian aquatic reptiles such as mosasaurs and plesiosaurs, which were the top marine predators of their time, became extinct by the end of the Cretaceous. The ichthyosaurs had disappeared from fossil records before the mass extinction occurred.

Archosaurs

The archosaur clade includes two surviving groups, crocodilians and birds, along with the various extinct groups of non-avian dinosaurs and pterosaurs.

Crocodyliforms

Ten families of crocodilians or their close relatives are represented in the Maastrichtian fossil records, of which five died out prior to the K–Pg boundary. Five families have both Maastrichtian and Paleocene fossil representatives. All of the surviving families of crocodyliforms inhabited freshwater and terrestrial environments—except for the Dyrosauridae, which lived in freshwater and marine locations. Approximately 50% of crocodyliform representatives survived across the K–Pg boundary, the only apparent trend being that no large crocodiles survived. Crocodyliform survivability across the boundary may have resulted from their aquatic niche and ability to burrow, which reduced susceptibility to negative environmental effects at the boundary. Jouve and colleagues suggested in 2008 that juvenile marine crocodyliforms lived in freshwater environments as do modern marine crocodile juveniles, which would have helped them survive where other marine reptiles became extinct; freshwater environments were not so strongly affected by the K–Pg extinction event as marine environments were.

Pterosaurs

One family of pterosaurs, Azhdarchidae, was definitely present in the Maastrichtian, and it likely became extinct at the K–Pg boundary. These large pterosaurs were the last representatives of a declining group that contained ten families during the mid-Cretaceous. Several other pterosaur lineages may have been present during the Maastrichtian, such as the ornithocheirids, pteranodontids, nyctosaurids, as well as, a possible tapejarid, though they are represented by fragmentary remains that are difficult to assign to any given group. While this was occurring, modern birds were undergoing diversification; traditionally it was thought that they replaced archaic birds and pterosaur groups, possibly due to direct competition, or they simply filled empty niches, but there is no correlation between pterosaur and avian diversities that are conclusive to a competition hypothesis, and small pterosaurs were present in the Late Cretaceous. In fact, at least some niches previously held by birds were reclaimed by pterosaurs prior to the K–Pg event.

Birds

Most paleontologists regard birds as the only surviving dinosaurs (see Origin of birds). It is thought that all non-avian theropods became extinct, including then-flourishing groups such as enantiornithines and hesperornithiforms. Several analyses of bird fossils show divergence of species prior to the K–Pg boundary, and that duck, chicken, and ratite bird relatives coexisted with non-avian dinosaurs. Large collections of bird fossils representing a range of different species provides definitive evidence for the persistence of archaic birds

Figure 91: *Tyrannosaurus was among the dinosaurs living on Earth before the extinction.*

to within 300,000 years of the K–Pg boundary. The absence of these birds in the Paleogene is evidence that a mass extinction of archaic birds took place there. A small fraction of the Cretaceous bird species survived the impact, giving rise to today's birds. The only bird group known for certain to have survived the K–Pg boundary is the Aves. Avians may have been able to survive the extinction as a result of their abilities to dive, swim, or seek shelter in water and marshlands. Many species of avians can build burrows, or nest in tree holes or termite nests, all of which provided shelter from the environmental effects at the K–Pg boundary. Long-term survival past the boundary was assured as a result of filling ecological niches left empty by extinction of non-avian dinosaurs.

Non-avian dinosaurs

Excluding a few controversial claims, scientists agree that all non-avian dinosaurs became extinct at the K–Pg boundary. The dinosaur fossil record has been interpreted to show both a decline in diversity and no decline in diversity during the last few million years of the Cretaceous, and it may be that the quality of the dinosaur fossil record is simply not good enough to permit researchers to distinguish between the options. There is no evidence that late Maastrichtian non-avian dinosaurs could burrow, swim, or dive, which suggests they were unable to shelter themselves from the worst parts of any environmental stress that occurred at the K–Pg boundary. It is possible that small dinosaurs (other than birds) did survive, but they would have been deprived of food, as herbivorous dinosaurs would have found plant material scarce and carnivores would have quickly found prey in short supply.

The growing consensus about the endothermy of dinosaurs (see dinosaur physiology) helps to understand their full extinction in contrast with their close relatives, the crocodilians. Ectothermic ("cold-blooded") crocodiles have very limited needs for food (they can survive several months without eating) while endothermic ("warm-blooded") animals of similar size need much more food to sustain their faster metabolism. Thus, under the circumstances of food chain disruption previously mentioned, non-avian dinosaurs died, while some crocodiles survived. In this context, the survival of other endothermic animals, such as some birds and mammals, could be due, among other reasons, to their smaller needs for food, related to their small size at the extinction epoch.

Whether the extinction occurred gradually or suddenly has been debated, as both views have support from the fossil record. A study of 29 fossil sites in Catalan Pyrenees of Europe in 2010 supports the view that dinosaurs there had great diversity until the asteroid impact, with more than 100 living species. More recent research indicates that this figure is obscured by taphonomical biases, however, and the sparsity of the continental fossil record. The results of this study, which were based on estimated real global biodiversity, showed that between 628 and 1,078 non-avian dinosaur species were alive at the end of the Cretaceous and underwent sudden extinction after the Cretaceous–Paleogene extinction event. Alternatively, interpretation based on the fossil-bearing rocks along the Red Deer River in Alberta, Canada, supports the gradual extinction of non-avian dinosaurs; during the last 10 million years of the Cretaceous layers there, the number of dinosaur species seems to have decreased from about 45 to approximately 12. Other scientists have made the same assessment following their research.

Several researchers support the existence of Paleocene non-avian dinosaurs. Evidence of this existence is based on the discovery of dinosaur remains in the Hell Creek Formation up to 1.3 m (4.3 ft) above and 40,000 years later than the K–Pg boundary. Pollen samples recovered near a fossilized hadrosaur femur recovered in the Ojo Alamo Sandstone at the San Juan River in Colorado, indicate that the animal lived during the Cenozoic, approximately 64.5 Ma (about 1 million years after the K–Pg extinction event). If their existence past the K–Pg boundary can be confirmed, these hadrosaurids would be considered a dead clade walking. Scientific consensus, however, is that these fossils were eroded from their original locations and then re-buried in much later sediments (also known as reworked fossils).

Mammals

All major Cretaceous mammalian lineages, including monotremes (egg-laying mammals), multituberculates, metatherians, eutherians, dryolestoideans, and gondwanatheres survived the K–Pg extinction event, although they suffered losses. In particular, metatherians largely disappeared from North America, and the Asian deltatheroidans became extinct. In the Hell Creek beds of North America, at least half of the ten known multituberculate species and all eleven metatherians species, are not found above the boundary. Multituberculates in Europe and North America survived relatively unscathed and quickly bounced back in the Palaeocene, but Asian forms were decimated, never again to represent a significant component on mammalian faunas.

Mammalian species began diversifying approximately 30 million years prior to the K–Pg boundary. Diversification of mammals stalled across the boundary. Current research indicates that mammals did not explosively diversify across the K–Pg boundary, despite the environment niches made available by the extinction of dinosaurs. Several mammalian orders have been interpreted as diversifying immediately after the K–Pg boundary, including Chiroptera (bats) and Cetartiodactyla (a diverse group that today includes whales and dolphins and even-toed ungulates), although recent research concludes that only marsupial orders diversified after the K–Pg boundary.

K–Pg boundary mammalian species were generally small, comparable in size to rats; this small size would have helped them find shelter in protected environments. In addition, it is postulated that some early monotremes, marsupials, and placentals were semiaquatic or burrowing, as there are multiple mammalian lineages with such habits today. Any burrowing or semiaquatic mammal would have had additional protection from K–Pg boundary environmental stresses.

Evidence

North American fossils

In North American terrestrial sequences, the extinction event is best represented by the marked discrepancy between the rich and relatively abundant late-Maastrichtian palynomorph record and the post-boundary fern spike.

At present the most informative sequence of dinosaur-bearing rocks in the world from the K–Pg boundary is found in western North America, particularly the late Maastrichtian-age Hell Creek Formation of Montana. Comparison with the older Judith River Formation (Montana) and Dinosaur Park Formation (Alberta), which both date from approximately 75 Ma, provides information on the changes in dinosaur populations over the last 10 million years

Figure 92: *Hell Creek Formation*

of the Cretaceous. However, these fossil beds are geographically limited, covering only part of one continent.

The middle–late Campanian formations show a greater diversity of dinosaurs than any other single group of rocks. The late Maastrichtian rocks contain the largest members of several major clades: *Tyrannosaurus*, *Ankylosaurus*, *Pachycephalosaurus*, *Triceratops*, and *Torosaurus*, which suggests food was plentiful immediately prior to the extinction.

In addition to rich dinosaur fossils, there are also plant fossils that illustrate the reduction in plant species across the K–Pg boundary. In the sediments below the K–Pg boundary the dominant plant remains are angiosperm pollen grains, but the boundary layer contains little pollen and is dominated by fern spores. More usual pollen levels gradually resume above the boundary layer. This is reminiscent of areas blighted by modern volcanic eruptions, where the recovery is led by ferns, which are later replaced by larger angiosperm plants.

Marine fossils

The mass extinction of marine plankton appears to have been abrupt and right at the K–Pg boundary. Ammonite genera became extinct at or near the K–Pg boundary; however, there was a smaller and slower extinction of ammonite genera prior to the boundary that was associated with a late Cretaceous marine regression. The gradual extinction of most inoceramid bivalves began well before the K–Pg boundary, and a small, gradual reduction in ammonite diversity occurred throughout the very late Cretaceous.

Further analysis shows that several processes were in progress in the late Cretaceous seas and partially overlapped in time, then ended with the abrupt mass extinction. The diversity of marine life decreased when the climate near the K–Pg boundary increased in temperature. The temperature increased about three to four degrees very rapidly between 65.4 and 65.2 million years ago, which is very near the time of the extinction event. Not only did the climate temperature increase, but the water temperature decreased, causing a drastic decrease in marine diversity.

Megatsunamis

The scientific consensus is that the asteroid impact at the K–Pg boundary left megatsunami deposits and sediments around the area of the Caribbean Sea and Gulf of Mexico, from the colossal waves created by the impact. These deposits have been identified in the La Popa basin in northeastern Mexico, platform carbonates in northeastern Brazil, in Atlantic deep-sea sediments, and in the form of the thickest-known layer of graded sand deposits, around 100 meters thick, in the Chicxulub crater itself, directly above the shocked granite ejecta.

The megatsunami has been estimated to be more than 100 metres (330 ft) tall, as the asteroid fell in an area of relatively shallow sea; in deep sea it would have been 4.6 kilometres (2.9 mi) tall.

Duration

The length of time taken for the extinction to occur is a controversial issue, because some theories about the extinction's causes require a rapid extinction over a relatively short period (from a few years to a few thousand years) while others require longer periods. The issue is difficult to resolve because of the Signor–Lipps effect; that is, the fossil record is so incomplete that most extinct species probably died out long after the most recent fossil that has been found. Scientists have also found very few continuous beds of fossil-bearing rock that cover a time range from several million years before the K–Pg extinction to a few million years after it. The sedimentation rate and thickness of K–Pg clay from three sites suggest short duration of event, perhaps less than ten thousand years. At one site in the Denver Basin of Colorado, the 'fern spike' lasted about one thousand years (no more than 71 thousand years); the earliest Cenozoic mammals appeared about 185 thousand years (no more than 570 thousand years) after the K–Pg boundary layer was deposited.

Chicxulub impact

Evidence for impact

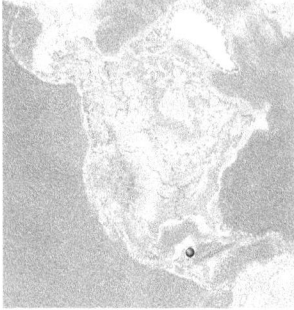

File:North_America_laea_relief_location_map.jpg

Location of Chicxulub crater, Mexico

In 1980, a team of researchers consisting of Nobel Prize–winning physicist Luis Alvarez, his son geologist Walter Alvarez, and chemists Frank Asaro and Helen Michel discovered that sedimentary layers found all over the world at the Cretaceous–Paleogene boundary contain a concentration of iridium many times greater than normal (30, 160, and 20 times in three sections originally studied). Iridium is extremely rare in Earth's crust because it is a siderophile element, and therefore, most of it sank along with the iron into Earth's core during planetary differentiation. As iridium remains abundant in most asteroids and comets, the Alvarez team suggested that an asteroid struck the Earth at the time of the K–Pg boundary. There were earlier speculations on the possibility of an impact event, but this was the first hard evidence.

This hypothesis was viewed as radical when first proposed, but additional evidence soon emerged. The boundary clay was found to be full of minute spherules of rock, crystallized from droplets of molten rock formed by the impact. Shocked quartz[205] and other minerals were also identified in the K–Pg boundary. The identification of giant tsunami beds along the Gulf Coast and the Caribbean also provided evidence, and suggested that the impact may have occurred nearby – as did the discovery that the K–Pg boundary became thicker in the southern United States, with meter-thick beds of debris occurring in northern New Mexico.

Further research identified the giant Chicxulub crater, buried under Chicxulub on the coast of Yucatán, as the source of the K–Pg boundary clay. Identified in 1990 based on work by geophysicist Glen Penfield in 1978, the crater is oval, with an average diameter of roughly 180 kilometres (110 mi), about the size calculated by the Alvarez team. The discovery of the crater – a necessary

Figure 93: *The K–Pg boundary exposure in Trinidad Lake State Park, in the Raton Basin of Colorado, shows an abrupt change from dark- to light-colored rock. White line added to mark the transition.*

prediction of the impact hypothesis – provided conclusive evidence for a K–Pg impact, and strengthened the hypothesis that it caused the extinction.

In a 2013 paper, Paul Renne of the Berkeley Geochronology Center reported that the date of the impact is 66.043±0.011 million years ago, based on argon–argon dating. He further posits that the mass extinction occurred within 32,000 years of this date.

In 2007, it was proposed that the impactor belonged to the Baptistina family of asteroids. This link has been doubted, though not disproved, in part because of a lack of observations of the asteroid and its family. It was recently discovered that 298 Baptistina does not share the chemical signature of the K–Pg impactor. Further, a 2011 Wide-field Infrared Survey Explorer (WISE) study of reflected light from the asteroids of the family estimated their break-up at 80 Ma, giving them insufficient time to shift orbits and impact Earth by 66 Ma.

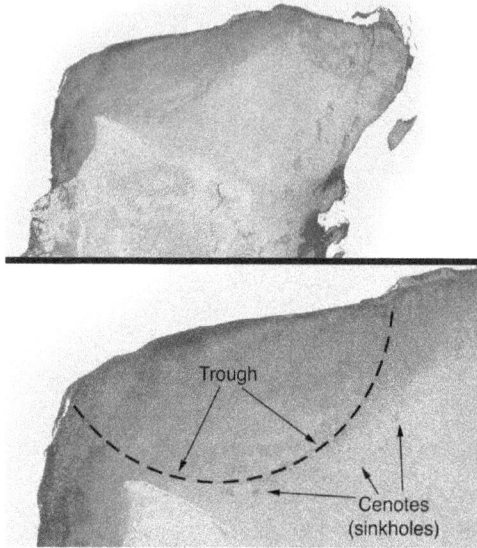

Figure 94: *Radar topography reveals the 180 km –wide (112 mi) ring of the Chicxulub Crater.*

Effects of impact

In March 2010, an international panel of 41 scientists reviewed 20 years of scientific literature and endorsed the asteroid hypothesis, specifically the Chicxulub impact, as the cause of the extinction, ruling out other theories such as massive volcanism. They had determined that a 10-to-15-kilometre (6.2 to 9.3 mi) asteroid hurtled into Earth at Chicxulub on Mexico's Yucatán Peninsula. The collision would have released the same energy as 100 teratonnes of TNT (420 ZJ) – more than a billion times the energy of the atomic bombings of Hiroshima and Nagasaki.

The Chicxulub impact caused a global catastrophe. Some of the phenomena were brief occurrences immediately following the impact, but there were also long-term geochemical and climatic disruptions that devastated the ecology.

The reentry of ejecta into Earth's atmosphere would include a brief (hours long) but intense pulse of infrared radiation, killing exposed organisms. A paper in 2013 by a prominent modeler of nuclear winter suggested that, based on the amount of soot in the global debris layer, the entire terrestrial biosphere might have burned, implying a global soot-cloud blocking out the sun and creating a nuclear winter effect. This is debated, however, with opponents arguing that local ferocious fires, probably limited to North America, fall short of global firestorms. This disagreement is termed the "Cretaceous-Palaeogene firestorm debate".

Aside from the hypothesized fire and/or nuclear winter effects, the impact would have created a dust cloud that blocked sunlight for up to a year, inhibiting photosynthesis. The asteroid hit an area of carbonate rock containing a large amount of combustible hydrocarbons and sulphur, much of which was vaporized, thereby injecting sulfuric acid aerosols into the stratosphere, which might have reduced sunlight reaching the Earth's surface by more than 50%, and would have caused acid rain. The resulting acidification of the oceans would kill many organisms that grow shells of calcium carbonate. At Brazos section, the paleo-sea surface temperature dropped as much as 7 °C for decades after the impact. It would take at least ten years for such aerosols to dissipate, and would account for the extinction of plants and phytoplankton, and subsequently herbivores and their predators. Creatures whose food chains were based on detritus would have a reasonable chance of survival, however. Freezing temperatures probably lasted for at least three years.

If widespread fires occurred, they would have increased the CO $_2$ content of the atmosphere and caused a temporary greenhouse effect once the dust clouds and aerosol settled, and, this would have exterminated the most vulnerable organisms that survived the period immediately after the impact.

Although most paleontologists now agree that an asteroid did hit the Earth at approximately the end of the Cretaceous, there is an ongoing dispute whether the impact was the sole cause of the extinctions.

2016 Chicxulub crater drilling project

In 2016, a scientific drilling project obtained deep rock core samples from the peak ring around the Chicxulub impact crater. The discoveries confirmed that the rock comprising the peak ring had been shocked by immense pressure and melted in just minutes from its usual state into its present form. Unlike seafloor deposits, the peak ring was made of granite originating much deeper in the earth, which had been ejected to the surface by the impact. Gypsum is a sulfate-containing rock usually present in the shallow seabed of the region; it had been almost entirely removed, vaporized into the atmosphere. Further, the event was immediately followed by a megatsunami[206] sufficient to lay down the largest known layer of sand separated by grain size directly above the peak ring.

These findings strongly support the impact's role in the extinction event. The impactor was large enough to create a 120 mile-wide (193 km) peak ring, to melt, shock, and eject deep granite, to create colossal water movements, and to eject an immense quantity of vaporized rock and sulfates into the atmosphere,

Figure 95: *The river bed at the Moody Creek Mine, 7 Mile Creek /
Waimatuku, Dunollie, New Zealand contains evidence of a devastat-
ing event on terrestrial plant communities at the Cretaceous-Paleogene
boundary, confirming the severity and global nature of the event.*

where they would have persisted for a long time. This worldwide dispersal
of dust and sulfates would have affected climate catastrophically, led to large
temperature drops, and devastated the food chain.

Alternative hypotheses

Though the concurrence of the end-Cretaceous extinctions with the Chicxulub
asteroid impact strongly supports the impact hypothesis, some scientists continue to suggest that other causes may have contributed. In particular, volcanic
eruptions, climate change, sea level change, and other impact events have been
suggested to play a role. The end-Cretaceous event is the only mass extinction
that is known to be associated to an impact, and other large impacts, such as
the impact that created the Manicouagan reservoir, do not coincide with any
noticeable extinction event.

Deccan Traps

Before 2000, arguments that the Deccan Traps flood basalts caused the extinction were usually linked to the view that the extinction was gradual, as the flood basalt events were thought to have started around 68 Mya and lasted more than 2 million years. The most recent evidence shows that the traps erupted over a period of 800,000 years spanning the K–Pg boundary, and therefore may be responsible for the extinction and the delayed biotic recovery thereafter.

The Deccan Traps could have caused extinction through several mechanisms, including the release of dust and sulfuric aerosols into the air, which might have blocked sunlight and thereby reduced photosynthesis in plants. In addition, Deccan Trap volcanism might have resulted in carbon dioxide emissions that increased the greenhouse effect when the dust and aerosols cleared from the atmosphere.

In the years when the Deccan Traps hypothesis was linked to a slower extinction, Luis Alvarez (who died in 1988) replied that paleontologists were being misled by sparse data. While his assertion was not initially well-received, later intensive field studies of fossil beds lent weight to his claim. Eventually, most paleontologists began to accept the idea that the mass extinctions at the end of the Cretaceous were largely or at least partly due to a massive Earth impact. Even Walter Alvarez acknowledged that other major changes may have contributed to the extinctions.

Some geophysical models suggest a connection between the impact and the Deccan Traps. These models, combined with high-precision radiometric dating, suggest that the Chicxulub impact could have triggered some of the largest Deccan eruptions, and could have triggered eruptions at active volcanoes anywhere on Earth.

Multiple impact event

Other crater-like topographic features have also been proposed as impact craters formed in connection with Cretaceous-Paleogene extinction. This suggests the possibility of near-simultaneous multiple impacts, perhaps from a fragmented asteroidal object similar to the Shoemaker–Levy 9 impact with Jupiter. In addition to the 180 km (110 mi) Chicxulub Crater, there is the 24 km (15 mi) Boltysh crater in Ukraine (65.17±0.64 Ma), the 20 km (12 mi) Silverpit crater in the North Sea (59.5±14.5 Ma) possibly formed by bolide impact, and the controversial and much larger 600 km (370 mi) Shiva crater. Any other craters that might have formed in the Tethys Ocean would have been obscured by the northward tectonic drift of Africa and India.

Maastrichtian sea-level regression

There is clear evidence that sea levels fell in the final stage of the Cretaceous by more than at any other time in the Mesozoic era. In some Maastrichtian stage rock layers from various parts of the world, the later layers are terrestrial; earlier layers represent shorelines and the earliest layers represent seabeds. These layers do not show the tilting and distortion associated with mountain building, therefore the likeliest explanation is a "regression", a drop in sea level. There is no direct evidence for the cause of the regression, but the currently accepted explanation is that the mid-ocean ridges became less active and sank under their own weight.

A severe regression would have greatly reduced the continental shelf area, the most species-rich part of the sea, and therefore could have been enough to cause a *marine* mass extinction; however, this change would not have sufficed to cause the extinction of the ammonites. The regression would also have caused climate changes, partly by disrupting winds and ocean currents and partly by reducing the Earth's albedo and increasing global temperatures.

Marine regression also resulted in the loss of epeiric seas, such as the Western Interior Seaway of North America. The loss of these seas greatly altered habitats, removing coastal plains that ten million years before had been host to diverse communities such as are found in rocks of the Dinosaur Park Formation. Another consequence was an expansion of freshwater environments, since continental runoff now had longer distances to travel before reaching oceans. While this change was favorable to freshwater vertebrates, those that prefer marine environments, such as sharks, suffered.

Multiple causes

Proponents of multiple causation view the suggested single causes as either too small to produce the vast scale of the extinction, or not likely to produce its observed taxonomic pattern. In a review article, J. David Archibald and David E. Fastovsky discussed a scenario combining three major postulated causes: volcanism, marine regression, and extraterrestrial impact. In this scenario, terrestrial and marine communities were stressed by the changes in, and loss of, habitats. Dinosaurs, as the largest vertebrates, were the first affected by environmental changes, and their diversity declined. At the same time, particulate materials from volcanism cooled and dried areas of the globe. Then an impact event occurred, causing collapses in photosynthesis-based food chains, both in the already-stressed terrestrial food chains and in the marine food chains.

Recent work led by Sierra Peterson at Seymour Island, Antarctica, showed two separate extinction events near the Cretaceous-Paleogene boundary, with one correlating to Deccan Trap volcanism and one correlated with the Chicxulub impact. The team analyzed combined extinction patterns using a new clumped isotope temperature record from a hiatus-free, expanded K-Pg boundary section. They documented a 7.8±3.3 °C warming synchronous with the onset of Deccan Traps volcanism and a second, smaller warming at the time of meteorite impact. They suggest local warming may have been amplified due to simultaneous disappearance of continental or sea ice. Intra-shell variability indicates a possible reduction in seasonality after Deccan eruptions began, continuing through the meteorite event. Species extinction at Seymour Island occurred in two pulses that coincide with the two observed warming events, directly linking the end-Cretaceous extinction at this site to both volcanic and meteorite events via climate change.

Recovery and radiation

The K–Pg extinction had a profound effect on the evolution of life on Earth. The elimination of dominant Cretaceous groups allowed other organisms to take their place, spurring a remarkable series of adaptive radiations in the Paleogene. The most striking example is the replacement of dinosaurs by mammals. After the K–Pg extinction, mammals evolved rapidly to fill the niches left vacant by the dinosaurs. Also significant, within the mammalian genera, new species were approximately 9.1% larger after the K–Pg boundary.

Other groups also underwent major radiations. Based on molecular sequencing and fossil dating, Neoaves appeared to radiate after the K–Pg boundary. They even produced giant, flightless forms, such as the herbivorous *Gastornis* and Dromornithidae, and the predatory Phorusrhacidae. The extinction of Cretaceous lizards and snakes may have led to the radiation of modern groups such as iguanas, monitor lizards, and boas. On land, giant boid and enormous madtsoiid snakes appeared, and in the seas, giant sea snakes radiated. Teleost fish diversified explosively, filling the niches left vacant by the extinction. Groups appearing in the Paleocene and Eocene include billfish, tunas, eels, and flatfish. Major changes are also seen in Paleogene insect communities. Many groups of ants were present in the Cretaceous, but in the Eocene ants became dominant and diverse, with larger colonies. Butterflies diversified as well, perhaps to take the place of leaf-eating insects wiped out by the extinction. The advanced mound-building termites, *Termitidae*, also appear to have risen in importance.

Further reading

<templatestyles src="Template:Refbegin/styles.css" />

- Fortey, Richard (2005). *Earth: An Intimate History*[207]. New York: Vintage Books. ISBN 978-0-375-70620-2. OCLC 54537112[208].

External links

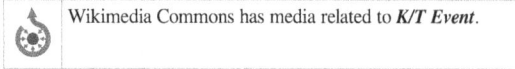

> Wikimedia Commons has media related to *K/T Event*.

- "The Great Chicxulub Debate 2004"[209]. Geological Society of London. 2004. Retrieved 2007-08-02.
- Kring DA (2005). "Chicxulub Impact Event: Understanding the K–T Boundary"[210]. NASA Space Imagery Center. Archived from the original[211] on June 29, 2007. Retrieved 2007-08-02.
- Cowen R (2000). "The K–T extinction"[212]. University of California Museum of Paleontology. Retrieved 2007-08-02.
- "What killed the dinosaurs?"[213]. University of California Museum of Paleontology. 1995. Retrieved 2007-08-02.
- Papers and presentations resulting from the 2016 Chicxulub drilling project[214]

<indicator name="featured-star"> ⭐ </indicator>

Chicxulub crater

<indicator name="featured-star"> ⭐ </indicator>

Chicxulub crater

Chicxulub impact structure

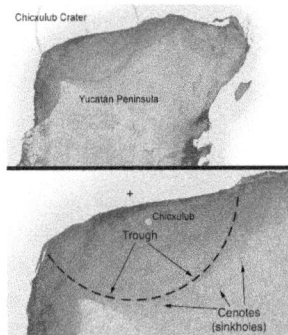

Imaging from NASA's Shuttle Radar Topography Mission STS-99 reveals part of the 180 km (110 mi) diameter ring of the crater. The numerous sinkholes clustered around the trough of the crater suggest a prehistoric oceanic basin in the depression left by the impact.

Impact crater/structure	
Confidence	Confirmed
Diameter	150 km (93 mi)
Depth	20 km (12 mi)
Impactor diameter	10–15 kilometres (6.2–9.3 mi)
Age	66.043 ± 0.011 Ma Cretaceous–Paleogene boundary
Exposed	No
Drilled	Yes
Bolide type	Carbonaceous chondrite
Location	
Coordinates	21°24′0″N 89°31′0″W[215]Coordinates: 21°24′0″N 89°31′0″W[215]
Country	▌∙▌ Mexico
State	Yucatán

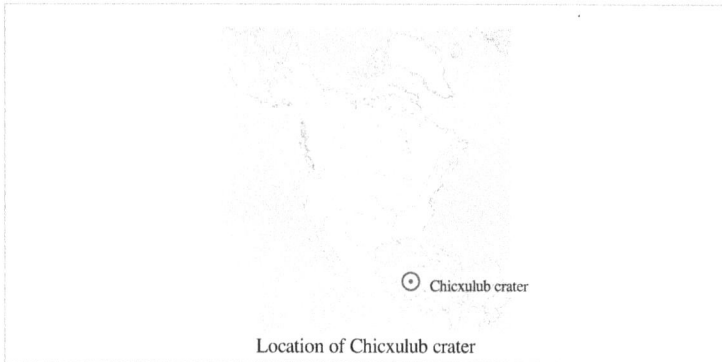

Location of Chicxulub crater

The **Chicxulub crater** (/'tʃiːkʃʊluːb/; Mayan: [tʃʼikʃuluɓ]) is an impact crater buried underneath the Yucatán Peninsula in Mexico. Its center is located near the town of Chicxulub, after which the crater is named. It was formed by a large asteroid or comet about 10 to 15 kilometres (6.2 to 9.3 miles) in diameter, the Chicxulub impactor, striking the Earth. The date of the impact coincides precisely with the Cretaceous–Paleogene boundary (K–Pg boundary), slightly less than 66 million years ago, and a widely accepted theory is that worldwide climate disruption from the event was the cause of the Cretaceous–Paleogene extinction event, a mass extinction in which 75% of plant and animal species on Earth became extinct, including all non-avian dinosaurs.

The crater is estimated to be 150 kilometres (93 miles) in diameter and 20 km (12 mi) in depth, well into the continental crust of the region of about 10–30 km (6.2–18.6 mi) depth. It is the second largest confirmed impact structure on Earth and the only one whose peak ring is intact and directly accessible for scientific research.

The crater was discovered by Antonio Camargo and Glen Penfield, geophysicists who had been looking for petroleum in the Yucatán during the late 1970s. Penfield was initially unable to obtain evidence that the geological feature was a crater and gave up his search. Later, through contact with Alan Hildebrand in 1990, Penfield obtained samples that suggested it was an impact feature. Evidence for the impact origin of the crater includes shocked quartz, a gravity anomaly, and tektites in surrounding areas.

In 2016, a scientific drilling project drilled deep into the peak ring of the impact crater, hundreds of meters below the current sea floor, to obtain rock core samples from the impact itself. The discoveries were widely seen as confirming current theories related to both the crater impact and its effects.

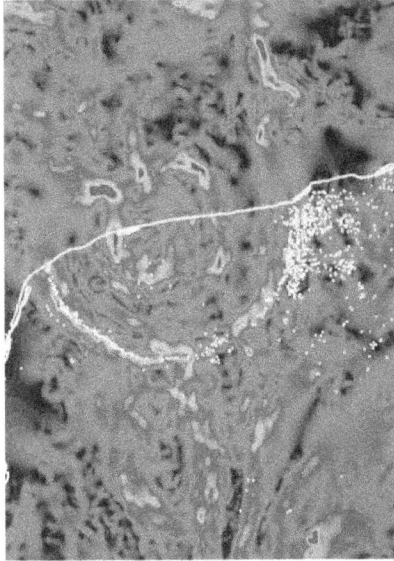

Figure 96: *Gravity anomaly map of the Chicxulub impact structure. The coastline is shown as a white line. A striking series of concentric features reveals the location of the crater. White dots represent water-filled sinkholes (solution-collapse features common in the limestone rocks of the region) called cenotes after the Maya word dzonot. A dramatic ring of cenotes is associated with the largest peripheral gravity-gradient feature. The origin of the cenote ring remains uncertain, although the link to the underlying buried crater seems clear.*

Discovery

In 1978, geophysicists Glen Penfield and Antonio Camargo were working for the Mexican state-owned oil company Petróleos Mexicanos, or Pemex, as part of an airborne magnetic survey of the Gulf of Mexico north of the Yucatán peninsula.[216] Penfield's job was to use geophysical data to scout possible locations for oil drilling.[217] In the data, Penfield found a huge underwater arc with "extraordinary symmetry" in a ring 70 km (40 mi) across.[218] He then obtained a gravity map of the Yucatán made in the 1960s. A decade earlier, the same map suggested an impact feature to contractor Robert Baltosser, but he was forbidden to publicize his conclusion by Pemex corporate policy of the time.[219] Penfield found another arc on the peninsula itself, the ends of which pointed northward. Comparing the two maps, he found the separate arcs formed a circle, 180 km (110 mi) wide, centered near the Yucatán village

Chicxulub; he felt certain the shape had been created by a cataclysmic event in geologic history.

Pemex disallowed release of specific data but let Penfield and company official Antonio Camargo present their results at the 1981 Society of Exploration Geophysicists conference.[220] That year's conference was underattended and their report attracted scant attention. Coincidentally, many experts in impact craters and the K–Pg boundary were attending a separate conference on Earth impacts. Although Penfield had plenty of geophysical data sets, he had no rock cores or other physical evidence of an impact.

He knew Pemex had drilled exploratory wells in the region. In 1951, one bored into what was described as a thick layer of andesite about 1.3 kilometres (4,300 ft) down. This layer could have resulted from the intense heat and pressure of an Earth impact, but at the time of the borings it was dismissed as a lava dome—a feature uncharacteristic of the region's geology. Penfield tried to secure site samples, but was told such samples had been lost or destroyed. When attempts at returning to the drill sites and looking for rocks proved fruitless, Penfield abandoned his search, published his findings and returned to his Pemex work.

At the same time, in 1980, geologist Walter Alvarez and his father, Nobel Prize-winning scientist Luis Walter Alvarez, put forth his hypothesis that a large extraterrestrial body had struck Earth. In 1981, unaware of Penfield's discovery, University of Arizona graduate student Alan R. Hildebrand and faculty adviser William V. Boynton published a draft Earth-impact theory and sought a candidate crater.[221] Their evidence included greenish-brown clay with surplus iridium containing shocked quartz grains and small weathered glass beads that looked to be tektites.[222] Thick, jumbled deposits of coarse rock fragments were also present, thought to have been scoured from one place and deposited elsewhere by a megatsunami resulting from an Earth impact. Such deposits occur in many locations but seem concentrated in the Caribbean basin at the K–Pg boundary.[223] So when Haitian professor Florentine Morás discovered what he thought to be evidence of an ancient volcano on Haiti, Hildebrand suggested it could be a telltale feature of a nearby impact.[224] Tests on samples retrieved from the K–Pg boundary revealed more tektite glass, formed only in the heat of asteroid impacts and high-yield nuclear detonations.

In 1990, *Houston Chronicle* reporter Carlos Byars told Hildebrand of Penfield's earlier discovery of a possible impact crater.[225] Hildebrand contacted Penfield in April 1990 and the pair soon secured two drill samples from the Pemex wells, stored in New Orleans.[226] Hildebrand's team tested the samples, which clearly showed shock-metamorphic materials.

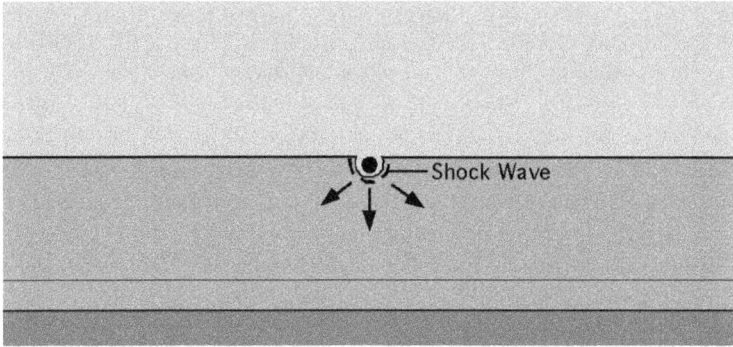

Figure 97: *An animation showing the impact, and subsequent crater formation (University of Arizona, Space Imagery Center).*

A team of California researchers including Kevin Pope, Adriana Ocampo, and Charles Duller, surveying regional satellite images in 1996, found a cenote (sinkhole) ring centered on Chicxulub that matched the one Penfield saw earlier; the cenotes were thought to be caused by subsidence of bolide-weakened lithostratigraphy around the impact crater wall.[227] More recent evidence suggests the actual crater is 300 km (190 mi) wide, and the 180 km ring is in fact an inner wall of it.[228]

Impact specifics

Researchers at the University of Glasgow dated tektite samples from the impact as 66,038,000 ± 11,000 years old.

The Chicxulub impactor had an estimated diameter of 15 kilometres (9.3 mi), and delivered an estimated energy of 10 billion Hiroshima A-bombs (about 1×10^{23} joules, or 100,000 EJ). By contrast, the most powerful man-made explosive device ever detonated, the Tsar Bomba, had an energy of only 210 petajoules (2.10×10^{17} joules, the yield of 50 megatons of TNT).[229] The object dug a hole 100 kilometres (62 mi) wide and 30 kilometres (19 mi) deep, leaving a crater mainly under the sea and covered by 600 metres (2,000 ft) of sediment by the 21st century.

Effects

The impact would have caused a megatsunami over 100 metres (330 ft) tall that would have reached all the way to what are now Texas and Florida. The height of the tsunami was limited by the relatively shallow sea in the area of the impact; in deep ocean it would have been 4.6 kilometres (2.9 mi) tall. A cloud of super-heated dust, ash and steam would have spread from the crater as the impactor burrowed underground in less than a second.[230] Excavated material along with pieces of the impactor, ejected out of the atmosphere by the blast, would have been heated to incandescence upon re-entry, broiling the Earth's surface and possibly igniting wildfires; meanwhile, colossal shock waves would have triggered global earthquakes and volcanic eruptions.[231] Fossil evidence for an instantaneous die-off of diverse animals was found in a soil layer only 10 centimetres (3.9 in) thick in New Jersey some 5,000 kilometres (3,100 mi) away from the impact site, indicating that death and burial under debris occurred suddenly and quickly over wide distances on land.

The emission of dust and particles could have covered the entire surface of the Earth for several years, possibly a decade, creating a harsh environment for living things. The shock production of carbon dioxide caused by the destruction of carbonate rocks would have led to a sudden greenhouse effect.[232] Over a decade or longer, sunlight would have been blocked from reaching the surface of the Earth by the dust particles in the atmosphere, cooling the surface dramatically. Photosynthesis by plants would also have been interrupted, affecting the entire food chain.[233,234] A model of the event developed by Lomax et al. (2001) suggests that net primary productivity (NPP) rates may have increased to higher than pre-impact levels over the long term because of the high carbon dioxide concentrations.

In February 2008, a team of researchers led by Sean Gulick at the University of Texas at Austin's Jackson School of Geosciences used seismic images of the crater to determine that the impactor landed in deeper water than was previously assumed. They argued that this would have resulted in increased sulfate aerosols in the atmosphere. According to the press release, that "could have made the impact deadlier in two ways: by altering climate (sulfate aerosols in the upper atmosphere can have a cooling effect) and by generating acid rain (water vapor can help to flush the lower atmosphere of sulfate aerosols, causing acid rain)." This was borne out by the results of a drilling project in 2016 which found that sulfate-containing rocks found in the area were not found in the peak ring (the rocks found were from deep within the earth's crust instead), the interpretation being that they had been vaporized by the impact and dispersed into the atmosphere.

A long-term local effect of the impact was the creation of the Yucatán sedimentary basin which "ultimately produced favorable conditions for human settlement in a region where surface water is scarce."

Geology and morphology

In their 1991 paper, Hildebrand, Penfield, and company described the geology and composition of the impact feature.[235] The rocks above the impact feature are layers of marl and limestone reaching to a depth of almost 1,000 m (3,300 ft). These rocks date back as far as the Paleocene.[236] Below these layers lie more than 500 m (1,600 ft) of andesite glass and breccia. These andesitic igneous rocks were only found within the supposed impact feature, as is shocked quartz. The K–Pg boundary inside the feature is depressed to 600 to 1,100 m (2,000 to 3,600 ft) compared with the normal depth of about 500 m (1,600 ft) measured 5 km (3 mi) away from the impact feature.[237] Along the edge of the crater are clusters of cenotes or sinkholes, which suggest that there was a water basin inside the feature during the Neogene period, after the impact. The groundwater of such a basin would have dissolved the limestone and created the caves and cenotes beneath the surface.[238] The paper also noted that the crater seemed to be a good candidate source for the tektites reported at Haiti.[239]

Astronomical origin of asteroid

In September 2007, a report published in *Nature* proposed an origin for the asteroid that created the Chicxulub crater. The authors, William F. Bottke, David Vokrouhlický, and David Nesvorný, argued that a collision in the asteroid belt 160 million years ago resulted in the Baptistina family of asteroids, the largest surviving member of which is 298 Baptistina. They proposed that the "Chicxulub asteroid" was also a member of this group. The connection between Chicxulub and Baptistina is supported by the large amount of carbonaceous material present in microscopic fragments of the impactor, suggesting the impactor was a member of a rare class of asteroids called carbonaceous chondrites, like Baptistina. According to Bottke, the Chicxulub impactor was a fragment of a much larger parent body about 170 km (106 mi) across, with the other impacting body being around 60 km (37 mi) in diameter.[240,241] In 2011, new data from the Wide-field Infrared Survey Explorer revised the date of the collision which created the Baptistina family to about 80 million years ago. This makes an asteroid from this family highly improbable to be the asteroid that created the Chicxulub crater, as typically the process of resonance and collision of an asteroid takes many tens of millions of years. In 2010, another hypothesis was offered which implicated the newly discovered asteroid P/2010 A2, a member of the Flora family of asteroids, as a possible remnant cohort of the K/Pg impactor.

Chicxulub and mass extinction

The Chicxulub Crater lends support to the theory postulated by the late physicist Luis Alvarez and his son, geologist Walter Alvarez, that the extinction of numerous animal and plant groups, including non-avian dinosaurs, may have resulted from a bolide impact (the Cretaceous–Paleogene extinction event). Luis and Walter Alvarez, at the time both faculty members at the University of California, Berkeley, postulated that this enormous extinction event, which was roughly contemporaneous with the postulated date of formation for the Chicxulub crater, could have been caused by just such a large impact.[242] The age of the rocks marked by the impact shows that this impact structure dates from roughly 66 million years ago, the end of the Cretaceous period, and the start of the Paleogene period. It coincides with the K–Pg boundary, the geological boundary between the Cretaceous and Paleogene. The impact associated with the crater is thus implicated in the Cretaceous–Paleogene extinction event, including the worldwide extinction of non-avian dinosaurs. This conclusion has been the source of controversy. In March 2010, forty-one experts from many countries reviewed the available evidence: 20 years' worth of data spanning a variety of fields. They concluded that the impact at Chicxulub triggered the mass extinctions at the K–Pg boundary.[243,244] In 2013 a study compared isotopes in impact glass from the Chicxulub impact with the same isotopes in ash from the boundary where the extinction event occurred in the fossil record; the study concluded that the impact glasses were dated at 66.038 ± 0.049 Ma, and the deposits immediately above the discontinuity in the geological and fossil record was dated to 66.019 ± 0.021 Ma, the two dates being within 19,000 years of each other, or almost exactly the same within experimental error. The theory is now widely accepted by the scientific community. Some critics, including paleontologist Robert Bakker, argue that such an impact would have killed frogs as well as dinosaurs, yet the frogs survived the extinction event.[245] Gerta Keller of Princeton University argues that recent core samples from Chicxulub prove the impact occurred about 300,000 years *before* the mass extinction, and thus could not have been the causal factor.[246] However, this conclusion is unsupported by radioactive dating and sedimentology.

The main evidence of such an impact, besides the crater itself, is contained in a thin layer of clay present in the K–Pg boundary across the world. In the late 1970s, the Alvarezes and colleagues reported that it contained an abnormally high concentration of iridium.[247] Iridium levels in this layer reached 6 parts per billion by weight or more compared to 0.4 for the Earth's crust as a whole;[248] in comparison, meteorites can contain around 470 parts per billion of this element.[249] It was hypothesized that the iridium was spread into the atmosphere when the impactor was vaporized and settled across the Earth's surface amongst other material thrown up by the impact, producing the layer of iridium-enriched clay.[250] Similarly, an iridium anomaly in core samples from the Pacific Ocean suggested the Eltanin impact of about 2.5 million years ago.

Multiple impact hypothesis

In recent years, several other craters of around the same age as Chicxulub have been discovered, all between latitudes 20°N and 70°N. Examples include the disputed Silverpit crater in the North Sea[251] and the Boltysh crater in Ukraine.[252] Both are much smaller than Chicxulub, but are likely to have been caused by objects many tens of meters across striking the Earth.[253] This has led to the hypothesis that the Chicxulub impact may have been only one of several impacts that happened nearly at the same time. Another possible crater thought to have been formed at the same time is the larger Shiva crater, though the structure's status as an impact crater is contested.[254]

The collision of Comet Shoemaker–Levy 9 with Jupiter in 1994 demonstrated that gravitational interactions can fragment a comet, giving rise to many impacts over a period of a few days if the comet should collide with a planet. Comets undergo gravitational interactions with the gas giants, and similar disruptions and collisions are very likely to have occurred in the past.[255] This scenario may have occurred on Earth at the end of the Cretaceous,[256] though Shiva and the Chicxulub craters might have been formed 300,000 years apart.

In late 2006, Ken MacLeod, a geology professor from the University of Missouri, completed an analysis of sediment below the ocean's surface, bolstering the single-impact theory. MacLeod conducted his analysis approximately 4,500 kilometres (2,800 mi) from the Chicxulub crater to control for possible changes in soil composition at the impact site, while still close enough to be affected by the impact. The analysis revealed there was only one layer of impact debris in the sediment, which indicated there was only one impact.[257] Multiple-impact proponents such as Gerta Keller regard the results as "rather hyper-inflated" and do not agree with the conclusion of MacLeod's analysis,[258] arguing that there might only be gaps of hours to days between impacts in a multiple-impact scenario (cf. Shoemaker-Levy 9) which would not leave a detectable gap in deposits.

Core samples (2016 drilling project)

Chicxulub is the only known Earth crater with a remaining impact peak ring, but it is under 600 m (2,000 ft) of sediment. During April and May 2016, a joint IODP-ICDP Mission Specific Platform Expedition no. 364 obtained the first offshore core samples from the peak ring, the central zone of the crater.

During Expedition 364, DES drillers on the *L/B Myrtle* collected core samples to enable ECORD Science Party members to study how the peak ring formed and calculate the total impact energy.

Their target depth was 1,500 m (4,900 ft) below the bottom of the ocean, but they reached an acceptable 1,335 m. Sample preparation and analysis are being performed at Bremen, Germany.

It was announced in November 2016 that pink granite, usually found deep in the Earth's crust, had been found in drilling samples.[259] It suggests the impact was so great it shocked and melted rocks found deep in the crust, causing them to shoot up before falling back down to produce the peak rings. The granite samples were also found to be lighter and weaker than normal granite, a result of the shock and extreme conditions of the impact. The findings confirmed that the rock comprising the peak ring had originated deep in the earth, and was ejected to the surface. It had been subjected to immense pressures and forces and had been melted by heat and shocked by pressure from its usual state into its present form in just minutes; the fact that the peak ring was made of granite was also significant, since granite is not a rock found in sea-floor deposits, originating much deeper in the earth, and had been ejected to the surface by the immense pressures of impact. Gypsum, a sulfate-containing rock that *is* usually present in the shallow seabed of the region, had been almost entirely removed and likely vaporized to enter the atmosphere, an event immediately followed by a megatsunami sufficient to lay down the largest-known layered bed of sand, around 100 m deep and separated by grain size, directly above the peak ring. These types of sand deposits are caused by extreme water movement, where the larger and heavier sand grains settle first, followed by lighter and smaller grains.

Taken together, analyses indicate that the impactor was large enough to create a 120-mile peak ring, to melt, shock and eject granite from many miles within the earth, to create colossal water movements, and to eject an immense quantity of vaporized rock and sulfates into the atmosphere, where they would have persisted over years to decades. This global dispersal of dust and sulfates would have led to a sudden and catastrophic effect on the climate worldwide, large temperature drops, and devastated the food chain. The researchers stated that the impact generated an environmental calamity that extinguished life, but it also induced a vast subsurface hydrothermal system that became an oasis for the recovery of life.[260]

A program on British television[261] described that the drilling revealed, from top down: thick Cenozoic limestone; a graded sediment deposit from one tsunami, over 100 m thick; the impact melted basement granite from the Earth's midcrust and shocked quartz. The peak ring itself did not contain the calcium sulphate that the rocks in the area around contain, leading the program makers to conclude that all the calcium sulphate in the crater area had been vaporized into the atmosphere and had become a dense sulphur dioxide veil stopping the sunlight. As additional clues of the resulting megatsunami represented in a New Jersey quarry, a dense marine bone bed was found on the Cretaceous–Paleogene boundary containing a mixture of dead sea animals with little or no damage from scavengers or predators. Also related to this tsunami was a dense dinosaur bone bed on the Cretaceous–Paleogene boundary found in Patagonia.

References

<templatestyles src="Template:Refbegin/styles.css" />

- Adamsky, Viktor; Smirnov, Yuri (1994). "Moscow's Biggest Bomb: the 50-Megaton Test of October 1961"[262] (PDF). *Cold War International History Project Bulletin* (4): 3, 19–21. Archived from the original[263] (PDF) on August 26, 2000.

- Alvarez, W.; Alvarez, L.W.; Asaro, F.; Michel, H.V. (1979). "Anomalous iridium levels at the Cretaceous/Tertiary boundary at Gubbio, Italy: Negative results of tests for a supernova origin". In Christensen, W.K.; Birkelund, T. *Cretaceous/Tertiary Boundary Events Symposium.* **2.** University of Copenhagen. p. 69.

- Bates, Robin (series producer), Chesmar, Terri and Baniewicz, Rich (associate producers) (1992). *The Dinosaurs! Episode 4: "Death of the Dinosaur"*[264] (TV-series). PBS Video, WHYY-TV.

  Bakker, Robert T. Interview: *The Dinosaurs: Death of the Dinosaur.* 1990, WHYY.

  Hildebrand, Alan. Interview: *The Dinosaurs: Death of the Dinosaur.* 1992, WHYY.

  Melosh, Gene. Interview: *The Dinosaurs: Death of the Dinosaur.* 1992, (1990): WHYY.

  Moras, Florentine. Interview: *The Dinosaurs: Death of the Dinosaur.* 1992, (filmed 1990): WHYY.

  Penfield, Glen. Interview: *The Dinosaurs: Death of the Dinosaur.* 1992, WHYY.

- Bottke, W.F.; Vokrouhlicky, D.; Nesvorny, D. (September 2007). "An asteroid breakup 160 Myr ago as the probable source of the K/T impactor"[265] (PDF). *Nature.* **449** (7158): 23–25. Bibcode: 2007Natur.449...48B[266]. doi: 10.1038/nature06070[267]. PMID 17805288[268]. Retrieved October 3, 2007.

- Bralower, Timothy J.; Paull, Charles K.; Leckie, R. Mark (April 1998). "The Cretaceous–Tertiary boundary cocktail: Chicxulub impact triggers margin collapse and extensive sediment gravity flows"[269] (PDF). *Geology*. **26** (4): 331–334. Bibcode: 1998Geo....26..331B[270]. doi: 10.1130/0091-7613(1998)026<0331:tctbcc>2.3.co;2[271]. Archived from the original[272] (PDF) on November 28, 2007. Retrieved September 25, 2007.
- Covey, C; et al. (1994). "Global climatic effects of atmospheric dust from an asteroid or comet impact on Earth". *Global and Planetary Change*. **9** (3–4): 263. Bibcode: 1994GPC.....9..263C[273]. doi: 10.1016/0921-8181(94)90020-5[274].
- Dunham, Will (November 30, 2006). "Single massive asteroid wiped out dinosaurs: study"[275]. *physadvice.net*. Archived from the original[276] on October 17, 2015. Retrieved September 29, 2007.
- Frankel, Charles (1999). *The End of the Dinosaurs: Chicxulub Crater and Mass Extinctions*. Cambridge University Press. p. 236. ISBN 978-0-521-47447-4.
- Grieve, R. (1975). "Petrology and Chemistry of the Impact Melt at Mistastin Lake Crater". *Geological Society of America Bulletin*. **86** (12): 1617–1629. Bibcode: 1975GSAB...86.1617G[277]. doi: 10.1130/0016-7606(1975)86<1617:PACOTI>2.0.CO;2[278].
- Hildebrand, Alan R.; Penfield, Glen T.; Kring, David A.; Pilkington, Mark; Zanoguera, Antonio Camargo; Jacobsen, Stein B.; Boynton, William V. (September 1991). "Chicxulub Crater; a possible Cretaceous/Tertiary boundary impact crater on the Yucatan Peninsula, Mexico"[279]. *Geology*. **19** (9): 867–871. Bibcode: 1991Geo....19..867H[280]. doi: 10.1130/0091-7613(1991)019<0867:CCAPCT>2.3.CO;2[281].
- Ingham, Richard (September 5, 2007). "Traced: The asteroid breakup that wiped out the dinosaurs"[282]. *AFP*. Google News. Archived from the original[283] on November 14, 2007. Retrieved September 27, 2007.
- Keller, Gerta; Adatte, Thierry; Berner, Zsolt; Harting, Markus; Baum, Gerald; Prauss, Michael; Tantawy, Abdel; Stueben, Doris (2007). "Chicxulub impact predates K–T boundary: New evidence from Brazos, Texas"[284] (PDF). *Earth and Planetary Science Letters*. **255** (3–4): 1–18. Bibcode: 2007E&PSL.255..339K[285]. doi: 10.1016/j.epsl.2006.12.026[286]. Archived from the original[287] (PDF) on June 23, 2007. Retrieved September 25, 2007.
- Kelley, Simon P.; Gurov, Eugene (2002). "The Boltysh, another end-Cretaceous impact"[288]. *Meteoritics & Planetary Science*. **37** (8): 1031–1043. Bibcode: 2002M&PS...37.1031K[289]. doi: 10.1111/j.1945-5100.2002.tb00875.x[290]. Archived from the original[291] on September 5, 2008.

- Kring, David A. (2003). "Environmental consequences of impact cratering events as a function of ambient conditions on Earth". *Astrobiology*. **3** (1): 133–152. Bibcode: 2003AsBio...3..133K[292]. doi: 10.1089/153110703321632471[293]. PMID 12809133[294].
- Kring, David A. "Discovering the Crater"[295]. *lpl.arizona.edu*. Archived from the original[296] on October 10, 2007. Retrieved October 12, 2007.
- Mason, Ben G.; Pyle, David M.; Oppenheimer, Clive (2004). "The size and frequency of the largest explosive eruptions on Earth". *Bulletin of Volcanology*. **66** (8): 735–748. Bibcode: 2004BVol...66..735M[297]. doi: 10.1007/s00445-004-0355-9[298].
- Mason, Moya K. (2007). "In Search of a Key Paper"[299]. *moyak.com*. Retrieved April 3, 2009.
- Mayell, Hillary (May 15, 2005). "Asteroid Rained Glass Over Entire Earth, Scientists Say"[300]. *National Geographic News*. Retrieved October 1, 2007.
- Mullen, Leslie (November 4, 2004). "Deep Impact – Shiva: Another K–T Impact?"[301]. *Astrobiology Magazine*. Retrieved September 29, 2007.
- Mullen, Leslie (October 21, 2004). "Did Multiple Impacts Pummel Earth 35 Million Years Ago?"[302]. *spacedaily.com*. Retrieved September 29, 2007.
- Perlman, David (September 6, 2007). "Scientists say they know where dinosaur-killing asteroid came from"[303]. *San Francisco Chronicle*. Retrieved October 3, 2007.
- Pope KO; Baines KH; Ocampo AC; Ivanov BA (1997). "Energy, volatile production, and climatic effects of the Chicxulub Cretaceous/Tertiary impact". *Journal of Geophysical Research*. **102** (E9): 245–64. Bibcode: 1997JGR...10221645P[304]. doi: 10.1029/97JE01743[305]. PMID 11541145[306].
- Pope KO; Ocampo AC; Kinsland GL; Smith R (1996). "Surface expression of the Chicxulub crater". *Geology*. **24** (6): 527–30. Bibcode: 1996Geo....24..527P[307]. doi: 10.1130/0091-7613(1996)024<0527:SEOTCC>2.3.CO;2[308]. PMID 11539331[309].
- Qivx Inc. (2003). "Periodic Table: Properties of Iridium"[310]. *qivx.com*. Archived from the original[311] on September 28, 2007. Retrieved September 25, 2007.
- Renne, PR; Ludwig, KR; Karner, DB (2000). "Progress and challenges in geochronology". *Science Progress*. **83**: 107–121. PMID 10800377[312].
- Rincon, Paul (March 4, 2010). "Dinosaur extinction link to crater confirmed"[313]. *BBC*. Retrieved March 5, 2010.
- Rojas-Consuegra, R.; M. A. Iturralde-Vinent; C. Díaz-Otero & D. García-Delgado (2005). "Significación paleogeográfica de la brecha basal del Límite K/T en Loma Dos Hermanas (Loma del Capiro), en Santa Clara,

provincia de Villa Clara. I Convención Cubana de Ciencias de la Tierra".
Geociencias. **8** (6): 1–9. ISBN 978-959-7117-03-2.

- Schulte, P.; Alegret, L.; Arenillas, I.; Arz, J. A.; Barton, P. J.; Bown, P.
  R.; Bralower, T. J.; Christeson, G. L.; et al. (5 March 2010). "The Chicx-
  ulub Asteroid Impact and Mass Extinction at the Cretaceous-Paleogene
  Boundary"[314]. *Science*. **327** (5970): 1214–1218. Bibcode: 2010Sci...
  327.1214S[315]. doi: 10.1126/science.1177265[316]. ISSN 1095-9203[317].
  PMID 20203042[318]. Retrieved March 5, 2010.

- Sharpton VL; Marin LE (1997). "The Cretaceous–Tertiary impact crater
  and the cosmic projectile that produced it". *Annals of the New York
  Academy of Sciences*. **822**: 353–80. Bibcode: 1997NYASA.822..353S[319].
  doi: 10.1111/j.1749-6632.1997.tb48351.x[320]. PMID 11543120[321].

- Stewart, S. A.; Allen, P.J. (2005). "3D seismic reflection mapping of
  the Silverpit multi-ringed crater, North Sea"[322]. *Geological Society of
  America Bulletin*. **117** (3): 354–368. Bibcode: 2005GSAB..117..354S[323].
  doi: 10.1130/B25591.1[324]. Archived from the original[325] on December 9,
  2011.

- Stewart S. A.; Allen P. J. (2002). "A 20-km-diameter multi-ringed
  impact structure in the North Sea". *Nature*. **418** (6897): 520–3. Bibcode: 2002Natur.418..520S[326]. doi: 10.1038/nature00914[327]. PMID
  12152076[328].

- Than, Ker (November 28, 2006). "Study: Single Meteorite Impact Killed
  Dinosaurs"[329]. *livescience.com*. Retrieved September 29, 2007.

- Verschuur; Gerrit L. (1996). *Impact!: The Threat of Comets and Asteroids*. Oxford University Press (U.S.). ISBN 978-0-19-511919-0.

- Web Elements (2007). "Geological Abundances"[330]. *webelements.com*.
  Retrieved September 26, 2007.

- Weinreb, David B. (March 2002). "Catastrophic Events in the History
  of Life: Toward a New Understanding of Mass Extinctions in the Fossil
  Record – Part I"[331]. *jyi.org*. Archived from the original[332] on October 18,
  2007. Retrieved October 3, 2007.

- Weisstein, Eric W. (2007). "Eric Weisstein's World of Physics – Roche
  Limit"[333]. *scienceworld.wolfram.com*. Retrieved September 5, 2007.

Further reading

- Schulte, P.; Alegret, L.; Arenillas, I.; et al. (2010). "The Chicxulub
  Asteroid Impact and Mass Extinction at the Cretaceous-Paleogene Boundary"[334] (PDF). *Science*. **327** (5970): 1214–18. Bibcode: 2010Sci...
  327.1214S[315]. doi: 10.1126/science.1177265[316]. ISSN 0036-8075[335].
  PMID 20203042[318]. Archived from the original[336] (PDF) on December
  9, 2011. Retrieved 9 December 2016.

External links

> Wikimedia Commons has media related to *Chicxulub crater.*

- Chicxulub Crater[337]
- Numerous sinkholes (Cenotes) marked around Chicxulub crater.[338] Opens in Google Earth
- NASA JPL: "A 'Smoking Gun' for Dinosaur Extinction"[339], March 6, 2003
- Chicxulub: Variations in the magnitude of the gravity field at sea level image[340] (Lunar and Planetary Institute, USRA)
- "Doubts On Dinosaurs"[341] – *Scientific American*
- Papers and presentations resulting from the 2016 Chicxulub drilling project[342]

Deccan Traps

Deccan Traps are a large igneous province located on the Deccan Plateau of west-central India (17°–24°N, 73°–74°E) and are one of the largest volcanic features on Earth. They consist of multiple layers of solidified flood basalt that together are more than 2,000 m (6,600 ft) thick, cover an area of c. 500,000 km^2 (200,000 sq mi), and have a volume of c. 1,000,000 km^3 (200,000 cu mi). Originally, the Deccan Traps may have covered c. 1,500,000 km^2 (600,000 sq mi),[343] with a correspondingly larger original volume.

Etymology

The term "trap" has been used in geology since 1785–1795 for such rock formations. It is derived from the Scandinavian word for stairs ("trappa") and refers to the step-like hills forming the landscape of the region.[344]

History

The Deccan Traps began forming 66.25 million years ago, at the end of the Cretaceous period. The bulk of the volcanic eruption occurred at the Western Ghats some 66 million years ago. This series of eruptions may have lasted less than 30,000 years in total.[345]

Figure 98: *The Western Ghats at Matheran in Maharashtra*

Figure 99: *Oblique satellite view of the Deccan Traps*

The original area covered by the lava flows is estimated to have been as large as 1.5 million km², approximately half the size of modern India. The Deccan Traps region was reduced to its current size by erosion and plate tectonics; the present area of directly observable lava flows is around 500,000 km² (200,000 sq mi).

Effect on mass extinctions and climate

The release of volcanic gases, particularly sulphur dioxide, during the formation of the traps contributed to climate change. Data points to an average drop in temperature of 2 °C in this period.

Because of its magnitude, scientists formerly speculated that the gases released during the formation of the Deccan Traps played a role in the Cretaceous–Paleogene (K–Pg) extinction event (also known as the Cretaceous–Tertiary extinction). It was theorized that sudden cooling due to sulfurous volcanic gases released by the formation of the traps and localised gas concentrations may have contributed significantly to the K–Pg, as well as other mass extinctions. However, the current consensus among the scientific community is that the extinction was triggered by the Chicxulub impact event in North America (which would have produced a sunlight-blocking dust cloud that killed much of the plant life and reduced global temperature, called an impact winter).

Work published in 2014 by geologist Gerta Keller and others on the timing of the Deccan volcanism suggests the extinction may have been caused by both the volcanism and the impact event.[346,347] This was followed by a similar study in 2015.

Petrology

Within the Deccan Traps at least 95% of the lavas are tholeiitic basalts. Other rock types present include: alkali basalt, nephelinite, lamprophyre and carbonatite.

Mantle xenoliths have been described from Kachchh (northwestern India) and elsewhere in the western Deccan.

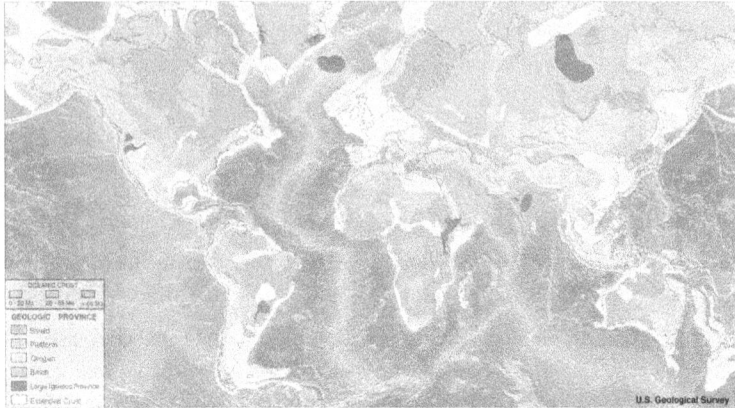

Figure 100: *The Deccan Traps shown as dark purple spot on the geologic map of India*

Figure 101: *Crystals of epistilbite and calcite in a vug in Deccan Traps basalt lava from Jalgaon District, Maharashtra*

Fossils

The Deccan Traps are famous for the beds of fossils that have been found between layers of lava. Particularly well known species include the frog *Oxyglossus pusillus* (Owen) of the Eocene of India and the toothed frog *Indobatrachus*, an early lineage of modern frogs, which is now placed in the Australian family Myobatrachidae.[348] The Infratrappean and Intertrappean Beds also contain fossil freshwater mollusks.[349]

Theories of formation

It is postulated that the Deccan Traps eruption was associated with a deep mantle plume. The area of long-term eruption (the hotspot), known as the Réunion hotspot, is suspected of both causing the Deccan Traps eruption and opening the rift that once separated the Seychelles plateau from India. Seafloor spreading at the boundary between the Indian and African Plates subsequently pushed India north over the plume, which now lies under Réunion island in the Indian Ocean, southwest of India. The mantle plume model has, however, been challenged.[350]

Data continue to emerge which supports the plume model. The motion of the Indian tectonic plate and the eruptive history of the Deccan traps show strong correlations. Based on data from marine magnetic profiles, a pulse of unusually rapid plate motion begins at the same time as the first pulse of Deccan flood basalts, which is dated at 67 million years ago. The spreading rate rapidly increased and reached a maximum at the same time as the peak basaltic eruptions. The spreading rate then dropped off, with the decrease occurring around 63 million years ago, by which time the main phase of Deccan volcanism ended. This correlation is seen as driven by plume dynamics.[351]

The Indian and African plates' motions have also been shown to be coupled, with the common element being the position of these plates relative to the location of the Réunion plume head. The onset of accelerated motion of India coincides with a large slowing of the rate of counterclockwise rotation of Africa. The close correlations between the plate motions suggest that they were both driven by the force of the Réunion plume.

Suggested link to impact events

Chicxulub crater

There is some evidence to link the Deccan Traps eruption to the asteroid impact which created the Chicxulub crater in the Mexican state of Yucatán. Although the Deccan Traps began erupting well before the impact, argon-argon dating suggests that the impact may have caused an increase in permeability that allowed magma to reach the surface and produced the most voluminous flows, accounting for around 70% of the volume. The combination of the asteroid impact and the resulting increase in eruptive volume may have been responsible for the mass extinctions that occurred at the time that separates the Cretaceous and Paleogene periods, known as the K–Pg boundary.

Shiva crater

A geological structure exists in the sea floor off the west coast of India has been suggested as a possible impact crater, in this context called the Shiva crater. It has also been dated at approximately 66 million years ago, potentially matching the Deccan traps. The researchers claiming that this feature is an impact crater suggest that the impact may have been the triggering event for the Deccan Traps as well as contributing to the acceleration of the Indian plate in the early Paleogene.[352] However, the current consensus in the Earth science community is that this feature is unlikely to be an actual impact crater.[353]

External links

Wikimedia Commons has media related to **Deccan Traps**.

- "Animated simulation by the Geodynamics group at the Geological Survey of Norway illustrating the Indian plate moving through the Indian Ocean"[354]. Archived from the original[355] on 23 July 2011.
- Scientist argues that volcanoes, not meteorite, killed dinosaurs[356]
- The Deccam Traps/Volcanism Theory[357]

Coordinates: 18°51′N 73°43′E[358]

Paleocene dinosaurs

The term **Paleocene dinosaurs** describes families or genera of non-avian dinosaurs that may have survived the Cretaceous–Paleogene extinction event, which occurred 66 million years ago. Although almost all evidence indicated that birds are the only dinosaur group that survived past the K–Pg boundary, there is some scattered evidence that some non-avian dinosaurs lived for a short period of time during the Paleocene epoch. The evidence for Paleocene non-avian dinosaurs is rare and remains controversial, although at least one non-neornithine ornithuran is known from the Paleocene, and it's known as *Qinornis*.

Implications

Several researchers have stated that some non-avian dinosaurs survived into the Paleocene and therefore the extinction of non-avian dinosaurs was gradual.[359] Their arguments were based on the finding of dinosaur remains in the Hell Creek Formation up to 1.3 m (4.3 ft) above (40,000 years later than) the K–Pg boundary. Similar reports have come from other parts of the world, including China.

There is possible evidence of a dead clade walking: in 2001, evidence was presented that pollen samples recovered near a fossilized hadrosaur femur recovered in the Ojo Alamo Sandstone at the San Juan River indicate that the animal lived during the Paleogene period, approximately 64.5 million years ago. Direct dating of bone has also been used to present an age of 64.8 ± 0.9 million years for one specimen. Many scientists, however, dismiss the "Paleocene non-avian dinosaurs" as reworked, that is, washed out of their original locations and then reburied in much later sediments. A compelling argument against reworking would be a complete or at least associated skeleton (e.g. more than one bone from the same individual) found above the K–Pg boundary. As yet no such finds have been reported.

The non-neornithine ornithuran *Qinornis*, is a peculiar fossil from China, that is dated as having 61 million years old, five million years after the K-Pg extinction event. This seems to be the very first indication that non-neornithine dinosaurs have survived for some millions of years after the extinction.

List of purported Paleogene dinosaur fossils

- Ojo Alamo Formation, New Mexico: Paleocene hadrosaurian.
- Takatika Grit, Chatham Islands: Paleocene Non-Avian theropods.

History of study

History of paleontology

Part of a series on
Paleontology

Paleontology Portal
Category

- $\frac{v}{t}$
- $\underline{e}^{360}$

The **history of paleontology** traces the history of the effort to understand the history of life on Earth by studying the fossil record left behind by living organisms. Since it is concerned with understanding living organisms of the past, paleontology can be considered to be a field of biology, but its historical development has been closely tied to geology and the effort to understand the history of Earth itself.

217

Figure 102: *Duria Antiquior – A more Ancient Dorset is a watercolor painted in 1830 by the geologist Henry De la Beche based on fossils found by Mary Anning. The late 18th and early 19th century was a time of rapid and dramatic changes in ideas about the history of life on earth.*

In ancient times, Xenophanes (570–480 BC), Herodotus (484–425 BC), Eratosthenes (276–194 BC), and Strabo (64 BC-24 AD) wrote about fossils of marine organisms, indicating that land was once under water. During the Middle Ages, fossils were discussed by Persian naturalist Ibn Sina (known as *Avicenna* in Europe) in *The Book of Healing* (1027), which proposed a theory of petrifying fluids that Albert of Saxony would elaborate on in the 14th century. The Chinese naturalist Shen Kuo (1031–1095) would propose a theory of climate change based on evidence from petrified bamboo.

In early modern Europe, the systematic study of fossils emerged as an integral part of the changes in natural philosophy that occurred during the Age of Reason. The nature of fossils and their relationship to life in the past became better understood during the 17th and 18th centuries, and at the end of the 18th century, the work of Georges Cuvier had ended a long running debate about the reality of extinction, leading to the emergence of paleontology- in association with comparative anatomy- as a scientific discipline. The expanding knowledge of the fossil record also played an increasing role in the development of geology, and stratigraphy in particular.

In 1822, the word "paleontology" was used by the editor of a French scientific journal to refer to the study of ancient living organisms through fossils, and the first half of the 19th century saw geological and paleontological activity become increasingly well organized with the growth of geologic societies and museums and an increasing number of professional geologists and fossil specialists. This contributed to a rapid increase in knowledge about the history of life on Earth, and progress towards definition of the geologic time scale largely based on fossil evidence. As knowledge of life's history continued to improve, it became increasingly obvious that there had been some kind of successive order to the development of life. This would encourage early evolutionary theories on the transmutation of species. After Charles Darwin published *Origin of Species* in 1859, much of the focus of paleontology shifted to understanding evolutionary paths, including human evolution, and evolutionary theory.

The last half of the 19th century saw a tremendous expansion in paleontological activity, especially in North America. The trend continued in the 20th century with additional regions of the Earth being opened to systematic fossil collection, as demonstrated by a series of important discoveries in China near the end of the 20th century. Many transitional fossils have been discovered, and there is now considered to be abundant evidence of how all classes of vertebrates are related, much of it in the form of transitional fossils. The last few decades of the 20th century saw a renewed interest in mass extinctions and their role in the evolution of life on Earth.[361] There was also a renewed interest in the Cambrian explosion that saw the development of the body plans of most animal phyla. The discovery of fossils of the Ediacaran biota and developments in paleobiology extended knowledge about the history of life back far before the Cambrian.

Prior to the 17th century

As early as the 6th century BC, the Greek philosopher Xenophanes of Colophon (570–480 BC) recognized that some fossil shells were remains of shellfish, which he used to argue that what was at the time dry land was once under the sea.[362] Leonardo da Vinci (1452–1519), in an unpublished notebook, also concluded that some fossil sea shells were the remains of shellfish. However, in both cases, the fossils were complete remains of shellfish species that closely resembled living species, and were therefore easy to classify.[363]

In 1027, the Persian naturalist, Ibn Sina (known as *Avicenna* in Europe), proposed an explanation of how the stoniness of fossils was caused in *The Book of Healing*. He modified an idea of Aristotle's, which explained it in terms of vaporous exhalations. Ibn Sina modified this into the theory of petrifying fluids (*succus lapidificatus*), which was elaborated on by Albert of Saxony in the 14th century and was accepted in some form by most naturalists by the 16th century.[364]

Shen Kuo (Chinese: 沈括) (1031–1095) of the Song Dynasty used marine fossils found in the Taihang Mountains to infer the existence of geological processes such as geomorphology and the shifting of seashores over time.[365] Using his observation of preserved petrified bamboos found underground in Yan'an, Shanbei region, Shaanxi province, he argued for a theory of gradual climate change, since Shaanxi was part of a dry climate zone that did not support a habitat for the growth of bamboos.[366]

As a result of a new emphasis on observing, classifying, and cataloging nature, 16th century natural philosophers in Europe began to establish extensive collections of fossil objects (as well as collections of plant and animal specimens), which were often stored in specially built cabinets to help organize them. Conrad Gesner published a 1565 work on fossils that contained one of the first detailed descriptions of such a cabinet and collection. The collection belonged to a member of the extensive network of correspondents that Gesner drew on for his works. Such informal correspondence networks among natural philosophers and collectors became increasingly important during the course of the 16th century and were direct forerunners of the scientific societies that would begin to form in the 17th century. These cabinet collections and correspondence networks played an important role in the development of natural philosophy.[367]

However, most 16th-century Europeans did not recognize that fossils were the remains of living organisms. The etymology of the word *fossil* comes from the Latin for things having been dug up. As this indicates, the term was applied to a wide variety of stone and stone-like objects without regard to whether they might have an organic origin. 16th-century writers such as Gesner and Georg Agricola were more interested in classifying such objects by their physical and mystical properties than they were in determining the objects' origins.[368] In addition, the natural philosophy of the period encouraged alternative explanations for the origin of fossils. Both the Aristotelian and Neoplatonic schools of philosophy provided support for the idea that stony objects might grow within the earth to resemble living things. Neoplatonic philosophy maintained that there could be affinities between living and non-living objects that could cause one to resemble the other. The Aristotelian school maintained that the seeds of living organisms could enter the ground and generate objects resembling those organisms.[369]

17th century

During the Age of Reason, fundamental changes in natural philosophy were reflected in the analysis of fossils. In 1665 Athanasius Kircher attributed giant bones to extinct races of giant humans in his *Mundus subterraneus*. In the

Figure 103: *Johann Jakob Scheuchzer tried to explain fossils using Biblical floods in his Herbarium of the Deluge (1709)*

same year Robert Hooke published *Micrographia*, an illustrated collection of his observations with a microscope. One of these observations was entitled "Of Petrify'd wood, and other Petrify'd bodies", which included a comparison between petrified and ordinary wood. He concluded that petrified wood was ordinary wood that had been soaked with "water impregnated with stony and earthy particles". He then suggested that several kinds of fossil sea shells were formed from ordinary shells by a similar process. He argued against the prevalent view that such objects were "Stones form'd by some extraordinary Plastick virtue latent in the Earth itself".[370] Hooke believed that fossils provided evidence about the history of life on Earth writing in 1668:

...if the finding of Coines, Medals, Urnes, and other Monuments of famous persons, or Towns, or Utensils, be admitted for unquestionable Proofs, that such Persons or things have, in former times had a being, certainly those Petrifactions may be allowed to be of equal Validity and Evidence, that there have formerly been such Vegetables or Animals... and are true universal Characters legible to all rational Men.[371]

Hooke was prepared to accept the possibility that some such fossils represented species that had become extinct, possibly in past geological catastrophes.

In 1667 Nicholas Steno wrote a paper about a shark head he had dissected. He compared the teeth of the shark with the common fossil objects known as tongue stones. He concluded that the fossils must have been shark teeth. Steno then took an interest in the question of fossils, and to address some

Figure 104: *Illustration from Steno's 1667 paper shows a shark head and its teeth along with a fossil tooth for comparison.*

of the objections to their organic origin he began studying rock strata. The result of this work was published in 1669 as *Forerunner to a Dissertation on a solid naturally enclosed in a solid*. In this book, Steno drew a clear distinction between objects such as rock crystals that really were formed within rocks and those such as fossil shells and shark teeth that were formed outside of those rocks. Steno realized that certain kinds of rock had been formed by the successive deposition of horizontal layers of sediment and that fossils were the remains of living organisms that had become buried in that sediment. Steno who, like almost all 17th century natural philosophers, believed that the earth was only a few thousand years old, resorted to the Biblical flood as a possible explanation for fossils of marine organisms that were far from the sea.[372]

Despite the considerable influence of *Forerunner*, naturalists such as Martin Lister (1638–1712) and John Ray (1627–1705) continued to question the organic origin of some fossils. They were particularly concerned about objects such as fossil Ammonites, which Hooke claimed were organic in origin, that did not resemble any known living species. This raised the possibility of extinction, which they found difficult to accept for philosophical and theological reasons.[373] In 1695 Ray wrote to the Welsh naturalist Edward Lluyd complaining of such views: "... there follows such a train of consequences, as seem to shock the Scripture-History of the novity of the World; at least they

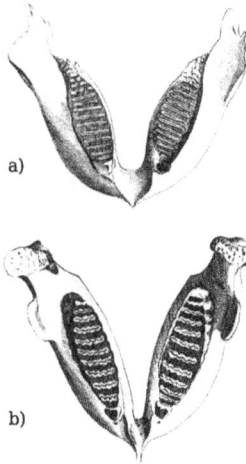

Cuvier's drawings of:
a) a mammoth's lower jaw and
b) an Indian elephant's

Figure 105: *A drawing comparing jaws was added in 1799 when Cuvier's 1796 presentation on living and fossil elephants was published.*

overthrow the opinion received, & not without good reason, among Divines and Philosophers, that since the first Creation there have been no species of Animals or Vegetables lost, no new ones produced."[374]

18th century

In his 1778 work *Epochs of Nature* Georges Buffon referred to fossils, in particular the discovery of fossils of tropical species such as elephants and rhinoceros in northern Europe, as evidence for the theory that the earth had started out much warmer than it currently was and had been gradually cooling.

In 1796 Georges Cuvier presented a paper on living and fossil elephants comparing skeletal remains of Indian and African elephants to fossils of mammoths and of an animal he would later name mastodon utilizing comparative anatomy. He established for the first time that Indian and African elephants were different species, and that mammoths differed from both and must be extinct. He further concluded that the mastodon was another extinct species that also differed from Indian or African elephants, more so than mammoths. Cuvier made another powerful demonstration of the power of comparative anatomy in paleontology when he presented a second paper in 1796 on a large fossil skeleton from Paraguay, which he named *Megatherium* and identified as

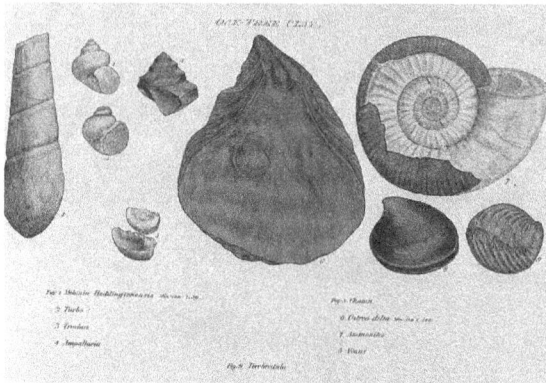

Figure 106: *Illustration from William Smith's 1815 Strata by Organized Fossils*

a giant sloth by comparing its skull to those of two living species of tree sloth. Cuvier's ground-breaking work in paleontology and comparative anatomy led to the widespread acceptance of extinction.[375] It also led Cuvier to advocate the geological theory of catastrophism to explain the succession of organisms revealed by the fossil record. He also pointed out that since mammoths and wooly rhinoceros were not the same species as the elephants and rhinoceros currently living in the tropics, their fossils could not be used as evidence for a cooling earth.

In a pioneering application of stratigraphy, William Smith, a surveyor and mining engineer, made extensive use of fossils to help correlate rock strata in different locations. He created the first geological map of England during the late 1790s and early 19th century. He established the principle of faunal succession, the idea that each strata of sedimentary rock would contain particular types of fossils, and that these would succeed one another in a predictable way even in widely separated geologic formations. At the same time, Cuvier and Alexandre Brongniart, an instructor at the Paris school of mine engineering, used similar methods in an influential study of the geology of the region around Paris.

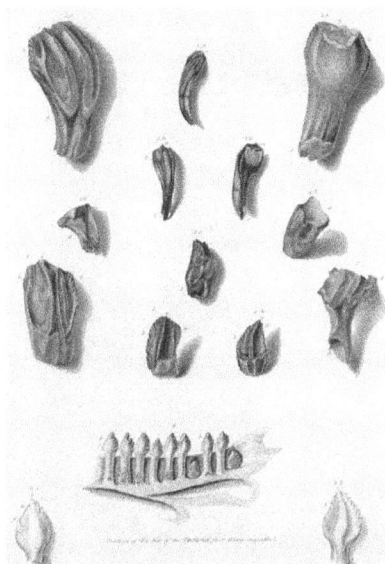

Figure 107: *Illustration of fossil Iguanodon teeth with a modern iguana jaw for comparison from Mantell's 1825 paper describing Iguanodon*

Early to mid-19th century

The age of reptiles

In 1808, Cuvier identified a fossil found in Maastricht as a giant marine reptile that would later be named *Mosasaurus*. He also identified, from a drawing, another fossil found in Bavaria as a flying reptile and named it *Pterodactylus*. He speculated, based on the strata in which these fossils were found, that large reptiles had lived prior to what he was calling "the age of mammals".[376] Cuvier's speculation would be supported by a series of finds that would be made in Great Britain over the course of the next two decades. Mary Anning, a professional fossil collector since age eleven, collected the fossils of a number of marine reptiles from the Jurassic marine strata at Lyme Regis. These included the first ichthyosaur skeleton to be recognized as such, which was collected in 1811, and the first two plesiosaur skeletons ever found in 1821 and 1823. Many of her discoveries would be described scientifically by the geologists William Conybeare, Henry De la Beche, and William Buckland.[377] It was Anning who observed that stony objects known as "bezoar stones" were often found in the abdominal region of ichthyosaur skeletons, and she noted that if such stones were broken open they often contained fossilized fish bones and scales as well

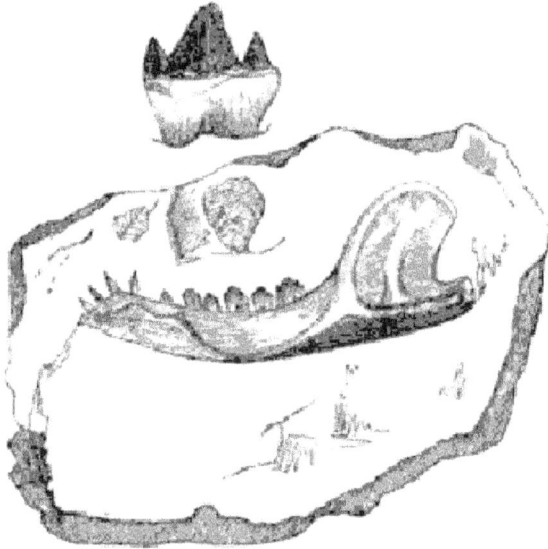

Figure 108: *Illustration of the fossil jaw of the Stonesfield mammal from Gideon Mantell's 1848 Wonders of Geology*

as sometimes bones from small ichthyosaurs. This led her to suggest to Buckland that they were fossilized feces, which he named coprolites, and which he used to better understand ancient food chains.[378]

In 1824, Buckland found and described a lower jaw from Jurassic deposits from Stonesfield. He determined that the bone belonged to a carnivorous land-dwelling reptile he called *Megalosaurus*. That same year Gideon Mantell realized that some large teeth he had found in 1822, in Cretaceous rocks from Tilgate, belonged to a giant herbivorous land-dwelling reptile. He called it *Iguanodon*, because the teeth resembled those of an iguana. All of this led Mantell to publish an influential paper in 1831 entitled "The Age of Reptiles" in which he summarized the evidence for there having been an extended time during which the earth had teemed with large reptiles, and he divided that era, based in what rock strata different types of reptiles first appeared, into three intervals that anticipated the modern periods of the Triassic, Jurassic, and Cretaceous.[379] In 1832 Mantell would find, in Tilgate, a partial skeleton of an armored reptile he would call *Hylaeosaurus*. In 1841 the English anatomist Richard Owen would create a new order of reptiles, which he called Dinosauria, for *Megalosaurus*, *Iguanodon*, and *Hylaeosaurus*.[380]

This evidence that giant reptiles had lived on Earth in the past caused great excitement in scientific circles,[381] and even among some segments of the general public.[382] Buckland did describe the jaw of a small primitive mammal, *Phascolotherium*, that was found in the same strata as *Megalosaurus*. This discovery, known as the Stonesfield mammal, was a much discussed anomaly. Cuvier at first thought it was a marsupial, but Buckland later realized it was a primitive placental mammal. Due to its small size and primitive nature, Buckland did not believe it invalidated the overall pattern of an age of reptiles, when the largest and most conspicuous animals had been reptiles rather than mammals.[383]

Paleobotany and the origin of the word *paleontology*

In 1828 Alexandre Brongniart's son, the botanist Adolphe Brongniart, published the introduction to a longer work on the history of fossil plants. Adolphe Brongniart concluded that the history of plants could roughly be divided into four parts. The first period was characterized by cryptogams. The second period was characterized by the appearance of the conifers. The third period brought emergence of the cycads, and the fourth by the development of the flowering plants (such as the dicotyledons). The transitions between each of these periods was marked by sharp discontinuities in the fossil record, with more gradual changes within the periods. Brongniart's work is the foundation of paleobotany and reinforced the theory that life on earth had a long and complex history, and different groups of plants and animals made their appearances in successive order.[384] It also supported the idea that the Earth's climate had changed over time as Brongniart concluded that plant fossils showed that during the Carboniferous the climate of Northern Europe must have been tropical.[385]

The increasing attention being paid to fossil plants in the first decades of the 19th century would trigger a significant change in the terminology for the study of past life. The editor of the influential French scientific journal, *Journal de Physique*, a student of Cuvier's named Henri Marie Ducrotay de Blainville, coined the term "paleozoologie" in 1817 to refer to the work Cuvier and others were doing to reconstruct extinct animals from fossil bones. However, Blainville began looking for a term that could refer to the study of both fossil animal and plant remains. After trying some unsuccessful alternatives, he hit on "palaeontologie" in 1822. Blainville's term for the study of the fossilized organisms quickly became popular and was anglicized into "paleontology".[386] The term "paleobotany" was coined in 1884 and "palynology" in 1944.

Catastrophism, uniformitarianism and the fossil record

In Cuvier's landmark 1796 paper on living and fossil elephants, he referred to a single catastrophe that destroyed life to be replaced by the current forms. As a result of his studies of extinct mammals, he realized that animals such as *Palaeotherium* had lived before the time of the mammoths, which led him to write in terms of multiple geological catastrophes that had wiped out a series of successive faunas.[387] By 1830, a scientific consensus had formed around his ideas as a result of paleobotany and the dinosaur and marine reptile discoveries in Britain.[388] In Great Britain, where natural theology was very influential in the early 19th century, a group of geologists that included Buckland, and Robert Jameson insisted on explicitly linking the most recent of Cuvier's catastrophes to the biblical flood. Catastrophism had a religious overtone in Britain that was absent elsewhere.[389]

Partly in response to what he saw as unsound and unscientific speculations by William Buckland and other practitioners of flood geology, Charles Lyell advocated the geological theory of uniformitarianism in his influential work *Principles of Geology*.[390] Lyell amassed evidence, both from his own field research and the work of others, that most geological features could be explained by the slow action of present-day forces, such as vulcanism, earthquakes, erosion, and sedimentation rather than past catastrophic events.[391] Lyell also claimed that the apparent evidence for catastrophic changes in the fossil record, and even the appearance of directional succession in the history of life, were illusions caused by imperfections in that record. For instance he argued that the absence of birds and mammals from the earliest fossil strata was merely an imperfection in the fossil record attributable to the fact that marine organisms were more easily fossilized. Also Lyell pointed to the Stonesfield mammal as evidence that mammals had not necessarily been preceded by reptiles, and to the fact that certain Pleistocene strata showed a mixture of extinct and still surviving species, which he said showed that extinction occurred piecemeal rather than as a result of catastrophic events.[392] Lyell was successful in convincing geologists of the idea that the geological features of the earth were largely due to the action of the same geologic forces that could be observed in the present day, acting over an extended period of time. He was not successful in gaining support for his view of the fossil record, which he believed did not support a theory of directional succession.[393]

Transmutation of species and the fossil record

Jean Baptiste Lamarck used fossils in his arguments for his theory of the transmutation of species in the early 19th century.[394] Fossil finds, and the emerging evidence that life had changed over time, fueled speculation on this topic during the next few decades.[395] Robert Chambers used fossil evidence in his 1844

Figure 109: *Geologic time scale from an 1861 book by Richard Owen shows the appearance of major animal types.*

popular science book *Vestiges of the Natural History of Creation*, which advocated an evolutionary origin for the cosmos as well as for life on earth. Like Lamarck's theory it maintained that life had progressed from the simple to the complex.[396] These early evolutionary ideas were widely discussed in scientific circles but were not accepted into the scientific mainstream.[397] Many of the critics of transmutational ideas used fossil evidence in their arguments. In the same paper that coined the term dinosaur Richard Owen pointed out that dinosaurs were at least as sophisticated and complex as modern reptiles, which he claimed contradicted transmutational theories.[398] Hugh Miller would make a similar argument, pointing out that the fossil fish found in the Old Red Sandstone formation were fully as complex as any later fish, and not the primitive forms alleged by *Vestiges*.[399] While these early evolutionary theories failed to become accepted as mainstream science, the debates over them would help pave the way for the acceptance of Darwin's theory of evolution by natural selection a few years later.[400]

Geological time scale and the history of life

Geologists such as Adam Sedgwick, and Roderick Murchison continued, in the course of disputes such as The Great Devonian Controversy, to make advances in stratigraphy. They described newly recognized geological periods, such as the Cambrian, the Silurian, the Devonian, and the Permian. Increasingly, such progress in stratigraphy depended on the opinions of experts with specialized knowledge of particular types of fossils such as William Lonsdale (fossil corals), and John Lindley (fossil plants) who both played a role in the Devonian controversy and its resolution.[401] By the early 1840s much of the geologic time scale had been developed. In 1841, John Phillips formally divided the geologic column into three major eras, the Paleozoic, Mesozoic, and Cenozoic, based on sharp breaks in the fossil record.[402] He identified the three periods of the Mesozoic era and all the periods of the Paleozoic era except the Ordovician. His definition of the geological time scale is still used today.[403] It remained a relative time scale with no method of assigning any of the periods' absolute dates. It was understood that not only had there been an "age of reptiles" preceding the current "age of mammals", but there had been a time (during the Cambrian and the Silurian) when life had been restricted to the sea, and a time (prior to the Devonian) when invertebrates had been the largest and most complex forms of animal life.

Expansion and professionalization of geology and paleontology

This rapid progress in geology and paleontology during the 1830s and 1840s was aided by a growing international network of geologists and fossil specialists whose work was organized and reviewed by an increasing number of geological societies. Many of these geologists and paleontologists were now paid professionals working for universities, museums and government geological surveys. The relatively high level of public support for the earth sciences was due to their cultural impact, and their proven economic value in helping to exploit mineral resources such as coal.[404]

Another important factor was the development in the late 18th and early 19th centuries of museums with large natural history collections. These museums received specimens from collectors around the world and served as centers for the study of comparative anatomy and morphology. These disciplines played key roles in the development of a more technically sophisticated form of natural history. One of the first and most important examples was the Museum of Natural History in Paris, which was at the center of many of the developments in natural history during the first decades of the 19th century. It was founded in 1793 by an act of the French National Assembly, and was based on an extensive royal collection plus the private collections of aristocrats confiscated during the French revolution, and expanded by material seized in French military conquests during the Napoleonic Wars. The Paris museum was the professional base for Cuvier, and his professional rival Geoffroy Saint-Hilaire. The English anatomists Robert Grant and Richard Owen both spent time studying

Figure 110: *Photograph of the second Archaeopteryx skeleton to be found, taken in 1881 at the Natural History Museum, Berlin*

there. Owen would go on to become the leading British morphologist while working at the museum of the Royal College of Surgeons.[405,406]

Late 19th century

Evolution

Charles Darwin's publication of the *On the Origin of Species* in 1859 was a watershed event in all the life sciences, especially paleontology. Fossils had played a role in the development of Darwin's theory. In particular he had been impressed by fossils he had collected in South America during the voyage of the Beagle of giant armadillos, giant sloths, and what at the time he thought were giant llamas that seemed to be related to species still living on the continent in modern times.[407] The scientific debate that started immediately after the publication of *Origin* led to a concerted effort to look for transitional fossils and other evidence of evolution in the fossil record. There were two areas where early success attracted considerable public attention, the transition between reptiles and birds, and the evolution of the modern single-toed horse.[408] In 1861 the first specimen of *Archaeopteryx*, an animal with both teeth and feathers and a mix of other reptilian and avian features, was discovered in a

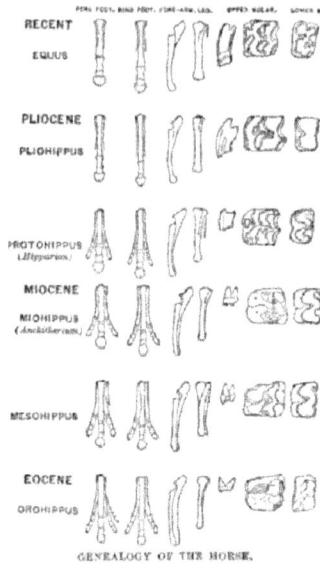

Figure 111: *Diagram by O.C. Marsh of the evolution of horse feet and teeth, reproduced in T. H. Huxley's 1876 book, Professor Huxley in America*

limestone quarry in Bavaria and described by Richard Owen. Another would be found in the late 1870s and put on display at the Natural History Museum, Berlin in 1881. Other primitive toothed birds were found by Othniel Marsh in Kansas in 1872. Marsh also discovered fossils of several primitive horses in the Western United States that helped trace the evolution of the horse from the small 5-toed *Hyracotherium* of the Eocene to the much larger single-toed modern horses of the genus *Equus*. Thomas Huxley would make extensive use of both the horse and bird fossils in his advocacy of evolution. Acceptance of evolution occurred rapidly in scientific circles, but acceptance of Darwin's proposed mechanism of natural selection as the driving force behind it was much less universal. In particular some paleontologists such as Edward Drinker Cope and Henry Fairfield Osborn preferred alternatives such as neo-Lamarckism, the inheritance of characteristics acquired during life, and orthogenesis, an innate drive to change in a particular direction, to explain what they perceived as linear trends in evolution.[409]

There was also great interest in human evolution. Neanderthal fossils were discovered in 1856, but at the time it was not clear that they represented a different species from modern humans. Eugene Dubois created a sensation with his discovery of Java Man, the first fossil evidence of a species that seemed clearly intermediate between humans and apes, in 1891.[410]

Developments in North America

A major development in the second half of the 19th century was a rapid expansion of paleontology in North America. In 1858 Joseph Leidy described a *Hadrosaurus* skeleton, which was the first North American dinosaur to be described from good remains. However, it was the massive westward expansion of railroads, military bases, and settlements into Kansas and other parts of the Western United States following the American Civil War that really fueled the expansion of fossil collection.[411] The result was an increased understanding of the natural history of North America, including the discovery of the Western Interior Sea that had covered Kansas and much of the rest of the Midwestern United States during parts of the Cretaceous, the discovery of several important fossils of primitive birds and horses, and the discovery of a number of new dinosaur genera including *Allosaurus*, *Stegosaurus*, and *Triceratops*. Much of this activity was part of a fierce personal and professional rivalry between two men, Othniel Marsh, and Edward Cope, which has become known as the Bone Wars.[412]

Overview of developments in the 20th century

Developments in geology

Two 20th century developments in geology had a big effect on paleontology. The first was the development of radiometric dating, which allowed absolute dates to be assigned to the geologic timescale. The second was the theory of plate tectonics, which helped make sense of the geographical distribution of ancient life.

Geographical expansion of paleontology

During the 20th century, paleontological exploration intensified everywhere and ceased to be a largely European and North American activity. In the 135 years between Buckland's first discovery and 1969 a total of 170 dinosaur genera were described. In the 25 years after 1969 that number increased to 315. Much of this increase was due to the examination of new rock exposures, particularly in previously little-explored areas in South America and Africa.[413] Near the end of the 20th century the opening of China to systematic exploration for fossils has yielded a wealth of material on dinosaurs and the origin of birds and mammals.[414] Also study of the Chengjiang fauna, a Cambrian fossil site in China, during the 1990s has provided important clues to the origin of vertebrates.[415]

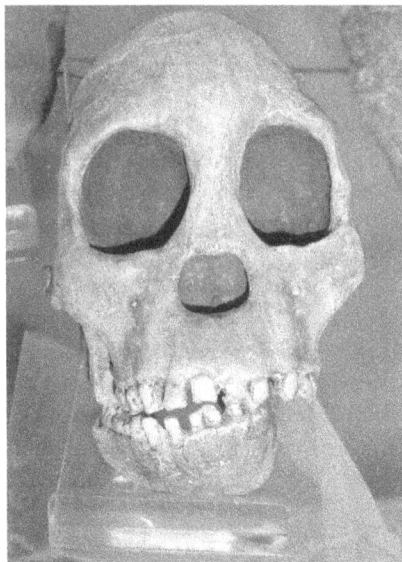

Figure 112: *Fossil of the Taung child discovered in South Africa in 1924*

Mass extinctions

The 20th century saw a major renewal of interest in mass extinction events and their effect on the course of the history of life. This was particularly true after 1980 when Luis and Walter Alvarez put forward the Alvarez hypothesis claiming that an impact event caused the Cretaceous–Paleogene extinction event, which killed off the non-avian dinosaurs along with many other living things. Also in the early 1980s Jack Sepkoski and David M. Raup published papers with statistical analysis of the fossil record of marine invertebrates that revealed a pattern (possibly cyclical) of repeated mass extinctions with significant implications for the evolutionary history of life.

Evolutionary paths and theory

Throughout the 20th century new fossil finds continued to contribute to understanding the paths taken by evolution. Examples include major taxonomic transitions such as finds in Greenland, starting in the 1930s (with more major finds in the 1980s), of fossils illustrating the evolution of tetrapods from fish, and fossils in China during the 1990s that shed light on the dinosaur-bird relationship. Other events that have attracted considerable attention have included the discovery of a series of fossils in Pakistan that have shed light on whale

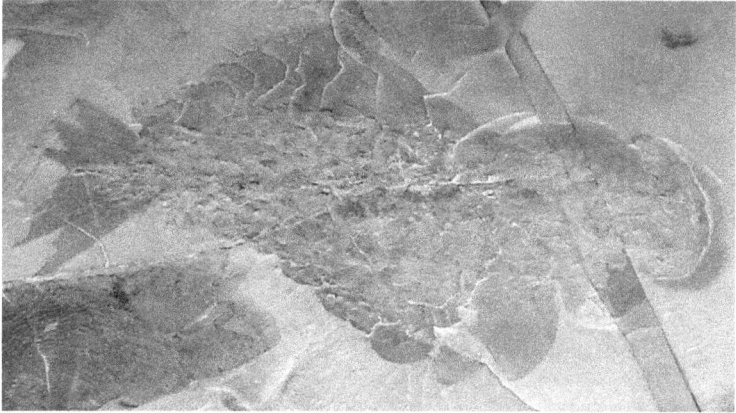

Figure 113: *A complete Anomalocaris fossil from the Burgess shale*

evolution, and most famously of all a series of finds throughout the 20th century in Africa (starting with Taung child in 1924) and elsewhere have helped illuminate the course of human evolution. Increasingly, at the end of the 20th century, the results of paleontology and molecular biology were being brought together to reveal detailed phylogenetic trees.

The results of paleontology have also contributed to the development of evolutionary theory. In 1944 George Gaylord Simpson published *Tempo and Mode in Evolution*, which used quantitative analysis to show that the fossil record was consistent with the branching, non-directional, patterns predicted by the advocates of evolution driven by natural selection and genetic drift rather than the linear trends predicted by earlier advocates of neo-Lamarckism and orthogenesis. This integrated paleontology into the modern evolutionary synthesis.[416] In 1972 Niles Eldredge and Stephen Jay Gould used fossil evidence to advocate the theory of punctuated equilibrium, which maintains that evolution is characterized by long periods of relative stasis and much shorter periods of relatively rapid change.[417]

Cambrian explosion

One area of paleontology that has seen a lot of activity during the 1980s, 1990s, and beyond is the study of the Cambrian explosion during which many of the various phyla of animals with their distinctive body plans first appear. The well-known Burgess Shale Cambrian fossil site was found in 1909 by Charles Doolittle Walcott, and another important site in Chengjiang China was found in 1912. However, new analysis in the 1980s by Harry B. Whittington, Derek Briggs, Simon Conway Morris and others sparked a renewed interest

Figure 114: *A Spriggina fossil from the Ediacaran*

and a burst of activity including discovery of an important new fossil site, Sirius Passet, in Greenland, and the publication of a popular and controversial book, *Wonderful Life* by Stephen Jay Gould in 1989.

Pre-Cambrian fossils

Prior to 1950 there was no widely accepted fossil evidence of life before the Cambrian period. When Charles Darwin wrote *The Origin of Species* he acknowledged that the lack of any fossil evidence of life prior to the relatively complex animals of the Cambrian was a potential argument against the theory of evolution, but expressed the hope that such fossils would be found in the future. In the 1860s there were claims of the discovery of pre-Cambrian fossils, but these would later be shown not to have an organic origin. In the late 19th century Charles Doolittle Walcott would discover stromatolites and other fossil evidence of pre-Cambrian life, but at the time the organic origin of those fossils was also disputed. This would start to change in the 1950s with the discovery of more stromatolites along with microfossils of the bacteria that built them, and the publication of a series of papers by the Soviet scientist Boris Vasil'evich Timofeev announcing the discovery of microscopic fossil spores in pre-Cambrian sediments. A key breakthrough would come when Martin Glaessner would show that fossils of soft bodied animals discovered by Reginald Sprigg during the late 1940s in the Ediacaran hills of Australia were in fact pre-Cambrian not early Cambrian as Sprigg had originally believed, making the Ediacaran biota the oldest animals known. By the end of the 20th century, paleobiology had established that the history of life extended back at least 3.5 billion years.

References

- Bowler, Peter J. (2003). Evolution:The History of an Idea. University of California Press. ISBN 0-520-23693-9.
- Bowler, Peter J. (1992). The Earth Encompassed:A History of the Environmental Sciences. W. W. Norton. ISBN 0-393-32080-4.
- Bowler, Peter J.; Iwan Rhys Morus (2005). *Making Modern Science*. The University of Chicago Press. ISBN 0-226-06861-7.
- Desmond, Adrian (1975). "The Discovery of Marine Transgressions and the Explanation of Fossils in Antiquity". American Journal of Science, Volume 275.
- Larson, Edward J. (2004). *Evolution: the remarkable history of scientific theory*. Modern Library. ISBN 0-679-64288-9.
- McGowan, Christopher (2001). The Dragon Seekers. Persus Publishing. ISBN 0-7382-0282-7.
- Everhart, Michael J. (2005). Oceans of Kansas: A Natural History of the Western Interior Sea. Indiana University Press. ISBN 0-253-34547-2.
- Greene, Marjorie; David Depew (2004). *The Philosophy of Biology:An Episodic History*. Cambridge University Press. ISBN 0-521-64371-6.
- Needham, Joseph (1986). Science and Civilization in China: Volume 3, Mathematics and the Sciences of the Heavens and the Earth. Caves Books Ltd. ISBN 0-253-34547-2.
- Robert Hooke (1665) *Micrographia*[418] The Royal Society
- Palmer, Douglas (2005) Earth Time: Exploring the Deep Past from Victorian England to the Grand Canyon. Wiley, Chichester. ISBN 978-0-470-02221-4
- Rudwick, Martin J.S. (1997). Georges Cuvier, Fossil Bones, and Geological Catastrophes. The University of Chicago Press. ISBN 0-226-73106-5.
- Prothero, Donald .R (2015). The Story of Life in 25 Fossils. Columbia University Press New York. ISBN 978-0-231-53942-5.
- Rudwick, Martin J.S. (1985). The Meaning of Fossils (2nd ed.). The University of Chicago Press. ISBN 0-226-73103-0.
- Rudwick, Martin J.S. (1985). The Great Devonian Controversy: The Shaping of Scientific Knowledge among Gentlemanly Specialists. The University of Chicago Press. ISBN 0-226-73102-2.

• Rudwick, Martin J.S. (2008). *Worlds Before Adam: The Reconstruction of Geohistory in the Age of Reform.* The University of Chicago Press. ISBN 0-226-73128-6.

• Zittel, Karl Alfred von (1901). *History of geology and palaentology to the end of the Nineteenth Century*[419]. Charles Scribner's Sons, London.

External links

• History of paleontology[420]
• History of palaeoentomology in Russia[421]
• Paleontology Milestones: Famous Paleontologists and Notable Contributions[422]
• History of Paleontology by P.D. Polly and R.L. Spang[423]

<indicator name="good-star"> ⊕ </indicator>t

Dinosaur renaissance

The **dinosaur renaissance**[424] was a small-scale scientific revolution that started in the late 1960s, and led to renewed academic and popular interest in dinosaurs. It was sparked by new discoveries and research indicating that dinosaurs may have been active and warm-blooded animals, rather than cold-blooded and sluggish as had been the prevailing view and description during the first half of the twentieth century.

The new view of dinosaurs was championed by John Ostrom, who argued that birds evolved from coelurosaurian dinosaurs, and particularly Robert Bakker who argued passionately that dinosaurs were warm-blooded in a way similar to modern mammals and birds. Bakker frequently portrayed his ideas as a renaissance of those popular in the late nineteenth century, referring to the period in between the Dinosaur Wars and the dinosaur renaissance as "the dinosaur doldrums".

The dinosaur renaissance led to a profound shift in thinking on nearly all aspects of dinosaur biology, including physiology, evolution, behaviour, ecology and extinction. It also led to many depictions of dinosaurs in popular culture.

Figure 115: *Robert Bakker lecturing at the Houston Museum of Natural Science*

Dinosaurs and the origin of birds

In the mid and latter parts of the nineteenth century, many scientists thought there was a close relationship between birds and dinosaurs—and that dinosaurs represented an intermediate stage between "reptiles" and birds.

Shortly after the 1859 publication of Charles Darwin's *The Origin of Species*, British biologist and evolution-defender Thomas Henry Huxley proposed that birds were descendants of dinosaurs. He cited skeletal similarities, particularly among dinosaurs, the "first bird"—*Archaeopteryx*—and modern birds.

However, in 1926, Gerhard Heilmann wrote his influential book *The Origin of Birds*,[425] in which he dismissed the dinosaur–bird link, based on the dinosaurs' supposed lack of a furcula.[426] Thereafter, the accepted hypothesis was that birds evolved from crocodylomorph and thecodont ancestors, rather than from dinosaurs. This removed dinosaurs from a central role in debates about the origin of living species, and may have contributed to the decline of academic interest in dinosaur evolution.

This situation persisted until 1964, when John Ostrom discovered a small carnivorous dinosaur which he named *Deinonychus antirrhopus*, a theropod whose skeletal resemblance to birds seemed unmistakable. This led Ostrom to argue that Huxley had been right, and that birds had indeed evolved from

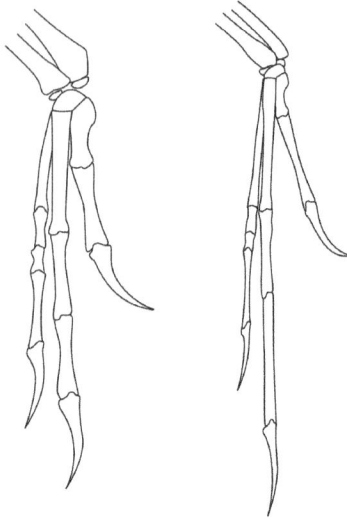

Figure 116: *The similarity of the hands of Deinonychus (left) and Archaeopteryx (right) led John Ostrom to revive the link between dinosaurs and birds.*

dinosaurs. Although it was *Deinonychus* that inspired Ostrom to connect birds with dinosaurs, very similar birdlike dinosaurs, such as *Velociraptor*, had been known for many decades, but no connection had been made. After Ostrom's discoveries, the idea that birds evolved from dinosaurs gained support among palaeontologists, and today it is almost universally accepted. Newer methods, such as cladistics, and the discovery of several feathered dinosaurs have helped confirm the relationship.

The relationship between dinosaurs and birds has led to considerable interest in dinosaur—particularly theropod—phylogeny, which is now far better understood.

Dinosaur monophyly

Initially, dinosaurs were thought to be a monophyletic group, comprising animals with a common ancestor not shared by other reptiles.Wikipedia:Citation needed However, Harry Seeley disagreed with this interpretation, and split the Dinosauria into two orders, the Saurischia ("lizard-hipped") and the Ornithischia ("bird-hipped"), which were seen as members of the Archosauria with no special relationship to each other. As such, the Dinosauria was no longer

Figure 117: *An 1897 painting of "Laelaps" (now Dryptosaurus) by Charles R. Knight. Bakker pointed to such restorations to demonstrate that in the 19th century it was widely accepted that dinosaurs may have been active and agile animals.*

seen as a scientific grouping, and "dinosaur" was reduced to being a popular term, without scientific meaning. This became the standard interpretation throughout much of the twentieth century.[427]

This changed in 1974, when Bakker and Peter Galton published a paper in *Nature*, arguing that not only were dinosaurs a natural monophyletic group, but that they should be raised to the status of a new class, which would also contain birds. Although initially this revival of dinosaur monophyly was controversial, the idea did gain acceptance, and since the rise of cladistic methodology, it has been nearly universally supported. The raising of the Dinosauria to class rank found less support, perhaps largely due to increasing use of phylogenetic taxonomy among vertebrate palaeontologists, in which ranks are entirely abandoned.

Warm-bloodedness and activity levels

In a series of scientific papers, books, and popular articles in the 1970s and 1980s, beginning with his 1968 paper *The superiority of dinosaurs*, Robert Bakker argued strenuously that dinosaurs were warm-blooded and active animals, capable of sustained periods of high activity. In most of his writings Bakker framed his arguments as new evidence leading to a revival of ideas popular in the late 19th century, frequently referring to an ongoing *dinosaur renaissance*. He used a variety of anatomical and statistical arguments to defend his case, the methodology of which was fiercely debated among scientists.

These debates sparked interest in new methods for ascertaining the palaeobiology of extinct animals, such as bone histology, which have been successfully applied to determining the growth-rates of many dinosaurs.

Today, it is generally thought that many or perhaps all dinosaurs had higher metabolic rates than living reptiles, but also that the situation is more complex and varied than Bakker originally proposed. For example, while smaller dinosaurs may have been true endotherms, the larger forms could have been inertial homeotherms, or many dinosaurs could have had intermediate metabolic rates.

New theories on dinosaur behaviour

The late 1960s also saw several new theories on the way dinosaurs behaved, often involving sophisticated social behaviour.

On the basis of trackways, Bakker argued that sauropod dinosaurs moved in structured herds, with the adults surrounding the juveniles in a protective ring. However, shortly afterwards this particular interpretation was challenged by Ostrom among others, although the venerable dinosaur track expert Roland T. Bird apparently agreed with Bakker.

The first rigorous study of dinosaur nesting behaviour came in the late 1970s, when palaeontologist Jack Horner showed that the duckbilled dinosaur *Maiasaura* cared for its young.

Changing portrayal of dinosaurs

The dinosaur renaissance changed not only scientific ideas about dinosaurs, but also their portrayal by artists. Bakker, himself a talented artist, often illustrated his ideas in a lively fashion. Indeed, Bakker's illustration[428] of *Deinonychus*, made for Ostrom's 1969 description, has become one of the most recognisable and iconic of dinosaur restorations.[429]

During the 1970s, restorations of dinosaurs shifted from being lizard-like, to being more mammal- and bird-like. Artists started to show dinosaurs in more active poses, and incorporating newer theories of dinosaur locomotion and behaviour. Tails that were widely shown as having been dragged behind a creature, were now shown uplifted, in order to balance the huge bodies while active.

Besides Bakker, key artists in this "new wave" were first Mark Hallett, Gregory S. Paul in the 1970s, and during the 1980s Doug Henderson and John Gurche.

Gregory Paul in particular defended and expanded on Bakker's ideas on dinosaur anatomy. He expounded a rigorous and detailed approach to dinosaur restoration, in which he often criticised the errors of the traditionalist approach. He also produced a large number of restorations showing small dinosaurs with feathers, and defended the idea in a number of articles and his book *Predatory Dinosaurs of the World*. His view was proven largely correct in the late 1990s with the discovery of several feathered dinosaurs. Paul's ideas and style have had a significant impact on dinosaur art, and likely will continue to do so for some time.

New extinction theories, the meteor impact

Traditionally paleontology had followed geology in preferring uniformitarian mechanisms, despite the promotion by Eugene Merle Shoemaker of the importance of catastrophic impacts. During the renaissance period Walter Alvarez and others found iridium in the Cretaceous–Tertiary boundary layer. Also the Chicxulub Crater, was identified and determined to be due to a meteor impact. These discoveries led to the acceptance and popularisation of the idea that the extinction had been caused by an impact event. This in turn undermined the assumption that dinosaurs had become extinct because they were inferior to mammals. Instead it suggested they had fallen prey to a random event which no large animal could have survived.

Cultural impacts

Bakker's non-technical articles and books, particularly *The Dinosaur Heresies*, have contributed significantly to the popularization of dinosaur science.

The Land Before Time was one of the first films to portray theropods in the correct horizontal pose, though the tripod pose was used more often.Wikipedia:Citation needed

The 1993 film version of *Jurassic Park* was perhaps the most significant event in raising public awareness of dinosaur renaissance theories. For the first time in a major film, dinosaurs were portrayed as intelligent, agile, warm-blooded animals, rather than lumbering monsters more common to older films. Jack Horner was a consultant, and the artwork of Gregory Paul, Mark Hallett, Doug Henderson, and John Gurche were used in pre-production. While the dinosaurs eventually shown in the films had various anatomical inaccuracies, all four of these artists are in the on-screen credits as "Dinosaur Specialists". Bakker himself was not consulted or credited, but his research is referenced by one of the characters in the film, and a Bakker look-alike appears in the sequel *The Lost World*.

Further reading

- Bakker, R. T. (1986). *The Dinosaur Heresies*. New York: William Morrow. ISBN 0-688-04287-2.
- Paul, G. S. (1988). *Predatory Dinosaurs of the World*. New York: Simon & Schuster. ISBN 0-671-61946-2.
- Czerkas, S. J.; Olson, E. C., eds. (1986). *Dinosaurs Past and Present, Volumes I and II*. Los Angeles: Natural History Museum of Los Angeles County. ISBN 0-938644-24-6.

Appendix

References

[1] Although dinosaurs are reptiles, views on them as being cold-blooded animals have changed in recent years; see physiology for more details.

[2] https://www.inverse.com/article/24268-dinosaur-chicken-gene-editing

[3] Padian, K. (2004). "Basal Avialae". In Weishampel, D.B.; Dodson, P.; Osmolska, H. (eds.). *The Dinosauria (Second ed.)*. Berkeley: University of California Press. pp. 210–231.

[4] Nesbitt, S. J., Barrett, P. M., Werning, S., Sidor, C. A., and A. J. Charig. (2012). "The oldest dinosaur? A Middle Triassic dinosauriform from Tanzania." *Biology Letters*.

[5] Lindow, B.E.K. (2011). "Bird Evolution Across the K–Pg Boundary and the Basal Neornithine Diversification." In Dyke, G. and Kaiser, G. (eds.)*Living Dinosaurs: The Evolutionary History of Modern Birds*, John Wiley & Sons, Ltd, Chichester, UK.

[6] Herculano Alvarenga, Washington Jones, and Andrés Rinderknecht (2010). The youngest record of phorusrhacid birds (Aves, Phorusrhacidae) from the late Pleistocene of Uruguay. Neues Jahrbuch für Geologie and Paläont. Abh, 256: 229–234; Stuttgart.

[7] Gerald Mayr (1009). Paleogene Fossil Birds

[8] Weishampel, D.B., Dodson, P., Oslmolska, H. (1990). "The Dinosauria". *University of California Press*. pp. 733.

[9] Norell, M., Gaffney, E.S., and Dingus, L. (2000). *Discovering dinosaurs: Evolution, extinction, and the lessons of prehistory*. University of California Press.

[10] Chiappe, L.M. and Witmer, L.M. (2002). *Mesozoic Birds: Above the Heads of Dinosaurs*. Berkeley: University of California Press.

[11] Hansell M (2000). *Bird Nests and Construction Behaviour*. University of Cambridge Press

[12] D. C. Deeming; G. Mayr (2018). "Pelvis morphology suggests that early Mesozoic birds were too heavy to contact incubate their eggs". Journal of Evolutionary Biology. in press. doi: 10.1111/jeb.13256.

[13] Varricchio, David J.; Horner, John J.; Jackson, Frankie D. (2002). "Embryos and eggs for the Cretaceous theropod dinosaur Troodon formosus". Journal of Vertebrate Paleontology. 22 (3): 564–576. doi:10.1671/0272-4634(2002)022[0564:EAEFTC]2.0.CO;2.

[14] Myers, T.S.; Fiorillo, A.R. (2009). "Evidence for gregarious behavior and age segregation in sauropod dinosaurs". Palaeogeography, Palaeoclimatology, Palaeoecology. 274: 96–104. doi: 10.1016/j.palaeo.2009.01.002.

[15] Godefroit, P., Sinitsa, S., Dhouailly, D., Bolotsky, Y., and Sizov, A. "Feather-like structures and scales in a Jurassic neornithischian dinosaur from Siberia." Program and Abstracts of the 73rd Meeting of the Society of Vertebrate Paleontology http://vertpaleo.org/PDFS/71/71353d57-1619-409e-9777-1f7c797d2ec6.pdf , October 2013.

[16] Archaeopteryx: a missing link http://www.ucmp.berkeley.edu/diapsids/birds/archaeopteryx.html. Berkeley: University of California. Museum of Paleontology.

[17] Dingus, L. and Rowe, T. (1998). *The Mistaken Extinction – Dinosaur Evolution and the Origin of Birds*. New York: W. H. Freeman.

[18] Paleobiogeography and biodiversity of Late Maastrichtian dinosaurs: how many dinosaur species went extinct at the Cretaceous-Tertiary boundary? - GeoScienceWorld http://bsgf.geoscienceworld.org/content/183/6/547

[19] Mullen, L. (2004). " Multiple Impacts http://www.astrobio.net/exclusive/1253/multiple-impacts". *Astrobiology Magazine*.

[20] Randall 2015.

[21] Benton, M.J. (2000). "A brief history of dinosaur paleontology". pp. 10–44, In Paul, G.S. (ed.). *The Scientific American book of dinosaurs*. St. Martin's Press, New York.

[22] Rupke, N. (1994). *Richard Owen: A Victorian Naturalist*. New Haven: Yale University Press.

[23] Bakker, R.T. (1986). *The Dinosaur Heresies*. New York: William Morrow.

[24] //tools.wmflabs.org/ftl/cgi-bin/ftl?st=&su=Dinosaurs&library=OLBP

[25] //tools.wmflabs.org/ftl/cgi-bin/ftl?st=&su=Dinosaurs

[26] //tools.wmflabs.org/ftl/cgi-bin/ftl?st=&su=Dinosaurs&library=0CHOOSE0

[27] http://www.worldcat.org/title/humongous-book-of-dinosaurs/oclc/36301321&referer=brief_results

[28] https://web.archive.org/web/20130529094636/http://www.cisneros-heredia.org/infotrans/usfq/ornitofauna/pdfs/zhou2004.pdf

[29] http://adsabs.harvard.edu/abs/2004NW.....91..455Z

[30] //doi.org/10.1007/s00114-004-0570-4

[31] //www.ncbi.nlm.nih.gov/pubmed/15365634

[32] http://www.cisneros-heredia.org/infotrans/usfq/ornitofauna/pdfs/zhou2004.pdf

[33] http://www.dinodatabase.com/

[34] http://www.gspauldino.com/

[35] http://skeletaldrawing.com/

[36] http://lhldigital.lindahall.org/cdm/landingpage/collection/dino

[37] http://dino.lindahall.org/

[38] http://www.bbc.co.uk/nature/life/dinosaur

[39] http://vimeo.com/74636204

[40] http://www.scientificamerican.com/article/how-dinosaurs-got-their-start-and-met-their-end-video/

[41] http://www.nhm.ac.uk/nature-online/life/dinosaurs-other-extinct-creatures/index.html

[42] http://www.dinosaurnews.org/

[43] http://www.ucmp.berkeley.edu/diapsids/dinosaur.html

[44] http://www.livescience.com/dinosaurs/

[45] http://www.enchantedlearning.com/subjects/dinosaurs/

[46] http://www.geol.umd.edu/~tholtz/dinoappendix/HoltzappendixWinter2010.pdf

[47] http://palaeo-electronica.org/

[48] Weishampel, Dodson & Osmolska, 2004, The Dinosauria

[49] Senter, P. (2007). "A new look at the phylogeny of Coelurosauria (Dinosauria: Theropoda)." *Journal of Systematic Palaeontology*, ()

[50] PC Sereno (1997) "The origin and evolution of dinosaurs" Annu. Rev. Earth Planet. Sci. 25:435-489

[51] Richard J. Butler, Paul Upchurch and David B. Norman (2008). The phylogeny of the ornithischian dinosaurs. Journal of Systematic Palaeontology, 6, pp 1-40 doi:10.1017/S1477201907002271

[52] Owens, 1842.

[53] Seeley, 1888. While the paper was published in 1888, it was first delivered in 1887.

[54] Benton, Michael 2004. The classification scheme is available online http://palaeo.gly.bris.ac.uk/benton/vertclass.html

[55] Weishampel, 2004

[56] http://adsabs.harvard.edu/abs/1887RSPS...43..165S

[57] //doi.org/10.1098/rspl.1887.0117

[58] Strauss, Bob."Why Were Dinosaurs So Big? The Facts and Theories Behind Dinosaur Gigantism". About Education. http://dinosaurs.about.com/od/dinosaurevolution/a/bigdinos.htm

[59] Carpenter, K. (2006). "Biggest of the big: a critical re-evaluation of the mega-sauropod *Amphicoelias fragillimus*." In Foster, J.R. and Lucas, S.G., eds., 2006, *Paleontology and Geology of the Upper Jurassic Morrison Formation*. New Mexico Museum of Natural History and Science Bulletin **36**: 131–138.

[60] Giant dinosaur slims down a bit. *BBC News* Science & Environment. https://www.bbc.co.uk/news/science-environment-40889321

[61] http://www.awf.org/wildlife-conservation/ostrich

[62] Xu, X., Zhao, Q., Norell, M., Sullivan, C., Hone, D., Erickson, G., Wang, X., Han, F. and Guo, Y. (2009). "A new feathered maniraptoran dinosaur fossil that fills a morphological gap in avian origin." *Chinese Science Bulletin*, 6 pages, accepted November 15, 2008.

[63] Which was the smallest dinosaur? http://www.technosaurs.ca/tag/default.aspx?id=114 Royal Tyrrell Museum. Last accessed 2008-05-23.

[64] Conservation International (Content Partner); Mark McGinley (Topic Editor). 2008. "Biological diversity in the Caribbean Islands." In: Encyclopedia of Earth. Eds. Cutler J. Cleveland (Washington, D.C.: Environmental Information Coalition, National Council for Science and the Environment). [First published in the Encyclopedia of Earth May 3, 2007; Last revised August 22, 2008; Retrieved November 9, 2009]. <http://www.eoearth.org/article/Biological_diversity_in_the_Caribbean_Islands>

[65] Wedel, M. 2013. A giant, skeletally immature individual of *Apatosaurus* from the Morrison Formation of Oklahoma http://svpca.org/years/2013_edinburgh/abstracts.pdf. The Annual Symposium of Vertebrate Palaeontology and Comparative Anatomy 2013:45.

[66] José L. Carballido; Diego Pol; Alejandro Otero; Ignacio A. Cerda; Leonardo Salgado ; Alberto C. Garrido ; Jahandar Ramezani ; Néstor R. Cúneo ; Javier M. Krause (2017). "A new giant titanosaur sheds light on body mass evolution among sauropod dinosaurs". Proceedings of the Royal Society B: Biological Sciences. 284 (1860): 20171219. doi:10.1098/rspb.2017.1219.

[67] Lacovara, K; Harris J., Lammana M., Novas F., Martinez R., and Amrosio, A. 2004. An enormous sauropod from the Maastrichtian Pari Aike Formation of southernmost Patagonia" *Journal of Vertebrate Paleontology* 24(3) Supplement, 81A

[68] Giant dinosaur slims down a bit. *BBC News* Science & Environment. https://www.bbc.co.uk/news/science-environment-40889321

[69] V. D. Diaz, X. P. Suberpiola, and J. L. Sanz. 2013. Appendicular skeleton and dermal armour of the Late Cretaceous titanosaur Lirainosaurus astibia (Dinosauria: Sauropoda) from Spain. Palaeontologia Electronica 16(2):19A

[70] Wilson. J. A. (2006): An Overview of Titanosaur Evolution and Phylogeny. En (Colectivo Arqueológico-Paleontológico Salense, Ed.): Actas de las III Jornadas sobre Dinosaurios y su Entorno. 169-190. Salas de los Infantes, Burgos, España. 169

[71] https://www.researchgate.net/publication/228465395_Rastrilladas_de_icnitas_teropodas_gigantes_del_Jurasico_Superior_Sinclinal_de_Iouaridene_Marruecos

[72] Supplementary Information http://www.sciencemag.org/content/suppl/2014/09/10/science.1258750.DC1/Ibrahim.SM.pdf

[73] Wood, The Guinness Book of Animal Facts and Feats. Sterling Pub Co Inc (1983),

[74] *CRC Handbook of Avian Body Masses* by John B. Dunning Jr. (Editor). CRC Press (1992), .

[75] Arizmendi, M.C.; Rodríguez-Flores, C.; Soberanes-González, C. (2010). Schulenberg, T.S., ed. "Short-crested Coquette (Lophornis brachylophus)" http://neotropical.birds.cornell.edu/portal/species/overview?p_p_spp=241691 *Neotropical Birds Online*. Ithaca: Cornell Lab of Ornithology.

[76] Powers, D. R. (1991). Diurnal variation in mass, metabolic rate, and respiratory quotient in Anna's and Costa's hummingbirds. Physiological Zoology, 850-870.

[77] Del Hoyo, J. Elliott, A. and Sargatal, J. (1999) Handbook of the Birds of the World Volume 5: Barn-owls to Hummingbirds Lynx Edicions, Barcelona

[78] audubonbirds https://archive.is/20130414075706/http://www.audubonbirds.org/species/Birds/Bumblebee-Hummingbird.html

[79]

[80] Naish, D. (2012). Happy 6th Birthday, Tetrapod Zoology (part II) http://blogs.scientificamerican.com/tetrapod-zoology/2012/01/25/happy-6th-birthday-tetrapod-zoology-part-ii/ Tetrapod Zoology, January 25, 2012.

[81]

[82] name=G.S.Paul2010

[83] http://www.tyrrellmuseum.com/media/HadrSymp2011Abstract.pdf

[84]

[85] Bakker, R. T. 1980. Dinosaur heresy-dinosaur renaissance; pp. 351-462 in R. D. K. Thomas and E. C. Olson (eds.), A Cold Look at the Warm-blooded Dinosaurs. AAAS Selected Symposia Series No. 28.

[86]

[87] Galton, Peter M.; Upchurch, Paul, 2004, "Stegosauria" In: Weishampel, David B.; Dodson, Peter; and Osmólska, Halszka (eds.): *The Dinosauria*, 2nd edition, Berkeley: University of California Press. Pp. 344-345

[88] http://www.livescience.com/animalworld/060301_big_carnivores.html

[89] http://www.geol.umd.edu/~tholtz/dinoappendix/HoltzappendixWinter2011.pdf

[90] https://dinosaurusblog.com/2016/08/01/dinosauri-rekordy/

[91] Skinner, Justin. "ROM Puts Oldest Dinosaur Eggs Ever Discovered on Display" http: //www.insidetoronto.com/news/local/article/812684--rom-puts-oldest-dinosaur-eggs-ever-discovered-on-display. insidetoronto.com. May 6, 2010.

[92] Moskvitch, Katia. "Eggs with the Oldest Known Embryos of a Dinosaur Found" https://www. bbc.co.uk/news/science-environment-11734616. BBC News. November 12, 2010.

[93] "First Discoveries," Carpenter (1999); page 5.

[94] "First Discoveries," Carpenter (1999); page 4.

[95]

[96] Simon, D. J. (2014). " Giant Dinosaur (theropod) Eggs of the Oogenus Macroelongatoolithus (Elongatoolithidae) from Southeastern Idaho: Taxonomic, Paleobiogeographic, and Reproductive Implications. http://scholarworks.montana.edu/xmlui/bitstream/handle/1/8693/ SimonD0814.pdf?sequence=1" (Doctoral dissertation, Montana State University, Bozeman).

[97] Laura E. Wilson, Karen Chin, Frankie D. Jackson, and Emily S. Bray. V. Paleobiology and eggs http://www.ucmp.berkeley.edu/science/eggshell/eggshell2.php. *UCMP Online Exhibits: Fossil Eggshell*

[98] The Palaeobiology Database http://www.paleodb.org/cgi-bin/bridge.pl?action= basicTaxonInfo&taxon_no=82906

[99] The Palaeobiology Database http://www.paleodb.org/cgi-bin/bridge.pl?action= checkTaxonInfo&taxon_no=67205

[100] The Palaeobiology Database http://www.paleodb.org/cgi-bin/bridge.pl?action= checkTaxonInfo&taxon_no=67198

[101] The Palaeobiology Database http://www.paleodb.org/cgi-bin/bridge.pl?action= basicTaxonInfo&taxon_no=81056

[102] The Palaeobiology Database http://www.paleodb.org/cgi-bin/bridge.pl?action= basicTaxonInfo&taxon_no=67185

[103] The Palaeobiology Database http://www.paleodb.org/cgi-bin/bridge.pl?action= basicTaxonInfo&taxon_no=81709

[104] The Palaeobiology Database http://www.paleodb.org/cgi-bin/bridge.pl?action= basicTaxonInfo&taxon_no=67183

[105] The Palaeobiology Database http://www.paleodb.org/cgi-bin/bridge.pl?action= basicTaxonInfo&taxon_no=98798

[106] The Palaeobiology Database http://www.paleodb.org/cgi-bin/bridge.pl?action= basicTaxonInfo&taxon_no=65584

[107] The Palaeobiology Database http://www.paleodb.org/cgi-bin/bridge.pl?action= basicTaxonInfo&taxon_no=67189

[108] The Palaeobiology Database http://www.paleodb.org/cgi-bin/bridge.pl?action= basicTaxonInfo&taxon_no=56741

[109] The Palaeobiology Database http://www.paleodb.org/cgi-bin/bridge.pl?action= basicTaxonInfo&taxon_no=67196

[110] The Palaeobiology Database http://www.paleodb.org/cgi-bin/bridge.pl?action= basicTaxonInfo&taxon_no=68519

[111] The Palaeobiology Database http://www.paleodb.org/cgi-bin/bridge.pl?action= checkTaxonInfo&taxon_no=65562

[112] The Palaeobiology Database http://www.paleodb.org/cgi-bin/bridge.pl?action= checkTaxonInfo&taxon_no=84312

[113] The Palaeobiology Database http://www.paleodb.org/cgi-bin/bridge.pl?action= checkTaxonInfo&taxon_no=67195

[114] The Palaeobiology Database http://www.paleodb.org/cgi-bin/bridge.pl?action= checkTaxonInfo&taxon_no=67290

[115] The Palaeobiology Database http://www.paleodb.org/cgi-bin/bridge.pl?action= checkTaxonInfo&taxon_no=65567

[116] The Palaeobiology Database http://www.paleodb.org/cgi-bin/bridge.pl?action= checkTaxonInfo&taxon_no=81708

[117] https://www.bbc.co.uk/news/science-environment-11734616

[118] http://adsabs.harvard.edu/abs/2001CRASE.332..647D

[119] //doi.org/10.1016/s1251-8050%2801%2901580-4

[120] http://adsabs.harvard.edu/abs/2005Sci...309..761R

[121] //doi.org/10.1126/science.1114942

[122] http://www.insidetoronto.com/news/local/article/812684--rom-puts-oldest-dinosaur-eggs-ever-discovered-on-display

[123] http://palaeo.gly.bris.ac.uk/palaeofiles/eggs/default.html

[124] Bakker, R.T. (1968). "The superiority of dinosaurs" *Discovery*, v. 3(2), p. 11-22

[125] http://jeb.biologists.org/content/184/1/63.full.pdf

[126] Full text currently online at and Detailed anatomical analyses can be found at

[127] This is also one of several topics featured in a post on Naish's blog, – note *Mirischia* was a coelurosaur, which Naish believes was closely related to *Compsognathus*.

[128] Ward, Peter (2006) *Out of thin air: Dinosaurs, birds, and earth's ancient atmosphere* https//books.google.com Pages 159–198, National Academies Press.

[129] News summary at

[130] But note that this paper's main subject is that the fossil provided strong evidence of a 4-chambered heart, which is not widely accepted.

[131] Chinsamy, Anusuya; and Hillenius, Willem J. (2004). "Physiology of nonavian dinosaurs". *The Dinosauria*, 2nd. 643–659.

[132] Note Kristina Rogers also published papers under her maiden name, Kristina Curry.

[133] Ricqles, A. J. de. (1974). *Evolution of endothermy: histological evidence*. Evolutionary Theory 1: 51–80

[134] Fastovsky & Weishampel 2009, p.258.

[135] Fastovsky & Weishampel 2009, p.260.

[136] Abstract also online at

[137]

[138] This was recognized not later than 1909: The arguments and many of the images are also presented in

[139] Fastovsky & Weishampel 2009, p.251.

[140] Fastovsky & Weishampel 2009, p.252.

[141] See also image at

[142] See also and

[143] http://tools.wmflabs.org/timescale/?Ma=115–105

[144] See also

[145] http://www.ploscollections.org/article/info%3Adoi%2F10.1371%2Fjournal.pone.0023339; jsessionid=4A4B8A5E7DD12BC3E642D5AE30B80069.ambra02

[146] Fastovsky & Weishampel 2009, p.255.

[147] The earliest clear evidence of hair or fur is in fossils of *Castorocauda*, from 164M years ago in the mid Jurassic, See also the news item at It has been argued since the 1950s at the latest that there may be evidence of hair in early-Triassic cynodonts such as *Thrinaxodon*: and but the foramina (small tunnels) in cynodont snout bones are ambiguous evidence at best, since similar foramina are found in a few living reptiles: and

[148] See also the explanation of this, with useful illustrations, at

[149] http://palaeo-electronica.org/1999_2/gigan/issue2_99.htm

[150] https://www.nytimes.com/library/national/science/042100sci-paleo-dinosaur.html

[151] http://www.adelaide.edu.au/adelaidean/issues/5501/news5550.html

[152] link https://archive.org/details/proceedingsofaca19acad

[153] For example in 1923, three years before Heilmans's book, Roy Chapman Andrews found a good *Oviraptor* fossil in *Mongolia*, but Henry Fairfield Osborn, who analyzed the fossil in 1924, misidentified the furcula as an interclavicle; described in

[154] In an *Oviraptor*: See the summary and pictures at

[155] _ full text currently online at This lists a large number of theropods in which furculae have been found, as well as describing those of *Suchomimus Tenerensis* and *Tyrannosaurus rex*.

[156] University of Maryland department of geology home page, "Theropoda I" on *Avetheropoda* http://www.geol.umd.edu/~tholtz/G104/10422ther.htm, 14 July 2006.

[157] **Scienceblogs:** *Limusaurus* is awesome http://scienceblogs.com/tetrapodzoology/2009/06/limusaurus_is_awesome.php .

[158] Developmental Biology 8e Online. Chapter 16: Did Birds Evolve From the Dinosaurs? http://8e.devbio.com/article.php?ch=16&id=161

[159] Vargas AO, Wagner GP and Gauthier, JA. 2009. Limusaurus and bird digit identity. Available from Nature Precedings http://hdl.handle.net/10101/npre.2009.3828.1

[160] Feduccia, A. (2012). *Riddle of the Feathered Dragons: Hidden Birds of China.* Yale University Press, ,

[161] Foth, C. (2012). "On the identification of feather structures in stem-line representatives of birds: evidence from fossils and actuopalaeontology." *Paläontologische Zeitschrift,*

[162] Chinsamy, Anusuya; and Hillenius, Willem J. (2004). "Physiology of nonavian dinosaurs". *The Dinosauria,* 2nd. 643–659.

[163] See commentary on the article https://www.theguardian.com/life/news/story/0,12976,1326559,00.html

[164] Also covers the Reproduction Biology paragraph in the Feathered dinosaurs and the bird connection section.

[165] Organ CL, Schweitzer MH, Zheng W, Freimark LM, Cantley LC, Asara JM, 2008, "Molecular phylogenetics of mastodon and *Tyrannosaurus rex*", *Science* **320**: 499

[166] Kaye TG, Gaugler G, Sawlowicz Z, 2008, "Dinosaurian soft tissues interpreted as bacterial biofilms", *PLoS ONE* **3**, e2808

[167] Peterson JE, Lenczewski ME, Scherer RP, 2010, "Influence of microbial biofilms on the preservation of primary soft tissue in fossil and extant archosaurs", *PLoS ONE* **5**, e13334

[168] Bern M, Phinney BS, Goldberg D, 2009, "Reanalysis of *Tyrannosaurus rex* mass spectra", *Journal of Proteome Research,* **8**: 4328–4332

[169] Cleland TP et al., 2015, "Mass spectrometry and antibody-based characterization of blood vessels from *Brachylophosaurus canadensis, Journal of Proteome Research* **14**: 5252–5262

[170] Michael Buckley, Stacey Warwood, Bart van Dongen, Andrew C. Kitchener, Phillip L. Manning, 2017, "A fossil protein chimera; difficulties in discriminating dinosaur peptide sequences from modern cross-contamination", *Proceedings of the Royal Society B* **284**: 20170544

[171] See also

[172] Feduccia, A. (1993).

[173] Cretaceous tracks of a bird with a similar lifestyle have been found -

[174] Videler, J.J. 2005: Avian Flight. Oxford University. Press, Oxford.

[175] Summarized at

[176] There is a video clip of a very young chick doing this at

[177] Summarized in

[178] Chatterjee, Sankar, Templin, R.J. (2004) "Feathered coelurosaurs from China: new light on the arboreal origin of avian flight" pp. 251-281. In Feathered Dragons: Studies on the Transition from Dinosaurs to Birds (P. J. Currie, E. B. Koppelhus, M. A. Shugar, and J. L. Wright (eds.). Indiana University Press, Bloomington.

[179] Samuel F. Tarsitano, Anthony P. Russell, Francis Horne1, Christopher Plummer and Karen Millerchip (2000) On the Evolution of Feathers from an Aerodynamic and Constructional View Point" *American Zoologist* 2000 40(4):676-686;

[180] Hopson, James A. "Ecomorphology of avian and nonavian theropod phalangeal proportions:Implications for the arboreal versus terrestrial origin of bird flight" (2001) From New Perspectives on the Origin and Early Evolution of Birds: Proceedings of the International Symposium in Honor of John H. Ostrom. J. Gauthier and L. F. Gall, eds. New Haven: Peabody Mus. Nat. Hist., Yale Univ. © 2001 Peabody Museum of Natural History, Yale University. All rights reserved.

[181] Paul, G.S. (2002). "Dinosaurs of the Air: The Evolution and Loss of Flight in Dinosaurs and Birds." Baltimore: Johns Hopkins University Press. page 257

[182] Parsons, William L.; Parsons, Kristen M. (2015). "Morphological Variations within the Ontogeny of Deinonychus antirrhopus (Theropoda, Dromaeosauridae)". PLoS ONE 10 (4). doi: 10.1371/journal.pone.0121476. e0121476.

[183] Joel D. Hutson & Kelda N. Hutson, 2018, "Retention of the flight-adapted avian finger-joint complex in the Ostrich helps identify when wings began evolving in dinosaurs", *Ostrich: Journal of African Ornithology* DOI: 10.2989/00306525.2017.1422566

[184] https://www.webcitation.org/5QU8U23Dq?url=http://ravenel.si.edu/paleo/paleoglot/files/Barsbold_83b.pdf

[185] http://apnews.excite.com/article/20140731/us-sci-shrinking-dinosaurs-a5c053f221.html

[186] https://doi.org/10.1016/S0748-3007(03)00069-0

[187] http://www.cumv.cornell.edu/pdf/Bostwick_2003.pdf

[188] http://www.dinosauria.com

[189] https://web.archive.org/web/20070209063731/http://dinosauria.com/jdp/archie/archie.htm

[190] https://web.archive.org/web/20060812210343/http://www.dinosauria.com/jdp/archie/dinoarch.htm

[191] https://doi.org/10.1126/science.1120331

[192] http://www.ucmp.berkeley.edu/diapsids/avians.html

[193] http://www.talkorigins.org/faqs/archaeopteryx.html

[194] http://www.amnh.org/exhibitions/dinosaurs-among-us

[195] http://news.nationalgeographic.com/2016/04/160405-dinosaurs-feathers-birds-museum-new-york-science/

[196] Foster, Michael; Lankester, E. Ray 1898–1903. *The scientific memoirs of Thomas Henry Huxley*. 4 vols and supplement. London: Macmillan.

[197] Kundrát, M. 2004. When did theropods become feathered? – evidence for pre-Archaeopteryx feathery appendages. Journal of Experimental Zoology (Mol. Dev. Evol.) 302B, 355-364.

[198] Hopp, Thomas J., Orsen, Mark J. (2004) "Feathered Dragons: Studies on the Transition from Dinosaurs to Birds. Chapter 11. Dinosaur Brooding Behavior and the Origin of Flight Feathers" Currie, Koppelhaus, Shugar, Wright. Indiana University Press. Bloomington, IN. USA.

[199] Norell, M. Xu, X. (2005) " The Varieties of Tyrannosaurs http://www.naturalhistorymag.com/htmlsite/master.html?http://www.naturalhistorymag.com/htmlsite/0505/0505_feature.html" Natural History Magazine May 2005.

[200] Zelenitsky, Darla K.; Therrien, Francois; Erickson, Gregory M.; DeBuhr, Christopher L.; Kobayashi, Yoshitsugu; Eberth, David A.; Hadfield, Frank (10/26/12). "Feathered Non-Avian Dinosaurs From North America Provide Insight into Wing Origins" *Science* 338 (510).

[201] http://www.ucmp.berkeley.edu/diapsids/avians.html

[202] http://www.bbc.co.uk/programmes/b099v33p

[203] The abbreviation is derived from the juxtaposition of **K**, the common abbreviation for the Cretaceous, which in turn originates from the correspondent German term *Kreide*, and **Pg**, which is the abbreviation for the Paleogene.

[204] The former designation includes the term 'Tertiary' (abbreviated as **T**), which is now discouraged as a formal geochronological unit by the International Commission on Stratigraphy.<ref>

[205] Shocked minerals have their internal structure deformed, and are created by intense pressures as in nuclear blasts and meteorite impacts.

[206] A *megatsunami* is a massive movement of sea waters, which can reach inland tens or hundreds of kilometers.

[207] https://books.google.com/books?id=8i8UzOYJlgUC

[208] //www.worldcat.org/oclc/54537112

[209] http://www.geolsoc.org.uk/chicxulub

[210] https://web.archive.org/web/20070629230804/http://www.lpl.arizona.edu/SIC/impact_cratering/Chicxulub/Chicx_title.html

[211] http://www.lpl.arizona.edu/SIC/impact_cratering/Chicxulub/Chicx_title.html

[212] http://www.ucmp.berkeley.edu/education/events/cowen1b.html

[213] http://www.ucmp.berkeley.edu/diapsids/extinction.html

[214] https://gsa.confex.com/gsa/2017AM/webprogram/Session43180.html

[215] //tools.wmflabs.org/geohack/geohack.php?pagename=Chicxulub_crater&params=21_24_0_N_89_31_0_W_type:landmark_scale:5000000_region:MX

[216] Verschuur, 20–21.

[217] Bates.

218

[219] Verschuur, 20.
[220] Weinreb.
[221] Mason.
[222] Hildebrand, Penfield, et al.
[223]
[224] Morás.
[225] Frankel, 50.
[226] Hildebrand interview.
[227] Pope, Baines, et al.
[228] Sharpton & Marin.
[229] Adamsky and Smirnov, 19.
[230] Melosh, interview.
[231] Melosh. "On the ground, you would feel an effect similar to an oven on broil, lasting for about an hour [...] causing global forest fires."
[232] Hildebrand, Penfield, et al.; 5.
[233] Perlman.
[234] Pope, Ocampo, et al.
[235] Hildebrand, Penfield, et al.; 1.
[236] Hildebrand, Penfield, et al.; 3.
[237] Hildebrand, Penfield, et al.; 4.
[238] Kring, "Discovering the Crater".
[239] Sigurdsson.
[240]
[241] Ingham.
[242] Alvarez, W. interview.
[243]
[244] Rincon.
[245] Kring, "Environment Consequences".
[246] Keller, et al.
[247] Alvarez.
[248] Web Elements.
[249] Quivx.
[250] Mayell.
[251] Stewart, Allen.
[252] Kelley, Gurov.
[253] Stewart.
[254] Mullen, "Shiva".
[255] Weisstein.
[256]
[257] Than.
[258] Dunham.
[259] Chicxulub and the Exploration of Large Peak-Ring Impact Craters through Scientific Drilling https://www.geosociety.org/gsatoday/science/G352A/GSATG352A.pdf (PDF). David A. Kring, Philippe Claeys, Sean P.S. Gulick, Joanna V. Morgan, and Gareth S. Collins. *The Geological Society of America.* 2017.
[260] Probing the impact-generated hydrothermal system in the peak ring of the Chicxulub crater and its potential as a habitat https://www.hou.usra.edu/meetings/lpsc2017/pdf/1212.pdf. (PDF) Barry J. Shaulis, Ulrich Riller, Charles Cockell, Marco J., and L. Coolen. *Lunar and Planetary Science XLVIII* (2017)
[261] *The Day the Dinosaurs Died*, BBC2 television, 1 July 2017, 6 to 7 pm
[262] https://web.archive.org/web/20000826213556/http://cwihp.si.edu/pdf/bull4a.pdf
[263] http://cwihp.si.edu/pdf/bull4a.pdf
[264] http://imdb.com/title/tt0103400/
[265] http://www.boulder.swri.edu/~bottke/Reprints/Bottke_2007_Nature_449_48_Baptistina_KT.pdf
[266] http://adsabs.harvard.edu/abs/2007Natur.449...48B

[267] //doi.org/10.1038/nature06070

[268] //www.ncbi.nlm.nih.gov/pubmed/17805288

[269] https://web.archive.org/web/20071128093102/http://www.geosc.psu.edu/people/faculty/personalpages/tbralower/Braloweretal1998.pdf

[270] http://adsabs.harvard.edu/abs/1998Geo....26..331B

[271] //doi.org/10.1130/0091-7613%281998%29026%3C0331%3Atctbcc%3E2.3.co%3B2

[272] http://www.geosc.psu.edu/people/faculty/personalpages/tbralower/Braloweretal1998.pdf

[273] http://adsabs.harvard.edu/abs/1994GPC.....9..263C

[274] //doi.org/10.1016/0921-8181%2894%2990020-5

[275] https://web.archive.org/web/20151017002003/http://geology.physadvice.net/2006/12/05/

[276] http://geology.physadvice.net/2006/12/05/

[277] http://adsabs.harvard.edu/abs/1975GSAB...86.1617G

[278] //doi.org/10.1130/0016-7606%281975%2986%3C1617%3APACOTI%3E2.0.CO%3B2

[279] http://geology.geoscienceworld.org/cgi/content/abstract/19/9/867

[280] http://adsabs.harvard.edu/abs/1991Geo....19..867H

[281] //doi.org/10.1130/0091-7613%281991%29019%3C0867%3ACCAPCT%3E2.3.CO%3B2

[282] https://web.archive.org/web/20071114031858/http://afp.google.com/article/ALeqM5jz3TGi2zcsmdYQDxwbdCwq2kanMA

[283] http://afp.google.com/article/ALeqM5jz3TGi2zcsmdYQDxwbdCwq2kanMA

[284] https://web.archive.org/web/20070623000329/http://geoweb.princeton.edu/people/faculty/keller/Keller_et_al_%20EPSL_2007.pdf

[285] http://adsabs.harvard.edu/abs/2007E&PSL.255..339K

[286] //doi.org/10.1016/j.epsl.2006.12.026

[287] http://geoweb.princeton.edu/people/faculty/keller/Keller_et_al_%20EPSL_2007.pdf

[288] https://web.archive.org/web/20080905133453/http://www.uark.edu/~meteor/abst37-8.htm#kelley

[289] http://adsabs.harvard.edu/abs/2002M&PS...37.1031K

[290] //doi.org/10.1111/j.1945-5100.2002.tb00875.x

[291] http://www.uark.edu/~meteor/abst37-8.htm#kelley

[292] http://adsabs.harvard.edu/abs/2003AsBio...3..133K

[293] //doi.org/10.1089/153110703321632471

[294] //www.ncbi.nlm.nih.gov/pubmed/12809133

[295] https://web.archive.org/web/20071010021337/http://www.lpl.arizona.edu/SIC/impact_cratering/Chicxulub/Discovering_crater.html

[296] http://www.lpl.arizona.edu/SIC/impact_cratering/Chicxulub/Discovering_crater.html

[297] http://adsabs.harvard.edu/abs/2004BVol...66..735M

[298] //doi.org/10.1007/s00445-004-0355-9

[299] http://www.moyak.com/papers/citation-searching.html

[300] http://news.nationalgeographic.com/news/2005/04/0415_050418_chicxulub.html

[301] http://www.spacedaily.com/news/deepimpact-04r.html

[302] http://www.spacedaily.com/news/deepimpact-04p.html

[303] http://www.sfgate.com/cgi-bin/article.cgi?f=/c/a/2007/09/06/MNVFRUVCK.DTL

[304] http://adsabs.harvard.edu/abs/1997JGR...10221645P

[305] //doi.org/10.1029/97JE01743

[306] //www.ncbi.nlm.nih.gov/pubmed/11541145

[307] http://adsabs.harvard.edu/abs/1996Geo....24..527P

[308] //doi.org/10.1130/0091-7613%281996%29024%3C0527%3ASEOTCC%3E2.3.CO%3B2

[309] //www.ncbi.nlm.nih.gov/pubmed/11539331

[310] https://web.archive.org/web/20070928011229/http://www.qivx.com/ispt/elements/ptw_077.php

[311] http://www.qivx.com/ispt/elements/ptw_077.php

[312] //www.ncbi.nlm.nih.gov/pubmed/10800377

[313] http://news.bbc.co.uk/2/hi/science/nature/8550504.stm

[314] http://www.sciencemag.org/cgi/content/abstract/327/5970/1214

[315] http://adsabs.harvard.edu/abs/2010Sci...327.1214S

[316] //doi.org/10.1126/science.1177265

[317] //www.worldcat.org/issn/1095-9203

[318] //www.ncbi.nlm.nih.gov/pubmed/20203042

[319] http://adsabs.harvard.edu/abs/1997NYASA.822..353S

[320] //doi.org/10.1111/j.1749-6632.1997.tb48351.x

[321] //www.ncbi.nlm.nih.gov/pubmed/11543120

[322] https://web.archive.org/web/20111209114719/http://www.gsajournals.org/perlserv/?request= get-document&doi=10.1130%2FB25591.1

[323] http://adsabs.harvard.edu/abs/2005GSAB..117..354S

[324] //doi.org/10.1130/B25591.1

[325] http://www.gsajournals.org/perlserv/?request=get-document&doi=10.1130%2FB25591.1

[326] http://adsabs.harvard.edu/abs/2002Natur.418..520S

[327] //doi.org/10.1038/nature00914

[328] //www.ncbi.nlm.nih.gov/pubmed/12152076

[329] http://www.livescience.com/animals/061128_dinosaur_extinct.html

[330] http://www.webelements.com/webelements/elements/text/Ir/geol.html

[331] https://web.archive.org/web/20071018153637/http://jyi.org/volumes/volume5/issue6/features/ weinreb.html

[332] http://www.jyi.org/volumes/volume5/issue6/features/weinreb.html

[333] http://scienceworld.wolfram.com/physics/RocheLimit.html

[334] https://web.archive.org/web/20111209132114/http://www.nd.edu/~cneal/CRN_Papers/ Schulte10_Sci_Chicxulub.pdf

[335] //www.worldcat.org/issn/0036-8075

[336] http://www3.nd.edu/~cneal/CRN_Papers/Schulte10_Sci_Chicxulub.pdf

[337] http://www.chicxulubcrater.org

[338] http://bbs.keyhole.com/ubb/download.php?Number=1226046

[339] http://www.jpl.nasa.gov/news/features.cfm?feature=8

[340] http://www.lpi.usra.edu/publications/slidesets/craters/slide_37.html

[341] http://www.scientificamerican.com/article.cfm?id=doubts-on-dinosaurs

[342] https://gsa.confex.com/gsa/2017AM/webprogram/Session43180.html

[343] https://newsoffice.mit.edu/2014/volcanic-eruption-dinosaur-extinction-1211 What really killed the dinosaurs? Before an asteroid wiped out the dinosaurs, Earth experienced a short burst of intense volcanism." Jennifer Chu | "MIT News Office," 11 December 2014

[344] Trap http://dictionary.reference.com/browse/trap at dictionary.reference.com

[345] " India's Smoking Gun: Dino-killing Eruptions https://www.sciencedaily.com/releases/2005/ 08/050810130729.htm." *ScienceDaily*, 10 August 2005.

[346] Keller, G., *Deccan volcanism, the Chicxulub impact, and the end-Cretaceous mass extinction: Coincidence? Cause and effect?*, in *Volcanism, Impacts, and Mass Extinctions: Causes and Effects*, GSA Special Paper 505, Pp. 29-55, 2014 abstract http://specialpapers.gsapubs.org/ content/early/2014/06/10/2014.2505_03.1.abstract

[347] Schoene, B., et al., *U-Pb geochronology of the Deccan Traps and relation to the end-Cretaceous mass extinction*, Science, 12 Nov. 2014, abstract http://www.sciencemag.org/cgi/ doi/10.1126/science.aaa0118

[348] http://tolweb.org/Myobatrachinae/16946

[349] Hartman, J.H., Mohabey, D.M., Bingle, M., Scholz, H., Bajpai, S., and Sharma, R., 2006, Initial survivorship of nonmarine molluscan faunas in end-Cretaceous Deccan intertrappean strata, India: Geological Society of America (annual meeting, Philadelphia) Abstracts with Programs, v. 38, no. 7, p. 143.

[350] Sheth, Hetu C. " The Deccan Beyond the Plume Hypothesis http://www.mantleplumes.org/ Deccan.html." *MantlePlumes.org*, 2006.

[351] S.C. Cande & D.R. Stegman; Indian and African plate motions driven by the push force of the Réunion plume head; Nature; Volume 475; pp. 47–52; (7 July 2011)

[352] Chatterjee, Sankar. " The Shiva Crater: Implications for Deccan Volcanism, India-Seychelles Rifting, Dinosaur Extinction, and Petroleum Entrapment at the KT Boundary http://gsa.confex. com/gsa/2003AM/finalprogram/abstract_58126.htm." Paper No. 60-8, Seattle Annual Meeting, November 2003.

[353] - original article at source http://www.astrobio.net/news/article1281.html

[354] https://web.archive.org/web/20110723122146/http://www.geodynamics.no/indexOld.htm

[355] http://www.geodynamics.no/indexOld.htm

[356] http://www.msnbc.msn.com/id/50119631/ns/technology_and_science-science/#.
UMJh4eQ0WSo

[357] http://hoopermuseum.earthsci.carleton.ca/saleem/volcanism.htm

[358] //tools.wmflabs.org/geohack/geohack.php?pagename=Deccan_Traps&params=18_51_N_73_
43_E_region:IN_type:landmark_scale:2500000

[359] National Geographic http://news.nationalgeographic.com/news/2009/05/090501-dinosaur-
lost-world_2.html

[360] //en.wikipedia.org/w/index.php?title=Template:Paleontology&action=edit

[361] Bowler Evolution: The History of an Idea pp. 351–352

[362] Desmond p. 692-697.

[363] Rudwick The Meaning of Fossils p. 39

[364] Rudwick The Meaning of Fossils p. 24

[365] Shen Kuo,Mengxi Bitan (梦溪笔谈 ; Dream Pool Essays) (1088)

[366] Needham, Volume 3, p. 614.

[367] Rudwick The Meaning of Fossils pp. 9–17

[368] Rudwick The Meaning of Fossils pp. 23–33

[369] Rudwick The Meaning of Fossils pp. 33–36

[370] Hooke Micrographia observation XVII

[371] Bowler The Earth Encompassed (1992) pp. 118–119

[372] Rudwick The Meaning of Fossils pp 72–73

[373] Rudwick The Meaning of Fossils pp 61–65

[374] Bowler The Earth Encompassed (1992) p. 117

[375] McGowan the dragon seekers pp. 3–4

[376] Rudwick Georges Cuvier, Fossil Bones and Geological Catastrophes p. 158

[377] McGowan pp. 11–27

[378] Rudwick, Martin Worlds Before Adam: The Reconstruction of Geohistory in the Age of Reform
(2008) pp. 154–155.

[379] Cadbury, Deborah The Dinosaur Hunters (2000) pp. 171–175.

[380] McGowan p. 176

[381] McGowan pp. 70–87

[382] McGowan p. 109

[383] McGowan pp. 78–79

[384] Rudwick The Meaning of Fossils pp. 145–147

[385] Bowler The Earth Encompassed (1992)

[386] Rudwick Worlds before Adam p. 48

[387] Rudwick The Meaning of Fossils pp. 124–125

[388] Rudwick The Meaning of Fossils pp. 156–157

[389] Rudwick The Meaning of Fossils pp. 133–136

[390] McGowan pp. 93–95

[391] McGowan pp. 100–103

[392] Rudwick The Meaning of Fossils pp. 178–184

[393] McGowan pp. 100

[394] Rudwick The Meaning of Fossils p. 119

[395] McGowan p. 8

[396] McGowan pp. 188–191

[397] Larson p. 73

[398] Larson p. 44

[399] Ruckwick The Meaning of fossils pp. 206–207

[400] Larson p. 51

[401] Rudwick The Great Devonian Controversy p. 94

[402] Larson pp. 36–37

[403] Rudwick The Meaning of Fossils p. 213

[404] Rudwick The Meaning of Fossils pp. 200–201

[405] Greene and Depew The Philosophy of Biology pp. 128–130

[406] Bowler and Morus *Making Modern Science* pp. 168–169
[407] Bowler *Evolution: The History of an Idea* p. 150
[408] Larson *Evolution* p. 139
[409] Larson pp. 126–127
[410] Larson pp. 145–147
[411] Everhart *Oceans of Kansas* p. 17
[412] The Bone Wars. From Wyoming Tales and Trails http://www.wyomingtalesandtrails.com/bonewars2.html Wyoming Tales and Trails.
[413] McGowan p. 105
[414] Bowler *Evolution* p. 349
[415] Prothero ch. 8
[416] Bowler *Evolution* p. 337
[417] Eldredge, Niles and S. J. Gould (1972). "Punctuated equilibria: an alternative to phyletic gradualism" http://www.blackwellpublishing.com/ridley/classictexts/eldredge.asp In T.J.M. Schopf, ed., *Models in Paleobiology*. San Francisco: Freeman Cooper. pp. 82–115. Reprinted in N. Eldredge *Time frames*. Princeton: Princeton Univ. Press, 1985. Available here .
[418] http://www.gutenberg.org/etext/15491
[419] https://archive.org/details/historyofgeology00zittrich
[420] http://www.strangescience.net
[421] http://palaeoentomolog.ru/english.html
[422] http://www.juliantrubin.com/schooldirectory/paleontologists.html
[423] http://mypage.iu.edu/~pdpolly/Papers/PollySpang_2002_HistPaleo.pdf
[424] The term has entered into common usage after an article of the same name by paleontologist Robert T. Bakker in *Scientific American*, in April 1975. Examples can be found here http://www.citypaper.com/news/story.asp?id=11282 and here https://web.archive.org/web/20060110100858/http://www.geotimes.org/jan06/feature_threedinofaces.html.
[425] Heilmann, G. 1926: *The Origin of Birds*. Witherby, London. (1972 Dover reprint)
[426] An assumption which is now known to have been incorrect.
[427] Romer A.S. 1956. *Osteology of the Reptiles. Chicago: University Chicago.* 772 p.
[428] https://web.archive.org/web/20090228070415/http://www.lindahall.org/events_exhib/exhibit/exhibits/dino/ost1969_l.shtml
[429] It is now known that the drawing is inaccurate in many respects, including the pubis being far too short, and the fact that feathers are lacking.

Article Sources and Contributors

The sources listed for each article provide more detailed licensing information including the copyright status, the copyright owner, and the license conditions.

Dinosaur *Source:* https://en.wikipedia.org/w/index.php?oldid=853721247 *License:* Creative Commons Attribution-Share Alike 3.0 *Contributors:* 4444hhhh, 564dude, A D Monroe III, Abyssal, AdamDeanHall, Adrianxw, Al-Andalus, Alaney2k, Alejandrocaro35, Alexbrn, Alumnum, Annihilannic, Ant, Anthony22, Arjayay, Ashorocetus, Attilios, BD2412, BDD, Bender235, Bgwhite, BobEnyart, Brandmeister, Cadmus90, Carson34, Chiswick Chap, ChongDae, ChrisTheWhaleKing, ClueBot NG, CodeBadger, Coreybchapman, Crazy object, CuriousMind01, Daask, DangerousJXD, DavideVeloria88, Dbachmann, Dcirovic, Dinan Blueje, Dinoguy2, Dinohk, Dinostuck, Dr J Alvarez, DrKay, Drbogdan, DuncanHill, Dunkleosteus77, Editor abcdef, Egsan Bacon, Electricburst1996, Etherjammer, Ewulp, Extrapolaris, FP2C, FabulousFerd, Falconfly, Fama Clamosa, Farsight001, Florian Blaschke, FunkMonk, Gaius Cornelius, Generallu2, Gigafan0731, GliderMaven, Grand'mere Eugene, Grassynoel, Hazhk, Headbomb, Hipporoo, Hmains, Holy Goo, How come why not, Htculln38, IJReid, Icensnow42, Ira Leviton, Isambard Kingdom, Jens Lallensack, Jfraatz, Jim1138, JohannSnow, Jss367, Just plain Bill, Karyn Devlin, Khajidha, Killdevil, Kintaro, Lightlowemon, LittleJerry, Loonball5, Lusotitan, Lythronaxargestes, MB298, MWAK, Magyar25, Mariomassone, MaryBowser, Materialscientist, MathKnight, MathKnight-at-TAU, Meganesia, Mgiganteus1, Micromesistius, Mike Rosoft, Mikedelsol, MineUser (MinecraftUser), Mrjulesd, Mx. Granger, Nagualdesign, Neuroforever, Niceguyedc, Od Mishehu, Ogress, Paine Ellsworth, PaleoGeekSquared, Paleomario66, Phieuxghazzieh, Plantdrew, Prot D, Pvmoutside, R. S. Shaw, RINOTIGER, Raptormimus456, Rashkeqamar, Red Director, Ricardo A. Olea, Richard.sutt, RichardWeiss, Rjwilmsi, RomanNumeralII, Rp2006, Rtkat3, SandyGeorgia, Saturn comes back around, Serols, Shaded0, Sigmaslash5, Silbad, Slate Weasel, Smalljim, Spicemix, Stefanpw, Stikkyy, TAnthony, TBustah, The name, TheLateDentarthurdent, TheNeutroniumAlchemist, Tholme, Thor Dockweiler, Thornsie, Tom.Reding, Trappist the monk, Tyvic, VexorAbVikipædia, Vsmith, WelcometoJurassicPark, WolfmanSF, Wubzy, YeOldeGentleman, Zagalejo, Zemant, Zeupar 1

Evolution of dinosaurs *Source:* https://en.wikipedia.org/w/index.php?oldid=851053335 *License:* Creative Commons Attribution-Share Alike 3.0 *Contributors:* AS, Abyssal, Apokryltaros, Atethnekos, Aurous One, Azcolvin429, Bongwarrior, Bustertank, Cadiomals, ClueBot NG, CuriousMind01, CyanoTex, David Gerard, DinoRhinoMammel, Drbogdan, Evangelos Giakoumatos, Fatapatate, Firsfron, Hoseumou, I dream of horses, J. Spencer, Jim1138, Jmv2009, John of Reading, Jss367, Kangfreud, Kevmin, Kintaro, Kjoonlee, Koavf, Kumioko (renamed), Leptictidium, Lithoderm, Lusotitan, Macdonaldross, Maharishi yogi, Mangostar, Marcraymond, Mario modesto, Mgiganteus1, Mikenorton, Mollwollfumble, Mscuthbert, Myasuda, NatureA16, No Swan So Fine, NotWith, Paul H., Peter M. Brown, Robin S, Rrburke, Rynosaur, SaberToothedWhale, Serols, Serpinium, Slightsmile, Smith609, Spotty11222, Sun Creator, Switchfootvio, Tintero, Tkjtkj, TwoTwoHello, Wavelength, Wetman, Woudloper, Zach Winkler, Zureks, 60 anonymous edits 47

Dinosaur classification *Source:* https://en.wikipedia.org/w/index.php?oldid=847157283 *License:* Creative Commons Attribution-Share Alike 3.0 *Contributors:* 4444hhhh, 61x62x61, Abhinav, Abyssal, Anclation~enwiki, Ant, Aspidel, Astropithicus, BD2412, Barneca, Ben van Vlierden, Cephal-odd, Chris the speller, Citation bot 1, Dcirovic, DeinonychusDinosaur999, Dinoguy2, Doc Tropics, DuncanHill, Firsfron, Gaius Cornelius, Griffinofwales, GrinBot~enwiki, Hoseumou, Ian Pitchford, Imorthodox23, J. Spencer, J.delanoy, Jntg4, Jusdafax, Keith Edkins, Koolrock, Kriv02, Kumioko (renamed), LilHelpa, MTSbot~enwiki, MWAK, Mark t young, Metaknowledge, Mgiganteus1, Mkl12, Mollwollfumble, NellieBly, Nuno Tavares, PaleoGeekSquared, Petter Bøckman, Philip Trueman, Phlebas, Playtime, Ptbotgourou, Quebec99, Rahk EX, RetiredUser2, Rholton, Rjwilmsi, Robin S, RupertMillard, Sheep81, Silver seren, Spotty11222, Srleffler, Steveoc 86, The Singing Badger, Thebigboi, Tonyxc600, Trappist the monk, Uncle Dick, Veledan, Vuerqex, Woudloper, Zureks, 85 anonymous edits 59

Dinosaur size *Source:* https://en.wikipedia.org/w/index.php?oldid=851388930 *License:* Creative Commons Attribution-Share Alike 3.0 *Contributors:* AB03, AManWithNoPlan, Alexander Davronov, Anasaitis, Anthony Appleyard, Apokryltaros, ArcaneHalveKnot, Ashorocetus, BLAZZE92, Bricksmashtv4, Brolyeuphyfusion, Byteflush, Cameron11598, Chrissymad, ClueBot NG, David.moreno72, Dcirovic, Dinoguy2, Doofinshmirts, Drbogdan, Edmarka, Eriorguez, Fanboyphilosopher, Fireflyfanboy, FriyMan, Fylindfotberserk, Gamma 124, Gigafan0731, Grand'mere Eugene, Grimphantom, GünniX, IJReid, Imminent77, Johnuniq, KoshVorlon, Kyle L. Fessenden, Lavalizard101, Lepricavark, Lythronaxargestes, Magioladitis, MarginalCost, Materialscientist, MathKnight, Meridas, Mgiganteus1, Mike.BRZ, Mikeblas, Mimifali, Nicholas liam marais, NinjaRobotPirate, Noblesix0607, Oaholroyd, Ojoceratops, Oshwah, PaleoGeekSquared, Plantdrew, Ponyo, Redom115, Rivertorch, Rjwilmsi, Spinosaurus75 (Dinosaur Fan), Sro23, TheVividen, Tomwiki2016, Torkoal22, Torvodon, VRB TO, WelcometoJurassicPark, WelcometoJurassicWorld, Wikid77, Wikishovel, Xiang180808, 169 anonymous edits 69

Dinosaur egg *Source:* https://en.wikipedia.org/w/index.php?oldid=848306188 *License:* Creative Commons Attribution-Share Alike 3.0 *Contributors:* 100110100, 2004mac, Abductive, Abyssal, Ashorocetus, BD2412, Bardielunit13, Baseball Watcher, Bastion Monk, BlueMoonset, Citation bot 1, ClueBot NG, Countmustard, DVdm, Darwin's Bulldog, Desktopdave, Dlrohrer2003, Doctorfluffy, Duivelwaan, Evangelos Giakoumatos, FunkMonk, Georgialh, Glasszone33, Hawkeye7, Headbomb, Hota44, J. Spencer, Jason Quinn, JediKnyghte, John of Reading, Khazar2, Kumioko (renamed), Kurousagi, Lavateraguy, Lemnaminor, M-le-mot-dit, Magioladitis, Mandarax, Meridas, Mgiganteus1, Middayexpress, Myasuda, Nadiatalent, Neitherday, Niceguyedc, Nikkimaria, Osado, PRehse, PigFlu Oink, Pinethicket, Qwfp, Rjwilmsi, Saintrain, Salvio giuliano, Soulbust, Takeaway, TexasAndroid, Tide rolls, Tony1, Unbuttered Parsnip, Wareditor2013, Wavelength, Widr, Woohookitty, 50 anonymous edits 87

Physiology of dinosaurs *Source:* https://en.wikipedia.org/w/index.php?oldid=849387711 *License:* Creative Commons Attribution-Share Alike 3.0 *Contributors:* 4444hhhh, A.Larionov, Abyssal, Adavidb, American In Brazil, Anrnusna, Auntof6, BD2412, BOTarate, Bender235, Billare, CapitalLetterBeginning, Cervical67, Charles Matthews, Chris the speller, CinchBug, Citation bot 1, ClueBot NG, CommonsDelinker, ContiAWB, Cuvette, Dan Gluck, Dcirovic, DemocraticLuntz, DinopediaR, Dropzink~enwiki, Eigenstatic, Epipelagic, FamAD123, Fickmaschine XXL, Firsfron, FunkMonk, Gazzster, George D. Watson, Gorthian, Graywords, HCA, HMallison, Henry Flower, Hoseumou, Illia Connell, J. Spencer, JayDee, Jessicapierce, JohannSnow, John of Reading, John.Conway, Jtambasco, Khazar2, Kintaro, Kjoonlee, Knowledgeable Raven, Kroush, Larrymcp, Leptictidium, LilHelpa, Lionhead99, MWAK, Majora4, Mandarax, Mark t young, Mfb, Mindmatrix, Miwanya, Mr.Taxonomist, Mrt3366, Nergaal, Nimbusania, Ohconfucius, Owozifa, PKT, Peterward2013, Petter Bøckman, Philcha, Poptrop02, R'n'B, Rainbow Shifter, Regaliceratops, Rich Farmbrough, Rjwilmsi, Sardanaphalus, SchreiberBike, Sct72, Sebastianblakehoward, Sheep81, Skizzik, Smith609, Spotty11222, Stevenlschanen, Steveprutz, SyaWgnignahCehT, Tabletop, Terrek, Theroadislong, Thumperward, Tony North, Tony1, Universaladdress, Vina-iwbot~enwiki, Vultur~enwiki, Wavelength, WolfmanSF, 77 anonymous edits 105

Origin of birds *Source:* https://en.wikipedia.org/w/index.php?oldid=853014734 *License:* Creative Commons Attribution-Share Alike 3.0 *Contributors:* Abce2, Abductive, Alansohn, Albertonykus, Alexander Vargas, Alphathon, Andrewman327, Animalparty, AnonMoos, Anrnusna, Anthony Appleyard, Attilios, B mazuki, BD2412, Battlekow, Bender235, Bkonrad, Bueller 007, CHW100, Caballero1967, Captain Occam, Chris the speller, Citation bot 1, ClueBot NG, Collieuk, CommonsDelinker, Conty~enwiki, CuriousMind01, CyberCorn Entropic, David Gerard, Dbachmann, Dcirovic, Demize, Dinoguy2, Diucón, Dmh~enwiki, Dobermanji, Dratman, Drbogdan, Drutt, Epicgenius, Epipelagic, Ettrig, Ewen, Falconfly, Ferahgo the Assassin, Firsfron, Firstbirdbeak, Floydian, FlyingAce, Focus, FunkMonk, Følelse, G.Kiruthikan, GermanJoe, GirasoleDE, Glacialfox, Grafen, HCA, Harizotoh9, Herostratus, J 1982, J. Spencer, JCSantos, Jbrougham, Jmv2009, Johnuniq, Jonesey95, Khazar2, Kintaro, Kumioko (renamed), Lambiam, Limulus, Ljosa, Look2See1, Lythronaxargestes, MWAK, Maias, Manul, Markunator, Meganesia, Mgiganteus1, Mike s, Mike.BRZ, Mindme, Mortee, Niceguyedc, Nick Number, Non-dropframe, NotWith, Omegaman99, Pzoot, Quebec99, Rainbow Shifter, Randy Kryn, Rich Farmbrough, Rjwilmsi, Robt Owen, Rufous-crowned Sparrow, Saintrain, SamX, SchreiberBike, Secondbirdbeak, SheriffIsInTown, Shirik, Shyamal, Simplexity22, Snowmanradio, Spicemix, Stephan Schulz, Sunrise, Tejendraji, The PIPE, The Thing That Should Not Be, Tktktk, TomS TDotO, Topilsky, Trappist the monk, Ucucha, Uwaga budowa, Vanished user 19794758563875, Vsmith, Writtenonsand, 86 anonymous edits 133

Feathered dinosaur *Source:* https://en.wikipedia.org/w/index.php?oldid=852988641 *License:* Creative Commons Attribution-Share Alike 3.0 *Contributors:* A2soup, AManWithNoPlan, Abyssal, Albertonykus, AldezD, Animalparty, Anrnusna, AnthonyW90, ArturoooGarcíaaa555, Ashorocetus, BD2412, BDD, Bgwhite, Blaylockjam10, CCevol2015, Caftaric, Ccevo2012, Ccevol2013, Chab CH, Chaoyangopterus, Chiswick Chap, ChiveFungi, Citynoise, ClueBot NG, CuriousMind01, Da Smallest Kitten, DangerZone1234, DangerousJXD, Dcirovic, Denn333, DerpyDuckAnimation, Dimeirex, Dinkytown, Dinoguy2, Donner60, Drbogdan, Editor abcdef, Eracekat, Eurodyne, Florian Blaschke, Formerlyanonymouseditor, Frankalbertson, FunkMonk, Gaddy1975, GeoGreg, GeoWriter, Geopersona, Hamish59, Harizotoh9, Headbomb, Hillbillyholiday, Illia Connell, InedibleHulk, Invertzoo, J. Spencer, JaneStillman, John, KLBot2, Kessler.254, Korny O'Near, Kwamikagami, Lalaharding, Lightlowemon, Look2See1, Lythronaxargestes, MWAK, Macrochelys, Magyar25, Manul, Markunator, Materialscientist, Me, Myself, and I are Here, Meganesia, Mrjulesd, NMaia, Nightscream, Nihiltres, NotWith, Obsidian Soul, Onanimus, Ornithodiez, Ost316, Paine Ellsworth, Paolodm, Petropoxy (Lithoderm Proxy), Ptbotgourou, Randy Kryn, Raptormimus456, Rjwilmsi, Saurusaurus, SchreiberBike, SchroCat, Serols, Shirt58, Simplexity22, Snori, SuperHero2111, The Mummy, Trappist the monk, Tucker915, Value321, Vsmith, Vuerqex, Wenlongtian, 91 anonymous edits 155

Cretaceous–Paleogene extinction event *Source:* https://en.wikipedia.org/w/index.php?oldid=853695914 *License:* Creative Commons Attribution-Share Alike 3.0 *Contributors:* 1201mis, 83d40m, Abyssal, Aerkem, Alanfdow, Alfie Gandon, Allisonmb, AndrewOne, Apokryltaros, ArishKanaan, Audaciter, BatteryIncluded, Bender235, Blapman65, BloodOfGods3298, Bobbyrob987, BolindazheShi, Bongwarrior, Boomer Vial, Boundarylayer, Braeden90000, CAPTAIN RAJU, CASSIOPEIA, Caftaric, Call - Me - Papi, CarloMartinelli, Chiswick Chap, Chris the speller, ChrisTheWhaleKing, ClueBot NG, Coreybchapman, Cornhead, CuriousEric, CuriousMind01, DadaNeem, David.moreno72, Dawnseeker2000, Dbreagornks, Dcirovic, Deacon Vorbis, DinosaursLoveExistence, DocWatson42, DrKay, Drbogdan, Duckduckstop, Dudley Miles, DuncanHill, Dunkleosteus54, El C, Eleassar, Epipelagic, Ericoides, FT2, Falconfly, Fama Clamosa, G0mx, GeoWriter, Geogene, Gilliam, Glevum, Gorthian, Ground Zero, Gulumeemee, HMohamud97, Hanif Al Husaini, Headbomb, Holy Goo, Hzsm, Isambard Kingdom, Ixfd64, J 1982, Jdwitts, Jim1138, JimVC3, Jinfengopteryx, John D. Croft, Julesd, Julietdeltalima, Juot, K6ka, Kinetic37, Krenair, LakesideMiners, LawrieM, Lazylaces, Lojbanist, Lugnuts, Lythronaxargestes, Magyar25, MarioProtIV, Mikenorton,

Image Sources, Licenses and Contributors

The sources listed for each image provide more detailed licensing information including the copyright status, the copyright owner, and the license conditions.

Image *Source:* https://en.wikipedia.org/w/index.php?title=File:Padlock-silver.svg *Contributors:* AzaToth, BotMultichill, BotMultichillT, Gurch, Jarekt, Kallerna, Multichill, Perhelion, Rd232, Riana, Sarang, Siebrand, Steinsplitter, 4 anonymous edits 1
Image *Source:* https://en.wikipedia.org/w/index.php?title=File:Dinosauria_montage_2.jpg *License:* Creative Commons Attribution 2.0 *Contributors:* Uploader: User:DrKay; based on selection at File:Various dinosaurs2.png User:Captmondo Tadek Kurpaski Hectonichus Agsft 1
Image *Source:* https://en.wikipedia.org/w/index.php?title=File:Red_Pencil_Icon.png *License:* Creative Commons Zero *Contributors:* User:Peter coxhead 1
Figure 1 *Source:* https://en.wikipedia.org/w/index.php?title=File:LA-Triceratops_mount-2.jpg *License:* Creative Commons Attribution-Sharealike 3.0 *Contributors:* User:MathKnight 4
Figure 2 *Source:* https://en.wikipedia.org/w/index.php?title=File:ם'אמספח-01.jpg *Contributors:* User:MathKnight 5
Figure 3 *Source:* https://en.wikipedia.org/w/index.php?title=File:Skull_diapsida_1.svg *License:* GNU Free Documentation License *Contributors:* derivative work: Gagea (talk) Skull_diapsida_1.png: Preto(m) 7
Figure 4 *Source:* https://en.wikipedia.org/w/index.php?title=File:Sprawling_and_erect_hip_joints_-_horizontal.svg *Contributors:* User:Fred the Oyster 8
Figure 5 *Source:* https://en.wikipedia.org/w/index.php?title=File:Marasuchus.JPG *License:* Public domain *Contributors:* HoopoeBaijiKite 10
Figure 6 *Source:* https://en.wikipedia.org/w/index.php?title=File:Herrerasaurusskeleton.jpg *License:* Creative Commons Attribution-Sharealike 2.0 *Contributors:* Zach Tirrell from Plymouth, USA 11
Figure 7 *Source:* https://en.wikipedia.org/w/index.php?title=File:Saurischia_pelvis.png *License:* Creative Commons Attribution-Sharealike 3.0 *Contributors:* User:AdmiralHood 13
Figure 8 *Source:* https://en.wikipedia.org/w/index.php?title=File:Tyrannosaurus_pelvis_left.jpg *License:* GNU Free Documentation License *Contributors:* User:Ballista 13
Figure 9 *Source:* https://en.wikipedia.org/w/index.php?title=File:Ornithischia_pelvis.png *License:* Creative Commons Attribution-Sharealike 3.0 *Contributors:* User:AdmiralHood 14
Figure 10 *Source:* https://en.wikipedia.org/w/index.php?title=File:Edmontosaurus_pelvis_left.jpg *License:* GNU Free Documentation License *Contributors:* en:User:Ballista, modified by Conty 14
Figure 11 *Source:* https://en.wikipedia.org/w/index.php?title=File:Dromaeosaurs.png *Contributors:* User:Fred Wierum 16
Figure 12 *Source:* https://en.wikipedia.org/w/index.php?title=File:Macronaria_scrubbed_enh.jpg *License:* GNU Free Documentation License *Contributors:* Богданов dmitrchel@mail.ru 17
Figure 13 *Source:* https://en.wikipedia.org/w/index.php?title=File:Ornithopods_jconway.jpg *License:* GNU Free Documentation License *Contributors:* Drawing by John Conway 18
Figure 14 *Source:* https://en.wikipedia.org/w/index.php?title=File:Largestdinosaursbysuborder_scale.png *License:* Creative Commons Attribution-Sharealike 3.0,2.5,2.0,1.0 *Contributors:* Matt Martyniuk 19
Figure 15 *Source:* https://en.wikipedia.org/w/index.php?title=File:Argentinosaurus_9.svg *License:* Public Domain *Contributors:* User:Slate Weasel 20
Figure 16 *Source:* https://en.wikipedia.org/w/index.php?title=File:Human-eoraptor_size_comparison(v2).png *License:* Creative Commons Attribution-Sharealike 2.5 *Contributors:* Dropzink 21
Figure 17 *Source:* https://en.wikipedia.org/w/index.php?title=File:Maiasaurusnest.jpg *License:* GNU Free Documentation License *Contributors:* Abyssal, Albertonykus, Dudo~commonswiki, Kevmin, Koobak, MGA73bot2, Wieralee 23
Figure 18 *Source:* https://en.wikipedia.org/w/index.php?title=File:Centrosaurus_dinosaur.png *License:* Public Domain *Contributors:* LadyofHats 24
Figure 19 *Source:* https://en.wikipedia.org/w/index.php?title=File:Lambeosaurus_magnicristatus_DB.jpg *Contributors:* Богданов dmitrchel@mail.ru 25
Figure 20 *Source:* https://en.wikipedia.org/w/index.php?title=File:Gniazdo_sieweczki_RB.JPG *License:* GNU Free Documentation License *Contributors:* User:Radomil 27
Figure 21 *Source:* https://en.wikipedia.org/w/index.php?title=File:Citipati_IGM_100_979.jpg *License:* Creative Commons Sharealike 1.0 *Contributors:* Dinoguy2 28
Figure 22 *Source:* https://en.wikipedia.org/w/index.php?title=File:Dino_bird_h.jpg *License:* Public Domain *Contributors:* Zina Deretsky, National Science Foundation 29
Figure 23 *Source:* https://en.wikipedia.org/w/index.php?title=File:Feathered_non-avian_Maniraptora.jpg *Contributors:* FunkMonk, Mariomassone 31
Figure 24 *Source:* https://en.wikipedia.org/w/index.php?title=File:Pneumatopores_on_the_left_ilium_of_the_theropod_Aerosteon_riocoloradensis.jpg *License:* Creative Commons Attribution 2.5 *Contributors:* Sereno PC, Martinez RN, Wilson JA, Varricchio DJ, Alcober OA, et al. 33
Figure 25 *Source:* https://en.wikipedia.org/w/index.php?title=File:Chicxulub_radar_topography.jpg *License:* Public Domain *Contributors:* NASA/JPL-Caltech 34
Figure 26 *Source:* https://en.wikipedia.org/w/index.php?title=File:William_Buckland_detail.png *License:* Public Domain *Contributors:* User:FunkMonk 37
Image *Source:* https://en.wikipedia.org/w/index.php?title=File:Edcope.jpg *Contributors:* UNIQ-ref-1-a69b4d4fb878f2af-QINU 38
Image *Source:* https://en.wikipedia.org/w/index.php?title=File:OthnielCharlesMarsh.jpg *License:* Public Domain *Contributors:* DrKay, Jarekt, Kilom691, Librotyrannus, Shizhao, Väsk, 1 anonymous edits 38
Figure 27 *Source:* https://en.wikipedia.org/w/index.php?title=File:Stego-marsh-1896-US_geological_survey.png *License:* Public Domain *Contributors:* Othniel Charles Marsh, uploaded by Firsfron & modified by anetode 38
Figure 28 *Source:* https://en.wikipedia.org/w/index.php?title=File:Dr._Bob_Bakker_with_Dino.jpg *License:* Creative Commons Attribution 2.0 *Contributors:* Ed Schipul 40
Figure 29 *Source:* https://en.wikipedia.org/w/index.php?title=File:Scipionyx_samniticus_232.jpg *License:* Creative Commons Attribution-Sharealike 3.0 *Contributors:* User:Ghedoghedo 41
Figure 30 *Source:* https://en.wikipedia.org/w/index.php?title=File:Iguanodon_Crystal_Palace.jpg *License:* Creative Commons Attribution-Sharealike 2.0 *Contributors:* Jes from Melbourne, Australia 42
Figure 31 *Source:* https://en.wikipedia.org/w/index.php?title=File:Triceratops-vs-T-Rex001.jpg *License:* Creative Commons Attribution 2.0 *Contributors:* Marcin Chady 43
Image *Source:* https://en.wikipedia.org/w/index.php?title=File:Commons-logo.svg *License:* logo *Contributors:* Anomie, Callanecc, CambridgeBayWeather, Jo-Jo Eumerus, RHaworth 45
Image *Source:* https://en.wikipedia.org/w/index.php?title=File:Wikiquote-logo.svg *License:* Public Domain *Contributors:* Rei-artur 45
Image *Source:* https://en.wikipedia.org/w/index.php?title=File:Wikisource-logo.svg *License:* Creative Commons Attribution-Sharealike 3.0 *Contributors:* ChrisiPK, Guillom, INeverCry, Jarekt, JuTa, Leyo, Lokal Profil, MichaelMaggs, NielsF, Rei-artur, Rocket000, Romaine, Steinsplitter 45
Image *Source:* https://en.wikipedia.org/w/index.php?title=File:Wikispecies-logo.svg *License:* Creative Commons Attribution-Sharealike 3.0 *Contributors:* (of code) cs:User:-xfi- 45
Image *Source:* https://en.wikipedia.org/w/index.php?title=File:Wiktionary-logo-en-v2.svg *Contributors:* User:Dan Polansky, User:Smurrayinchester 45
Image *Source:* https://en.wikipedia.org/w/index.php?title=File:Sound-icon.svg *License:* GNU Lesser General Public License *Contributors:* Crystal SVG icon set 45
Image *Source:* https://en.wikipedia.org/w/index.php?title=File:Cscr-featured.svg *License:* GNU Lesser General Public License *Contributors:* Anomie 46
Figure 32 *Source:* https://en.wikipedia.org/w/index.php?title=File:Evolution_of_dinosaurs_EN.svg *License:* GNU Free Documentation License *Contributors:* Evolution_of_dinosaurs_by_Zureks.svg: Zureks derivative work: Woudloper (talk) 48
Image *Source:* https://en.wikipedia.org/w/index.php?title=File:Dino_evol_1_modificated_ES.svg *License:* Public Domain *Contributors:* Dino_evol_1.jpg: Original uploader was Mollwollfumble at en.wikipedia derivative work: mario modesto (talk) 49
Image *Source:* https://en.wikipedia.org/w/index.php?title=File:Sauropod_Length.gif *License:* Public Domain *Contributors:* Mollwollfumble ... 51
Image *Source:* https://en.wikipedia.org/w/index.php?title=File:Sauropod_Skull_Length.gif *License:* Public Domain *Contributors:* Mollwollfumble 51
Image *Source:* https://en.wikipedia.org/w/index.php?title=File:Ceratops.gif *License:* Public Domain *Contributors:* Mollwollfumble 55

License

Index

Cattle, 90
Caudipteryx, 109, 138, 167
Caudofemoralis, 6
Cedarpelta bilbeyhallorum, 83, 84
Cell (biology), 146
Cellulose, 108
Cenote, 197, 199, 201
Cenozoic, 19, 69, 169, 230
Center of gravity, 112
Centrosaurinae, 67
Centrosaurus, 24
Cephalopod, 175
Cephalopoda, 175
Cerapoda, 62, 66
Ceratonykus oculatus, 79
Ceratopsia, 1, 3, 11, 19, 24, 30, 55, 57, 62, 67
Ceratopsian, 108, 126
Ceratopsidae, 57, 62, 67
Ceratopsoidea, 67
Ceratopsomorpha, 67
Ceratosauria, 10, 15, 52, 56, 60, 64, 110, 111, 126
Ceratosauridae, 60, 64
Ceratosaurus, 64
Cetaceans, 183
Cetartiodactyla, 183
Cetiosauridae, 18, 61, 63
Cetiosaurus, 51, 63
Chaetocercus heliodor, 78
Champsosaurus, 178
Changchunsaurus parvus, 80
Chang Qu, 36
Changyuraptor, 167
Chaoyangsaurus youngi, 82
Charadriiformes, 12
Charadrius, 27
Charles Darwin, 105, 134, 156, 219, 231, 236, 239
Charles Dickens, 44
Charles Doolittle Walcott, 235
Charles Lyell, 228
Charles R. Knight, 105, 107, 241
Charonosaurus jiayinensis, 79, 80
Chasmosaurinae, 67
Chasmosaurus belli, 82
Chasmosaurus russelli, 81
Chatham Islands, 215
Cheek, 10
Chemical element, 143
Chemistry, 19
Chicken, 27, 146
Chicxulub Crater, 34, 35, 169, 186, 188, 189, 191, **194**, 211, 214, 243
Chicxulub impactor, 169, 196, 199
Chicxulub, Yucatán, 186, 188, 196, 198
Chilantaisaurus tashuikouensis, 76, 77

China, 87, 215, 219, 233
China University of Geosciences, 160
Chinese dragon, 36
Chinese language, 220
Chipping Norton, 36
Chiroptera, 183
Chondrichthyes, 176
Chordate, 1
Chorion (egg), 91
Choristodera, 12, 173
Choristodere, 178
Christian Erich Hermann von Meyer, 134
Chromogisaurus novasi, 75
Chukar Partridge, 149
Circulatory system, 110
CITEREFRandall2015, 245
Citipati, 27, 28
Citipati (dinosaur), 88, 96, 145, 159, 167
Clade, 2, 12, 19, 47, 105, 140, 149, 173
Cladistic, 241
Cladistic analysis, 153
Cladistics, 39, 59, 138, 140, 143, 157, 240
Cladogram, 56, 166
Cladograms, 141
Class (biology), 3, 219, 241
Classification, 92
Clavicle, 30, 135, 157
Clavipectoral triangle, 6
Climate change, 172, 211, 218, 220
Cloaca, 29
Cnemial crest, 7
Coastal plain, 192
Coccolithophorids, 173
Coelophysidae, 56, 64, 126
Coelophysis, 15, 52, 64, 111
Coelophysoidea, 10, 15, 52, 60, 64
Coeluridae, 61, 110, 111, 126
Coelurosaur, 41, 112, 238, 249
Coelurosauria, 4, 10, 16, 52, 56, 61, 64, 140, 148, 152, 155, 167
Coelurus, 64
Coereba flaveola, 77
Coleoid, 175
Colepiocephale lambei, 83
Collagen, 42, 146
Collecting, 220
Coloradisaurus brevis, 75
Colorado, 187
Comet, 186, 196
Comet Shoemaker–Levy 9, 191, 203
Common basilisk, 149
Common descent, 9
Common guillemot, 26
Common ostrich, 16, 72
Commons:Category:Aves fossils, 154
Commons:Category:Chicxulub crater, 209